'Stéphanie Bijlmakers makes a unique analysis of the triangular relationship between Corporate Social Responsibility (CSR), human rights, and law. She critically revisits sources at various governance levels, from the UN Guiding Principles to the 2014 EU Directive on non-financial disclosure, culminating in a refreshing approach to corporate due diligence and CSR.'

Jan Wouters, Director, Leuven Centre for Global Governance Studies, KU Leuven, Belgium

'By a thorough and convincing analysis of the corporate responsibility to respect human rights as a global standard of expected conduct and a social norm, and its crystallization into various forms of international and national regulation, this book provides a welcome contribution to the understanding of human rights taking centre stage in a pluriform concept of corporate social responsibility as transnational law.'

Jan Eijsbouts (A.J.A.J.), Institute for Corporate Law, Governance and Innovation Policies, Maastricht University, the Netherlands

'With corporations' behaviour ever more disciplined by "Corporate Social Responsibility", Stéphanie Bijlmakers gives an authoritative insight into the law surrounding the discipline. While informed by the policy context of CSR, this volume takes a refreshingly legal viewpoint and therefore will be of great value to the scholarly and practising community alike.'

Geert Van Calster, Professor, Institute for European Law, KU Leuven, Belgium

'Stéphanie Bijlmakers' book covers an emerging field in the interface between public and private governance, between hard and soft law, and between national and international regulation of the impact of economic actors on society, in particular on human rights. It offers an innovative take on the issue of CSR and its increasing regulation through public and private law. The book will be of value to academics and practitioners, including corporate lawyers.'

Karin Buhmann, Professor of Business & Human Rights, Copenhagen Business School, Denmark

Corporate Social Responsibility, Human Rights, and the Law

Corporate Social Responsibility, Human Rights, and the Law examines the responsibilities of business enterprises for human rights from a legal perspective. It analyses the legal status of the 'corporate responsibility to respect human rights' as articulated by the United Nations Guiding Principles on Business and Human Rights (UNGPs). This concept currently reflects an international consensus and is promoted by the UN.

The book contemplates the various founding perspectives of the UNGPs, and how the integration of notions such as 'principled pragmatism' and 'polycentric governance' within its framework provides insights into the future course of law and policy, compliance, and corporate respect for human rights. The book thus takes a global focus, examining the interaction of Corporate Social Responsibility (CSR), human rights, and the law in a broader global governance context.

Setting out a possible future scenario for the legalization of the corporate responsibility to respect human rights that is informed by the UNGPs' founding perspectives and reflects current realities in the human rights landscape, this book will be of great interest to scholars of business ethics, international human rights law, and CSR more broadly.

Stéphanie Bijlmakers is an Affiliated Researcher at the Institute for Private International Law, KU Leuven, Belgium.

Routledge Research in Sustainability and Business

Contemporary Developments in Green Human Resource Management Research
Towards Sustainability in Action?
Douglas W.S. Renwick

Environmental Certification for Organisations and Products
Management Approaches and Operational Tools
Edited by Tiberio Daddi, Fabio Iraldo and Francesco Testa

Energy Law and the Sustainable Company
Innovation and Corporate Social Responsibility
Patricia Park and Duncan Park

Corporate Social Responsibility and Natural Resource Conflict
Kylie McKenna

Corporate Responsibility and Sustainable Development
Exploring the Nexus of Private and Public Interests
Edited by Lez Rayman-Bacchus and Philip R. Walsh

Sustainable Entrepreneurship and Social Innovation
Edited by Katerina Nicolopoulou, Mine Karatas-Ozkan, Frank Janssen and John Jermier

Corporate Social Responsibility, Human Rights, and the Law
Stéphanie Bijlmakers

Corporate Sustainability
The Next Steps Towards a Sustainable World
Jan Jaap Bouma and Teun Wolters

For more information about this series, please visit: www.routledge.com/Routledge-Research-in-Sustainability-and-Business/book-series/RRSB

Corporate Social Responsibility, Human Rights, and the Law

Stéphanie Bijlmakers

First published 2019
by Routledge

2 Park Square, Milton Park, Abingdon, Oxfordshire OX14 4RN
52 Vanderbilt Avenue, New York, NY 10017

Routledge is an imprint of the Taylor & Francis Group, an informa business

First issued in paperback 2020

British Library Cataloguing-in-Publication Data
A catalogue record for this book is available from the British Library

Library of Congress Cataloging-in-Publication Data
A catalog record has been requested for this book

ISBN: 978-0-8153-9923-0 (hbk)
ISBN: 978-0-367-45905-5 (pbk)

Typeset in Goudy
by Wearset Ltd, Boldon, Tyne and Wear

To my parents, Jos en Riny

Contents

Abbreviations

ATCA	Alien Tort Claims Act
BIT	Bilateral Investment Treaty
BHR	Business and Human Rights
CFREU	Charter of Fundamental Rights of the European Union
CJEU	Court of Justice of the European Union
CRC	Convention on the Rights of the Child
CSR	Corporate Social Responsibility
CtESCR	United Nations Committee on Economic, Social and Cultural Rights
CTN	Commission on Transnational Corporations
CtRC	United Nations Committee on the Rights of the Child
ECHR	European Convention on Human Rights
ECOSOC	United Nations Economic and Social Council
ECtHR	European Court of Human Rights
EP	European Parliament
EU	European Union
FRAME	Fostering Human Rights Among European Policies
GATT	General Agreement on Tariffs and Trade
GDP	Gross Domestic Product
GRI	Global Reporting Initiative
HRC	United Nations Human Rights Council
ICC	International Criminal Court
ICCPR	International Covenant on Civil and Political Rights
ICESCR	International Covenant on Economic, Social and Cultural Rights
ICJ	International Court of Justice
IFC	International Finance Corporation
ILO	International Labour Organization
ISO	International Organization for Standardization
MNE	Multinational Enterprise
MSF	Multi-stakeholder Forum
NAFTA	North American Free Trade Agreement
NAP	National Action Plan

NCP	National Contact Point
NGO	Non-Governmental Organization
NHRI	National Human Rights Institution
NIEO	New International Economic Order
OECD	Organisation for Economic Co-operation and Development
OHCHR	Office of the High Commissioner for Human Rights
OJ	Official Journal
SME	small and medium-sized enterprises
SRSG	Special Representative of the Secretary-General on the issue of human rights and transnational and other business enterprises
TEU	Treaty on European Union
TFEU	Treaty on the Functioning of the European Union
TNC	Transnational Corporation
TRIPS	Agreement on Trade-Related Aspects of Intellectual Property Rights
UDHR	Universal Declaration of Human Rights
UK	United Kingdom
UN	United Nations
UNCTAD	United Nations Conference on Trade and Development
UNGA	United Nations General Assembly
UNGC	United Nations Global Compact
UNGPs	United Nations Guiding Principles on Business and Human Rights
UN Norms	Norms on the responsibilities of transnational corporations and other business enterprises with regard to human rights
US	United States
WG BH	United Nations Working Group on Business and Human Rights
WTO	World Trade Organization

Introduction

Promoting human rights and responsible business practices opens up discussions on our view of business in today's globalized society, about Corporate Social Responsibility (CSR), and the role of the law in achieving compliance. These issues form the main themes of this book. The book explores how the responsibilities of business enterprises in relation to human rights have been defined, from a legal perspective. It focuses on the 'corporate responsibility to respect human rights', as articulated by the United Nations Guiding Principles on Business and Human Rights (UNGPs). This concept currently reflects an international consensus and is promoted by the UN. The definition and (legal) character of the corporate responsibility to respect human rights, and its human rights due diligence component in particular, are examined in detail. This concept relates to, but also differs and challenges, conventional understandings of CSR. It explores efforts by the EU and States to operationalize human rights due diligence into various areas of EU and national law and policy. This study sheds light on how and to what extent the codification of the UNGPs effectively implements CSR at national and EU level, and the implications thereof for Business and Human Rights (BHR). At the same time, the book contemplates the various perspectives that found the UNGPs, and how the integration of notions such as 'principled pragmatism' and 'polycentric governance' within its framework provides insights into the future course of law and policy, compliance, and corporate respect for human rights. The book thus takes a global focus, examining the interaction of CSR, human rights and the law in a broader global governance context.

Corporate social responsibility, human rights, and the law

Business enterprises have assumed a prominent role in the international arena. With operations and relations encompassing the entire globe, their activities have impacts on essential interests of an economic, financial, environmental and social nature. In the 1990s, the benefits of globalization were increasingly questioned. Concerns about unprecedented power of corporations and the perceived negative impact of their activities, including an alleged 'race to the bottom' in business regulations and a regulatory vacuum at the domestic and international level, triggered calls for business enterprises to assume greater governance responsibilities. The focus and aspirations of human rights shifted towards CSR initially.

A rich history of theories, approaches and terminologies on CSR has developed since the 1950s, when it was first introduced as a management idea.[1] CSR has responded dynamically to changes in evolving expectations and needs over time, and conceptions of CSR vary.[2,3] CSR gained new momentum and was reinforced by a CSR 'movement',[4] which resulted in a proliferation of a plethora of CSR regulatory initiatives ranging from principles, codes of conduct and norms to guidelines and framework conventions.[5] Business enterprises play an important role in the development of these initiatives, claiming to protect human rights in production processes and business activities.[6]

The notion of business enterprises having responsibilities towards human rights is thus not new to CSR scholarship. Human rights developed into a key social concern of CSR in the 1970s, although it was more narrowly defined then as encompassing labour and worker rights.[7] It is by now well established that human rights largely inform and define the social aspect of CSR. However, the CSR approach to human rights diverges considerably from the positivist approach based on the understanding of human rights as moral and legal entitlements with corresponding legally binding obligations. Conventional CSR narratives view human rights as an integral element of a broader CSR agenda, which covers substantive issues like environmental responsibilities, corruption, labour rights, consumer relations, workforce and community activities.[8] These conceptions hold, moreover, that human rights address corporate activities directly and are premised on the notion that it is not governments, but rather employees, investors, consumers and the public who should be the drivers and enforcers of CSR initiatives.[9] Despite these interactions between CSR and human rights, Wettstein notes, human rights have had a minimal role in shaping the general conceptions of CSR.[10]

Still today, many scholars continue to view business responsibilities as voluntary and company driven. CSR is depicted as voluntary not only in the sense of non-binding strictly legally speaking, but also discretionary in a moral sense, and thus 'hardly a "must" for companies'.[11] CSR has been traditionally referred to as obligations beyond the law and voluntary commitments of firms towards the societies in which they operate.[12] Whilst legal scholars take ('hard' law) obligations, compliance (through regulation) and corporate liability as point of departure, the CSR narrative has focused on 'softer' forms of responsibility, self-regulation and sustainability. Conventional conceptions of CSR perceive markets and business enterprises as belonging to the private domain, which is separated from the public domain, which is organized by the State.[13] The scarcity of domestic and international legal regulation imposing binding obligations upon business enterprises vis-à-vis a specified legal or natural person is thus often emphasized. This narrow approach to CSR, and its human rights aspect more specifically, has not only caused uncertainty about its exact scope, but it has also made scholars question the role of law in it.[14]

A new strand of discourse called Business and Human Rights (BHR) emerged in the 1990s.[15] BHR is a field that originated from legal scholarship and human rights advocacy and has developed independently from and in parallel to the debate on CSR,[16] hence the two fields are coterminous to an extent. BHR differs from the CSR discourse in important aspects. It treats human rights not as part of a broader agenda but as an end goal. Moreover, corporate conduct is benchmarked in light of key universal human rights principles that are codified in international treaties. BHR's primary concern is the quest of victims and impacted communities for corporate accountability for human rights abuses, including through selective human rights litigation. This quest shapes a distinct narrative for BHR, Ramasastry notes, one that drives companies away from corporate voluntarism and 'more into the realm of binding law, State-sponsored oversight, and the importance of access to remedy as a measure of corporate accountability'.[17]

Prominent BHR scholars led a standard-setting initiative within the former UN Commission on Human Rights of the Norms on the responsibilities of transnational corporations and other business enterprises with regards to human rights (UN Norms).[18] The authors of the UN Norms articulated human rights obligations[19] that were directly applicable to companies in regards to a limited set of human rights, which furthermore resembled State obligations.[20] The debate around the Norms turned divisive and polarized, and eventually failed to obtain the approval of the former UN Commission on Human Rights. This resulted in Prof. John Ruggie's appointment in 2005 as the UN Secretary-General's Special Representative on the issue of human rights and transnational and other business enterprises (the SRSG).

The SRSG developed a three-pillared UN 'Protect, Respect, Remedy' (PRR) Framework for a better functioning system for business and human rights governance on a global scale, which the UN Human Rights Council (the HRC) 'accepted' in 2008. The Framework comprises three core principles: the State duty to protect against human rights abuses by third parties, including business enterprises, the corporate responsibility to respect human rights and the need for effective access to remedies for victims of business-related abuses. The SRSG developed the UN Guiding Principles on Business and Human Rights (UNGPs) to serve as a platform for guidance and action to translate the abovementioned Framework to practice. The HRC 'endorsed' the UNGPs on 23 June 2011, marking the first time that the HRC and its predecessor, the UN Commission on Human Rights, had issued authoritative guidance on business and human rights.[21]

The UNGPs articulate a common definition of the corporate responsibility to respect human rights. This definition entails not only that business enterprises must comply with all applicable laws; it also includes a responsibility to respect internationally recognized human rights, wherever they operate. This is a negative responsibility to do no harm, yet it calls for affirmative 'due diligence' steps to identify, prevent and mitigate the human rights risks deriving from their operations and account for how these are addressed.[22] This responsibility is a soft norm[23] founded in social expectations, and thus, strictly speaking from a formalistic positivist perspective, of a non-legally binding nature. It therefore does not constitute, in and of itself, a legal definition of CSR, nor does it create international legal obligations for business enterprises as such.[24] However, such responsibility is not without any legal relevance.

The UNGPs and the corporate responsibility to respect have acquired an authoritative status. The SRSG began an active engagement effort to foster convergence around the UNGPs shortly after the HRC's acceptance of the PRR Framework in 2008.[25] Partially because of this effort, the UNGPs already found practical application in various instruments in 2011.[26] Following the HRC's endorsement of the UNGPs, an increasing number of international and national standard bodies have incorporated the UNGPs. These include the Organisation for Economic Co-operation and Development (OECD), the EU, the International Finance Corporation (IFC), the International Organization for Standardization (ISO) and the International Labour Organization (ILO). Also, businesses and other stakeholder groups have subscribed to the UNGPs.[27] This widespread uptake has been stimulated by the UN Working Group on Business and Human Rights (the WG BH)[28] and has largely proceeded through distribution networks, according to Finnemore and Sikkink, triggering a '"norm cascading" well beyond their institutional sphere of origin'.[29]

Objectives

An important theme of this book is the 'legalization' of business responsibilities related to human rights, which is examined within a broader global governance[30] context. The UNGPs have objectives that go well beyond classical legal obligations. These objectives can be best understood by reference to the SRSG's views and intentions, which this book explores through the SRSG's academic writings. The UNGPs integrate a number of the SRSG's perspectives. For instance, the notion of 'principled pragmatism', which guided the SRSG throughout this mandate, directs focus on the normative goal of protecting and promoting human rights and the institutional challenges that need to be overcome to achieve this goal. It also sheds light on the (practical) means to achieve it. The SRSG's understanding of the 'global public domain' sheds light on new actors and regulatory processes that have come to occupy the public sphere and the social role of these actors in creating CSR and BHR standards and expectations.

The UNGPs also incorporate the SRSG's perspective of 'polycentric governance'. The notion of 'polycentric governance'[31] refers to the multiple governance systems, in which the aforementioned actors participate, that shape business behaviour.[32] It also directs focus on how to address governance challenges through institutionalization and the coordination of the interactions between these governance systems. The UNGPs are situated in terms of 'polycentric' global governance and are characterized, too, as a polycentric governance system. Furthermore, the UNGPs reflect the complexities and dynamics of globalization. The UNGPs, by integrating these perspectives in a framework, can provide insights into the course of law and policy, the achievement of compliance and changes in business behaviour in relation to human rights.

A key research question that this book addresses is to what extent the codification of the UNGPs is effectively implementing CSR at national, supra- EU and international level, and its implications for BHR. The assumption is that if the UNGPs, by placing CSR at the centre of a polycentric system of global governance, succeed in bringing compliance – and achieving changes in the behaviour of the corporate world in relation to human rights, the corporate responsibility to respect human rights is bound to have more and more legal status – and renewed (both legal and non-legal) effects. The book finds that, whilst it is a matter of legal obligation for States to adopt the necessary rules and regulations to ensure businesses respect human rights in practice, the corporate responsibility to respect human rights already has and should acquire a more normative force, including by translation of such responsibility into a 'hard' (legally binding) norm at the national, regional and international level.

There are ever-increasing calls for a 'legislation' of human rights due diligence for companies at the national and supranational (EU) level. Further legal developments at the international level are anticipated with the creation, within the HRC, in 2013 of an intergovernmental working group with a mandate to develop an international legally binding instrument on business and human rights.

Definitions

This book adheres to the concept of CSR adopted by the EU Commission: 'the responsibility of enterprises for their impacts on society'.[33] This EU definition of CSR recognizes that apart from respect for applicable law, business enterprises should have in place a process to integrate, *inter alia*, human rights 'into their business operations and core strategy in close collaboration with their stakeholders'.[34] It identifies two key objectives for CSR: (1) 'maximising the creation of shared value for their owners/shareholders and for their other stakeholders and society at large'; and (2) 'identifying, preventing and mitigating their possible adverse impacts'.[35]

For the purpose of this book, the terms CSR and corporate responsibility (CR) are used interchangeably. CSR is, after all, a comprehensive responsibility for all actions and impacts (social, environmental, economic).[36] Moreover, CSR and the corporate responsibility to respect human rights are interlinked. To the extent that CSR's social aspect is informed by, and mirrors the corporate responsibility to respect human rights as defined by the UNGPs, CSR and the corporate responsibility to respect human rights can be said to interact and overlap.[37]

Both concepts can be subject to conceptual renewal, as a result of their interaction, the influence these concepts have on each other's development, and evolving circumstances. Moreover, effectively implementing CSR has implications for BHR in practice. This might not always be fully understood. For instance, the SRSG has drawn attention to the fact that the underlying notion of the shared value paradigm, which is 'compliance with the law and ethical standards, as well as mitigating any harm caused by business', is problematic in practice.[38]

This book adheres to a broad understanding of 'business' as including any type of business. The term 'business' is used interchangeably with 'corporation' or 'business enterprise' throughout the book. This corresponds with the SRSG's understanding that, since all business enterprises can have adverse human rights impacts, the corporate responsibility to respect human rights applies 'fully and equally to all business enterprises'.[39] The UNGPs reflect this notion.[40]

Structure

Chapter 1 describes the evolution of the regulatory landscape on CSR and BHR from a legal perspective. It traces the origins back to the 1970s when the first steps were taken towards individual and industry-wide codes of conduct, international standards and cooperation. It notes the agenda of the business community to promote voluntary approaches and the notion of CSR. As the media continued to bring to public attention the unpunished corporate human rights abuses, thereby exposing the limitations of voluntary approaches, justification for mandating CSR and businesses' human rights responsibilities increased. This chapter describes notes the emergence of the BHR discourse and how the quest by victims for legal corporate accountability and access to remedies led States towards a legalization of businesses' responsibilities in relation to human rights. This is followed by an analysis of the initiative of the UN Norms, which preceded the UNGPs and from whose failure the SRSG drew important conclusions. The chapter sheds light on the significance and justifications of attempts at 'legalizing' the business responsibilities for human rights during the previous decades.

Chapter 2 analyses the work of the SRSG in developing the UNGPs, in order to advance towards a more effective global regime for the prevention of, and remedy for, business-related human rights harm, including specific legal measures. This chapter rests on the assumption that in order to understand why and how the UNGPs came about and its potential for fostering change, we should take into account the broader global governance context. Since it is the SRSG who developed the UNGPs, it is important to understand the SRSG's views and intentions. The UNGPs' objectives can only be properly ascertained by reference to the SRSG's approach of 'principled pragmatism' and understanding of CSR as a key component of 'polycentric' governance. The SRSG situates the UNGPs in terms of 'polycentric' global governance and characterizes the UNGPs, too, as a polycentric governance system.

Chapter 3 sets out a scenario for the 'legalization' of the corporate responsibility to respect human rights. It examines the legal nature of the UNGPs as a soft law document, and the SRSG's conception of the corporate responsibility to respect human rights, as a responsibility that is differentiated yet complementary to the duty of States, and furthermore embedded in a global policy context. The UNGPs are set out to promote a regulatory dynamic under which the public and private governance systems (public, civil, and corporate) would become better aligned and perform mutually reinforcing roles. This chapter notes how this regulatory dynamic potentially affects and coordinates the regulation of business conduct. It sees compliance (i.e. factual adherence) by business enterprises to the corporate responsibility to respect human rights as motivated by a number of factors. It argues that if the UNGPs are effectively embedded in the evolving regulatory ecosystem in the business and human rights space,[41] the corporate responsibility to respect human rights, as it is currently conceived, should also further evolve. It sets out the scenario of this norm acquiring 'binding-ness' and normative force, including the (selective) translation of such responsibility into 'hard' (legally binding) norms at the national, regional and international level.

Chapter 4 examines the corporate responsibility to respect human rights from a legal perspective. It focuses on the concept of human rights due diligence and its (legal) character as a standard of conduct and form of compliance. This involves an analysis of the interpretations of this concept and an evaluation of differences and similarities between this concept and other (legal) due diligence concepts used in various areas of law, including the duty of care concept under certain national (tort) laws of non-contractual obligations. The balancing act that the human rights due diligence concept entails will be explored further through a parallelism with the due diligence obligations that are applicable to States under international human rights law. The chapter will reflect on the functionality of the human rights due diligence concept in enabling and promoting future legal developments within legal systems. More specifically, it examines the potential of this concept to drive analytical improvements in, and facilitate convergence across, national laws affecting business behaviour. The human rights due diligence concept may be viewed as a reformatory concept, bound to fruitfully redefine the standards of due diligence that different areas of the legal order currently set out for business enterprises and thus also contribute to the reconceptualization of such laws.

Chapter 5 explores EU action to promote responses to the UNGPs. It focuses on how and to what extent the UNGPs have been codified in EU law and policy and this codification is effectively implementing CSR, and business responsibilities for human rights, at EU and national level. The European Commission issued the Communication 'A renewed EU Strategy 2011–14 for Corporate Social Responsibility' (the EU CSR Strategy) on 25 October 2011. This communication provides the European Commission's internal policy framework for the promotion of CSR, and business respect for human rights, and sets out a renewed European Strategy for CSR.[42] This chapter argues that there is scope for the EU to increase its level of engagement with the UNGPs. It also notes that the substance of the efforts of the EU and the regulatory responses by the EU, States, business enterprises and other actors to the UNGPs provide indication of evolving CSR standards and practices. To the extent that the EU, by codifying the UNGPs in EU law and policies, succeed in bringing effective implementation of CSR at EU and national level, the corporate responsibility to respect human rights already has and should further take on more normative force and binding-ness in the EU context.

Chapter 6 examines the legal implications of giving effect to the corporate responsibility to respect human rights as defined in the UNGPs through EU and national mandatory disclosure legislation. The focus is on Directive 2014/95/EU, of 22 October 2014, as regards disclosure of non-financial and diversity information by certain large undertakings and groups ('the Directive'). The chapter analyses the so-called 'indirect' and 'direct' effect of the Directive. It concludes that by enacting the Directive, the EU opted for a type of legal instrument that has potentially sweeping implications in the rights of stakeholders when it comes to the disclosure obligations of corporations. However, as will be explained, in particular, in relation to the 'comply or explain' framework, it is uncertain whether the *content* of the Directive will contribute to furthering the rights of stakeholders. This chapter also argues that the Directive, in the light of its objectives and pursuant to well-established case law supporting a purposive interpretation of secondary EU legislation, should have certain extraterritorial effects.

The conclusion presents the key findings and the main argument that if the UNGPs, by placing CSR at the centre of a polycentric system of global governance, succeed in bringing compliance – and achieving changes in the behaviour of the corporate world in relation to human rights, the corporate responsibility to respect human rights is bound to have more and more legal status – and renewed (both legal and non-legal) effects.

Methodology

This book resorts to a combination of desk-top research and comparative studies. It conducts a study of primary sources (i.e. legislation and case law at the national, regional and international level) to find, organize and interpret legal standards, practices and developments that are relevant for the regulation of the corporate responsibility to respect human rights as defined in the UNGPs.

The book conducts a study of the principle sources of primary and secondary EU law (i.e. Regulations, Directives and Decisions) as well as the rulings which the Court of Justice of the European Union (CJEU) has rendered in this context. The EU Commission issued a communication setting out a renewed CSR Strategy in 2011. Relevant considerations are that this Communication presented a renewed EU definition of CSR, the EU aim of seeking policy alignment with the global approaches to CSR, the commitment of the EU to the implementation of the UNGPs, as well as the renewed Agenda for Action for 2011–2014, which encompasses regulatory actions besides voluntary actions to promote CSR. The European Commission's departure from the entirely voluntary approach to CSR policy it adopted in several previous initiatives revived hopes for further regulatory developments supportive of business respect for human rights in the EU context.

In European countries, issues core to CSR, like healthcare and education, have been considered part of the government agenda and have been objects of regulation.[43] Some aspects of CSR are already objects of EU regulation, such as reporting obligations, misleading advertising, unfair commercial practices and public procurement standards. Many of these regulations can be applied directly by judges in domestic courts.[44] Also, in the light of the EU's large internal market, its role in foreign direct investment and community values, its stance on CSR can influence business enterprises and suppliers from every region in the world.[45]

Two comparative studies are conducted

First, the *elements* of the human rights due diligence component of the corporate responsibility to respect, as defined in the UNGPs, are examined. The study will analyse these elements in comparison to legal definitions of due diligence that have been used in other areas of law (e.g. civil law, company law, securities law and, of course, international human rights law). Such comparison can result in an enhanced understanding of these elements and hence, the (legal) character of the corporate responsibility to respect human rights as a standard of conduct.

Second, on the basis of these findings, the legal *definitions* of CSR as identified in the policies and laws adopted within the respective legal systems will be examined. This will involve a comparison between the corporate responsibility to respect human rights, as defined in the UNGPs, and the definitions of CSR encountered in EU policy and legislation. The similarities and differences in concepts to the UNGPs and implications will be examined on the basis of a study of secondary sources (i.e. academic journal articles, books, policy documents etc.), elaborating upon the legal context and origins of the respective legislation or measures and the legal system more generally.

Notes

1 *See, e.g.* Archi B. Carroll & Kareem M. Shabana, *The Business Case for Corporate Social Responsibility: A Review of Concepts, Research and Practice*, 12(1) International Journal of Management Reviews, 86–88 (2010). Rangan Kasturi, et al., Business Solutions for the Global Poor: Creating Social and Economic Value (Jossey-Bass 2007).

2 Liesbeth F. Enneking, Foreign Direct Liability and Beyond: Exploring the Role of Tort Law in Promoting International Corporate Social Responsibility and Accountability, 382 (Eleven International Publishing 2012).

3 Anita Ramasastry, *Corporate Social Responsibility Versus Business and Human Rights: Bridging the Gap Between Responsibility and Accountability*, 14(2) Journal of Human Rights, 237–259 (2015).

4 Michael R. Macleod, *Emerging Investor Networks and the Construction of Corporate Social Responsibility*, 34 The Journal of Corporate Citizenship, 69–96 (2009).

5 Deborah Leipziger, The Corporate Social Responsibility Code Book (Greenleaf Publishing 2003).

6 CRS has not only left a mark on management literature, the phenomenon has been analysed philosophically, sociologically, economically, psychologically and even aesthetically. O. Alvar Elbing, *The Value Issue of Business: The Responsibility of the Businessman*, 13(1) The Academy of Management Journal, 79–89 (1970).

7 Florian Wettstein, *From Side Show to Main Act: Can Business and Human Rights Save Corporate Responsibility*, *in* Business and Human Rights: From Principles to Practise (Dorothe Baumann-Pauly & Justine Nolan eds., Taylor & Francis 2016).
8 *Communication from the Commission Concerning Corporate Social Responsibility: A Business Contribution to Sustainable Development*, COM(2002) 347 final (2 July 2002).
9 *Id.*
10 Ramasastry, *supra* note 3, at 237–259.
11 Wettstein, *supra* note 7, at 80.
12 Andrew Crane, et al., The Oxford Handbook of Corporate Social Responsibility (Oxford University Press 2009).
13 Wettstein, *supra* note 7, at 80.
14 J.A. Zerk, Multinationals and Corporate Social Responsibility: Limitations and Opportunities in International Law (Cambridge University Press 2006).
15 Ramasastry, *supra* note 3, at 237–259.
16 Wettstein, *supra* note 7, at 80.
17 Ramasastry, *supra* note 3, at 238.
18 The UN Norms had been developed by a Working Group on business and human rights established in 1998 under the auspices of the Sub-Commission on the Promotion and Protection of Human Rights, a subsidiary body of the former Human Rights Commission. Sub-Commission on the Promotion and Protection of Human Rights, Norms on the responsibilities of transnational corporations and other business enterprises with regard to human rights, E/CN.4/Sub.2/2003/12/Rev.2, approved by U.N. Sub-Commission on the E/CN.4/Sub.2/2003/L.11 at 52 (13 Aug. 2003).
19 Ramasastry, *supra* note 3, at 244. David Weissbrodt & Muria Kruger, *Norms on the Responsibilities of Transnational Corporations and Other Business Enterprises with Regard to Human Rights*, 97 The American Journal of International Law 901, 912 (2003).
20 Sub-Commission on the promotion and protection of human rights Res. 2003/16, Responsibilities of transnational corporations and other business enterprises with regard to human rights, U.N. Doc. E/CN.4/Sub.2/2003/L.11 (13 Apr. 2003).
21 *See* J. Ruggie, *Regulating Multinationals: The UN Guiding Principles, Civil Society, and International Legalization* (Regulatory Policy Program, Working Paper RPP-2015–04, 2015).
22 Michael Kerr, et al., Corporate Social Responsibility: A Legal Analysis, at 15 (LexisNexis 2009).
23 Soft norms are 'shared expectations of how particular actors are to conduct themselves in given circumstances'. J. Ruggie, *The Social Construction of the UN Guiding Principles on Business and Human Rights*, 13 (Corporate Responsibility Initiative, Working Paper No. 67, 2017).
24 John Ruggie has clearly stated that, in his view, business enterprises presently do not have direct human rights obligations under international law. The emphasis is therefore placed in the corporate 'responsibility', rather than a 'duty' to respect, and in 'social expectations' rather than 'legal obligations'. *Id.*
25 The SRSG has noted:

> [...] they illustrate the desirability of engaging intermediaries to achieve greater normative and regulatory coherence, large-scale effects, and more robust outcomes – intermediaries that, in this particular case, have more direct links to and influence over corporate conduct than the UN alone.
>
> John Ruggie, *Global Governance and 'New Governance Theory': Lessons from Business and Human Rights*, 20(1) Global Governance, 12 (2014)

26 The SRSG provided a document identifying various instances of practical applications of the PRR Framework at that point in time, *see* Special Representative of the United Nations Secretary-General for business & human rights, Applications of the

U.N. 'Protect, Respect and Remedy' Framework (30 June 2011), http://business-humanrights.org/sites/default/files/media/documents/applications-of-framework-jun-2011.pdf.

27 *See*, John Ruggie, *Opinion: Business and Human Rights – The Next Chapter* (7 Mar. 2013).

28 The WG BH was created in 2011 with a mandate to promote the effective implementation and dissemination of the UNGPs. The efforts of the WG BH can be considered a variant of 'orchestration', which was at the heart of the UNGPs' implementation strategy according to Ruggie. Ruggie, *supra* note 25, at 11.

29 Ruggie, *supra* note 23.

30 This book adheres to the SRSG's definition of global governance:

> *Governance*, at whatever level of social organization it occurs, refers to the systems of authoritative norms, rules, institutions, and practices by means of which any collectivity, from local to the global, manages its common affairs. *Global Governance* is generally defined as an instance of govern*ance* in the absence of govern*ment*.
>
> J. Ruggie, *supra* note 25, at 5

31 Vincent Ostrom, Charles Tiebout and Robert Warren (1961) first introduced the concept of 'polycentricity', in the words of Nobel Prize winner Elinor Ostrom:

> In their effort to understand whether the activities of a diverse array of public and private agencies engaged in providing and producing of public services in metropolitan areas was chaotic, as charged by other scholars – or potentially a productive arrangement. 'Polycentric' connotes many centers of decision making that are formally independent of each other. Whether they actually function independently, or instead constitute an interdependent system of relations, is an empirical question in particular cases. To the extent that they take each other into account in competitive relationships, enter into various contractual and cooperative undertakings or have recourse to central mechanisms to resolve conflicts, the various political jurisdictions in a metropolitan area may function in a coherent manner with consistent and predictable patterns of interacting behavior. To the extent that this is so, they may be said to function as a 'system'.
>
> Elinor Ostrom, Beyond Markets and States: Polycentric Governance of Complex Economic Systems, Prize Lecture (8 Dec. 2009), www.nobelprize.org/nobel_prizes/economic-sciences/laureates/2009/ostrom_lecture.pdf

Vincent Ostrom, et al., *The Organization of Government in Metropolitan Areas: A Theoretical Inquiry*, 55(4) The American Political Science Review, 831–832 (1961).

32 The SRSG has identified three distinct governance systems that shape business conduct. First, there is the system of public law and policy, national and international. Second, a civil governance system engages external stakeholders that are affected by, or have an interest in, multinationals. Third, the corporate governance system 'internalizes elements of the other two'. John Gerard Ruggie, Just Business Multinational Corporations and Human Rights, 43 (W.W. Norton & Company 2013).

33 *Communication from the Commission to the European Parliament, the Council, the European Economic and Social Committee and the Committee of the Regions: A Renewed EU Strategy 2011–14 for Corporate Social Responsibility*, COM (2011) 681 final, at 6 (25 Oct. 2011).

34 *Id.* at 6.

35 *Id.* at 5–6.

36 *Id.* at 6–7.

37 Indeed, the European Commission recognizes human rights as a prominent aspect of CSR that business enterprises should address, and indicates that it seeks policy

consistency with global approaches in promoting CSR, *inter alia*, the UNGPs. The EU definition of CSR appears to be broadly aligned with the expectations set out in the UNGPs. *See* Chapter 6.

38 J. Ruggie, Making Globalization Work for All: Achieving the Sustainable Development Goals through Business Respect for Human Rights (Nov. 2016), www.shiftproject.org/resources/viewpoints/globalization-sustainable-development-goals-business-respect-human-rights/.

39 Special Representative on the Issue of Human Rights and Transnational Corporations and Other Business Enterprises, *Guiding Principles on Business and Human Rights: Implementing the United Nations 'Protect, Respect and Remedy' Framework*. U.N.Doc. A/HRC/17/31, Commentary to GP 14 (21 Mar. 2011) (by John Ruggie).

40 The UNGPs indicate that '[T]he responsibility of business enterprises to respect human rights applies to all business enterprises regardless of their size, sector, operational context, ownership and structure'. *Id.* GP 14.

41 J. Ruggie, A.SK Social Science Award 2017 WZB Berlin Social Science Center Acceptance Speech (14 Oct. 2017), https://business-humanrights.org/sites/default/files/documents/John%20Ruggie%20acceptance%20speech_Berlin%202017.pdf.

42 Commission Staff Working Document on Implementing the UN Guiding Principles on Business and Human Rights – State of Play, 6, SWD (2015) 144 final (14 July 2015).

43 Crane, *supra* note 12.

44 Cf. *e.g.* Case 213/89 Factortame, 1990, E.C.R. I-02433.

45 Kerr, et al., *supra* note 22, at 568.

1 The legalization of business responsibilities for human rights in the evolving field of CSR and business and human rights

Introduction

This chapter describes the evolution of the field of CSR and business and human rights from a legal perspective. The origins are traced back to the 1970s when the first steps were taken to international standards, cooperation and individual and industry-wide codes of conduct. It notes the agenda of the business community to promote voluntary approaches and the notion of CSR. The continued exposure by the media of corporate human rights abuses, and thereby also the limitations of voluntary approaches, increased justification for mandating CSR and businesses' human rights responsibilities. The chapter describes the emergence of the BHR discourse and how the quest by victims for legal corporate accountability and access to remedies led States towards a legalization of business responsibilities in relation to human rights. This is followed by an analysis of the initiative of the UN Norms, an attempt to create legally binding human rights obligations for companies that preceded the UNGPs and from whose failure the SRSG drew important conclusions. The aim of this chapter is to reflect on the significance and justifications of legalizing corporate responsibilities for human rights during the previous decades.

The 1970s: international codes of conduct

The 1970s witnessed increasing concerns about the overarching power of Multinational Enterprises (MNEs) on the national development agendas of countries at different stages of development.[1] The power of MNEs was reflected in their size and geographical spread. Their sales in goods and services amounted to billions of dollars. They exceeded the size of the domestic economies of most of the 150 countries existing at the time. While headquartered in developed countries, the majority of MNEs had affiliates in many developing countries across the world. MNEs employed a large percentage of the global workforce. Their production-distribution systems extended globally. MNEs had significant financial resources at their disposal for research and innovation. Due to the capabilities of companies to satisfy the needs of both advanced and developing countries, their operations where perceived as important attributes to greater interdependence in international economic relations.[2]

While the expansion of MNEs was a welcome development to some,[3] most developing countries perceived it as a threat to their economic and social development and possibly, to their democracy.[4] A concern of newly emerging colonial States was that the asymmetry in economic relations among States and companies would create new dependencies and restrictions on their national autonomy. The hope was that by inviting the influx of large companies, business would lead to the creation of wealth, jobs, tax revenues, technological innovation, scientific know-how, and more generally, economic growth and development. These benefits were not necessarily forthcoming, however. Policies of export restrictions, repatriation of profits and intra-company transfer pricing resulted in earnings to flow out of the country, and the costs for technology, consumer goods and healthcare to rise.[5]

Reaping the benefits of increased economic activity could come at a significant political and social cost for developing countries. Social tensions could run high over labour rights[6] and growing inequalities. Political misconduct by business enterprises was also not uncommon. Companies were known to leverage governments in case of conflicting interests, sometimes having the latter act under direct instructions of the foreign diplomacy of the home countries of the corporations.[7]

The perceived threat of companies encroaching on national affairs left leaders of developing countries at unease. The 1970s witnessed strategic manoeuvring by these countries to consolidate international controls over the conduct of business enterprises through different forums at the international level. The issue of MNEs was integral to a broader agenda advocated by developing countries to found a New International Economic Order (NIEO). The purpose of the NIEO was agreed at the Bandung Conference in 1955.[8] The NIEO was propelled on the UN agenda with support from the G77, after which it received official backing by the UN General Assembly (UNGA). The 1974 Declaration for the Establishment of a New International Economic Order first introduced the concept of the NIEO and outlined a list of core principles upon which the new order was to be founded. These principles alluded to the sovereign equality of States, broadest cooperation of all States based on equity, full and equal participation in solving world economic problems, and full, permanent sovereignty of every State over its national resources and all economic activities.[9,10]

The Plan of Action and The Charter on Economic Rights and Duties of States were passed at the same time. Article 1 of the Charter stipulated:

> Every State has the sovereign and inalienable right to choose its economic system as well as it political, social and cultural systems in accordance with the will of its people, without outside interference, coercion or threat in any form whatsoever.[11]

The Charter recognized the right of States to regulate and control foreign investment and the activities of transnational corporations within its national jurisdiction, including through nationalization and expropriation of foreign property, and to settle disputes before domestic courts.[12] The Plan of Action called for the development and implementation of an international code of conduct to regulate business enterprises.

Through a strong, joint representation within G77, developing countries raised their concerns at the United Nations Conference on Trade and Development (UNCTAD), which was established in 1963. UNCTAD issued various reports and resolutions, and developed codes addressing two practices that could impact negatively on the economic development of developing countries: a special technology transfer draft code,[13] as well as principles and rules governing the use and control of restrictive business practices.[14] These codes were part of the first international codes of conduct that aimed to regulate the transnational operations and practices of these companies and their relations with States, and in particular 'host' states.

The UN started a process to establish a multilateral framework, the Transnational Code of Conduct. This was after alleged corporate involvement in efforts by the US to destabilize regimes in Iran, Guatemala and Chile in the 1950s and 1970s.[15] MNCs became an item on the agenda of the United Nations Economic and Social Council (ECOSOC) in 1972, after the Chilean representative addressed ECOSOC earlier that year, denouncing the US International Telephone and Telegraph Company (ITTC) for its interference in Chilean internal politics.[16,17] ECOSOC requested the appointment of a Group of Immanent Persons to study the role and impact of business enterprises.[18] Upon the Group's recommendations, the Commission on Transnational Corporations (CTN) was created in 1974 in the form of an intergovernmental forum.[19] The CTN chairman presented the first formulations of the UN Code of Conduct in 1979.[20] The text addressed three subjects: the activities of transnational enterprises, their treatment by the countries in which they operated and intergovernmental cooperation. The final draft of the UN draft code of conduct, which was issued in 1991,[21] did not feature any human rights.[22] After a lengthy and costly process, negotiations were suspended in 1992. No consensus could be achieved due to opposition to the initiative by most industrialized home-state governments and transnational corporations (TNCs).[23]

Attempts to develop issue-specific agreements were more successful and resulted in the adoption of, *inter alia*, the Tripartite Declaration of Principles concerning Multinational Enterprises and Social Policy (ILO Tripartite Declaration) and the OECD Guidelines for MNEs.

The ILO adopted the Tripartite Declaration in 1977.[24] This declaration was non-legally binding and invited the governments of the State Members of the ILO, the employers' and workers' organizations in these host and home countries and MNEs operating in their territories to observe a set of principles in the areas of employment, training, conditions of work and life, and industrial relations. These principles offered guidance on appropriate laws, policies, measures and actions that these actors may take to further social progress. They are founded on the international labour conventions and recommendations that the ILO developed since 1919, which are referenced in the text.[25] States that joined the ILO Tripartite Declaration were urged to ratify these conventions and recommendations if they had not done so already.

The aim of the ILO Tripartite Declaration was to provide principles and recommendations to governments, MNEs and workers 'to encourage the positive contribution that MNEs can make to economic and social progress and to minimize and resolve the difficulties to which their various operations may give rise'.[26] The ILO Tripartite Declaration recognizes that MNEs make an important contribution

> to the promotion of economic and social welfare; to the improvement of living standards and the satisfaction of basic needs; to the creation of employment opportunities, both directly and indirectly; and to the enjoyment of basic human rights, including freedom of association, throughout the world.[27]

However, the ILO Tripartite Declaration also warned that 'the advances made by multinational enterprises in organizing their operations beyond the national framework may lead to abuse of concentrations of economic power and to conflicts with national policy objectives and with the interest of the workers'.[28]

The ILO Tripartite Declaration calls on MNEs 'to fully take into account' and to act 'in harmony with' the established general policy objectives of the countries in which they operate, especially the development priorities and social aims of these countries.[29] To this effect, consultations must be held between the MNEs, the government and the national employers' and workers' organizations in these countries. Governments of home countries 'should promote good social practice in accordance with this Declaration of Principles'. These governments, in so doing, must give 'regard to the social and labour law, regulations and practices in host countries as well as to relevant international standards'.[30] Both home and host countries should be prepared to have consultations with each other on these issues when need arises. The Declaration is structured around five areas, for which recommendations on particular themes are developed: (i) general policies; (ii) employment; (iii) training; (iv) conditions of work and life; (v) industrial relations.[31]

The first edition of the OECD Guidelines for MNEs was adopted on 21 June 1976 in the context of negotiations on international investment matters.[32] The Guidelines aimed to help ensure harmony between MNEs' operations and the national policies of the countries in which they operated and to consolidate relations of mutual confidence between MNEs and States.[33] The underlying rationale was the improvement of the international investment climate. The OECD Guidelines for MNEs were adopted in an Annex to an OECD Declaration on international investment and MNEs. This Declaration introduced policy principles to strengthen the cooperation and consultation between member countries with regards to issues related to both international investment and MNEs.[34] One of these policy principles was the issuance of a set of joint recommendations by the members of the OECD to MNEs operating in their territory to observe the Guidelines as annexed thereto, the OECD Guidelines for MNEs.

Governments identified a common interest in encouraging the positive contributions of MNEs to social progress and to minimize and resolve problems that could arise due to their international structure and to contribute to improving the foreign investment climate.[35] The OECD Guidelines for MNEs were intended as part of a framework comprising interrelated and complementary instruments. The OECD Council promulgated two other decisions simultaneously, as part of this framework, relating to national treatment for foreign-controlled entities and international investment incentives and disincentives.[36]

The OECD Guidelines for MNEs were thus adopted by States as joint recommendations to the MNEs that operated in their territories. The Guidelines introduced international standards on the activities of MNEs. They established that enterprises should 'take fully into account established general policy objectives of Member countries in which they operate [...] in particular, give due consideration to those countries' aims and priorities with regards to economic and social process'. It also addressed the disclosure of information, competition, financing, taxation, employment and industrial relations, and science and technology. The Guidelines sought to correct[37] the conduct of MNEs, but did not levy sanctions for non-compliance. While their promotion by States was mandatory, the Guidelines stipulate that observance by MNEs was 'voluntary and not legally enforceable'.[38]

In a separate decision related to intergovernmental consultation procedures, the Council established a follow-up and consultation procedure allowing for discussions on the application of the Guidelines by individual MNEs. The purpose of the consultations was not to evaluate the individual conduct of MNEs, but to express views, and to provide understanding and clarification of the Guidelines that would inform the 1979 review of the Guidelines.[39] The Commission was not authorized to issue conclusions on the conduct of individual enterprises.[40] In 1984, the Members of the OECD agreed to establish a complaints mechanism in each government, the so-called National Contact Points (NCPs), that were tasked to not only promote the OECD Guidelines, but also 'to contribute to the solution of problems that may arise' related to the observance of the Guidelines.[41]

Another international initiative to regulate the conduct of business enterprises was adopted in 1977, the (then) EEC code for South Africa (also known as the 'Anti-Apartheid code'). The 'Anti-Apartheid code' was a foreign policy document[42] setting the expectation that MNEs uphold specified industrial relations, employment and social policies with regards to their 'Black African' employees. The purpose was to mitigate the effect of apartheid and segregation policies in South Africa.[43]

In 1981, the World Health Organization (WHO) launched the International Code of Marketing of Breast Milk Substitutes. This international code was narrowly focused on infant formula. The WHO enacted the code on the face of evidence that certain Western business enterprises, including Nestle, employed intense advertising and marketing methods to promote instant formula in developing countries.[44] These methods, which encompassed mass campaigning, free samples and the so-called 'mother-craft nurses' promoting the formula at health care facilities, failed to inform about the conditions under which the instant formula could be used safely and effectively. Due to poverty, illiteracy and unsanitary conditions, misuse became common, and this transformed the infant formula into a potentially hazardous substance.[45]

These first international codes of conduct articulate principles as applicable governments and transnational corporations in order to improve relations between each other in the areas of investment and economic development.[46] States were the primary addresses of the codes, and the recommendations by States set out in these codes addressed business enterprises indirectly. The codes were an attempt to achieve greater coherency in domestic policies related to business enterprises and foreign direct investment. Where these codes were meant to regulate the responsibilities of business enterprises in relation to human rights, this was only with regards to a limited range of labour and workers' rights. Negotiated within multilateral settings and between States, the codes had an international-governmental and public character.[47] These successes have been attributed, in part, to the membership composition,[48] and business participation in these processes. Business enterprises were generally excluded from participating, not without consequences.[49]

The 1980s-1990s: globalization and the CSR movement

The regulatory challenges posed by globalization: closing the gaps

The concerns about powerful MNEs having negative impacts on national development agendas subsided in the 1980s.[50] The 1980s was a decade of economic regulatory reforms and shifts in regulatory approaches.[51] State policies in the 1960s and early 1970s were set out to control and regulate the activities of business enterprises and foreign direct investment.[52] By the early 1980s, policies had shifted towards neoliberalist-inspired de-regulatory, market-friendly policies and processes. 'De-regulation' involved the withdrawal of the State from certain areas of the economy by relaxing or removing regulations and the opening up of certain industries to competition.[53] The privatization[54] of certain government activities and the subcontracting of some of these to private service providers was part of this trend. Certain public regulatory functions were delegated to public bodies and agencies operating autonomously from government. This involved a transfer of regulatory authority from States to non-state actors.[55] 'De-regulation' at national level was accompanied by 're-regulation' that involved the strengthening of rules at multiple levels, from the local to the international, to facilitate and protect economic prerogatives.[56]

Nearing the end of the 1980s, neoliberal policies and reform programs were widespread.[57] These programs were generally associated with dis-embedding or economic liberalization.[58] Implementation varied in both the North and South, however, according to the model of capitalism and local and industrial contexts.[59] The reform programs accelerated after the collapse of the Soviet economic model in 1989.[60] They involved far-reaching State policies of privatization and de-regulation. These were promoted and, on occasion, imposed on debt-ridden countries by the International Monetary Fund and the World Bank as a condition for financial support, in certain cases with detrimental results.[61] These programs brought the 'market-fundamentalist'-inspired policies set out in the Washington Consensus to reality, also in the developing world.[62]

International regimes of trade, finance and investment, as organized through the mechanisms of the Bretton Woods Institutions and from 1995 onwards, the World Trade Organisation (WTO), created a permissive environment for the emergence of international transaction flows.[63] Controls on currency exchanges and capital movements were lifted. Cross-border financial and capital flows increased significantly.[64] Successive negotiation rounds of the former General Agreements on Trade and Tariffs (GATT) had facilitated free trade and the reduction of trade barriers. This contributed to increased trade in goods, services and capital. The global Foreign Direct Investment (FDI) regime through Bilateral Investment Treaties (BITs), Foreign Trade Agreements (FTAs), and other International Trade Agreements (ITAs) consolidated far-reaching, legally enforceable protections of investor's interests, creating favourable conditions for FDI investment flows.[65] Legal protections granted through the intellectual property regimes (e.g. the Agreement on Trade-Related Aspects of Intellectual Property Rights (TRIPS) agreement of the WTO) allowed enterprises to exploit and reap the economic benefits of their inventions, at least for a certain time period.[66]

These global regimes created favourable environments that allowed business enterprises to grow and their power to rise to unprecedented levels.[67] Advances in technology, transportations, telecommunications[68] and financial instruments reduced the costs of investing abroad. Changes in production systems and the vertical integration of production flows and transactional costs into companies created economic incentives to engage in profit-creating activities abroad.[69] Business enterprises served as vehicles for the movement of foreign capital, currency and management to all corners of the world. Their cross-border investments drove the flow of capital, goods and ideas on a global scale. By linking different production sites and locations, business enterprises contributed to wider patterns of social, political and economic integration. Companies experienced incremental growth in size, geographical spread, economic power and influence.[70]

While business enterprises had been perceived in the 1970s as evil creatures eager to make profits at any cost, by the 1980s and 1990s they were viewed more positively as embodiments of progress, competitiveness and globalization.[71] This perception corresponded to the underlying neoliberal policies according to which business enterprises, as a source of jobs, capital, technology and investment, made significant contributions to national economic growth. This growth could potentially promote the socioeconomic conditions conducive to the realization of a wide range of human rights, including the economic rights to an adequate standard of living and the right to development.[72,73] Such positive impacts were far from self-evident, though. As studies have shown, economic growth would not automatically translate into progress,[74] and, in fact, could potentially have detrimental effects on human rights.[75]

Globalization has been paired with disparities in the distribution of these benefits globally, and to developing countries in particular. There were established concerns that developing 'host' States were in a worse position to mitigate the adverse effects of globalization.[76] In the pursuit of a neoliberal reform agenda and economic prosperity, certain countries lacked the economic and/or political incentives or capacity to impose and enforce human rights on business enterprises. Institutional capacity to discipline powerful corporations could be lacking as a result of corruption, a weak rule of law and/or weak democratic control.[77] Resource-rich countries in development frequently suffered the so-called 'resource curse' and ended up 'blighted by inequality and bad governance'.[78] Implementation gaps more generally have been attributed to States' changing regulatory role and an alleged loss of capacity to steer the market forces and capital flows that globalization unleashed towards public interest objectives.[79]

By the time globalization entered into an advanced stage, in the 1990s, its true negative effects[80] had become increasingly visible. A series of events involving MNEs with high public profiles drew public attention to the adverse human rights impacts caused by these enterprises themselves, or more commonly, their involvement in human rights violations by other actors, including grave human rights violations by governments in high-risk areas. The 1984 Bhopal disaster is one example of an event causing poisonous gas to leak from a pesticide plant operated by Union Carbide India Ltd in Bhopal, resulting in over 7,000 deaths and hundreds of thousands injured. Other cases involving Shell, Rio Tinto, Nike and other large multinationals also exposed the prevalence of implementation gaps in domestic jurisdictions. States had ratified and committed to international human rights law and assumed a primary obligation to protect human rights against infringements by business enterprises. The willingness, capacity and autonomy[81] of States to govern in the interest of human rights seemed relegated to the interest and demands of business enterprises, investors and markets.

Business enterprises reaped great benefits from arranging their business activities and operations in ways that allowed them to escape the regulatory grip of any single State or group of States.[82] The corporate legal structures and mobility were used to their commercial advantage by descending their production, activities, operations and money to the most favourable regulatory regimes. Business enterprises engaged in strategic manoeuvring to take optimal advantage of variations between national regulatory regimes. Often combined with rent-seeking behaviour and cronyism, this exacerbated competition between States in certain cases. States sought to retain or attract foreign investment through loosening regulatory economic and social restraints on companies. Examples are exemptions from tax and labour laws and free trade conditions in export processing zones as well as favourable safety, labour and environmental regulations.[83] This raised concerns about the so-called race to the bottom, which is well documented in the literature, at least in theory.[84]

There were also concerns about the State capacity, and potentially autonomy to regulate in the public interest, being affected by the obligations and commitments of States under BITs and FTAs. After the first BIT was signed in 1959, the protection and promotion of FDI came to be governed through a multifaceted, multilayered and increasingly complex network of International Investment Agreements (IIAs).[85] This is in part because previous attempts to negotiate a multilateral investment treaty failed.[86] The triumph of the market capitalism model from the 1980s until the end of the 1990s triggered a surge in the number of BITs.[87] BITs afforded foreign investors, prima facie, extensive one-sided protections of their economic expectations without imposing obligations. These were guarded through an investor-to-state dispute mechanism agreed to by the parties.[88] The potential economic and political costs incurred by FDI arbitration potentially caused a 'regulatory chill' on national regulation. This meant that States were unwilling to enact regulation, design policies in the interest of human rights or to take on new human rights obligations in fear of costly lawsuits from investors.[89]

In the context of perceived and actual cases demonstrating negative effects of economic forces and actors on human rights, combined with the regulatory vacuum at the domestic and international level that left the adverse human rights impacts of business enterprises largely unattended to, a new wave of social activism ensued in an attempt to regain social control over these forces. An increasing number of international and globally active non-governmental organizations (NGOs)[90] began to target markets and business enterprises directly, rather than indirectly through states and conventional political means at the national level. Grass-root human rights NGOs demanded greater responsibility and accountability from business enterprises for their adverse human rights impacts. Technological developments facilitated widespread media coverage of corporate abuses on a global scale, giving greater visibility to NGOs' cause. NGOs became empowered with new tools and platforms to retrieve and distribute information, foster awareness, mobilize support and leverage public debates.

NGOs employed strategies and confrontational tactics[91] that went beyond traditional tools of awareness raising.[92] Examples are public chastisement, demonstrations, inflicting reputational damage, consumer boycotts,[93] shareholder activism and divestments. These were intended to incite business enterprises to change their behaviour, *inter alia*, by leveraging their cost-benefit analysis of non-compliance and to engage them in the creation of international codes. Significant economic, political and moral pressures came to bear on business enterprises and mounted as consumers, investors and trade unions also became more diligent in evaluating their social performance.[94] There was a tendency for NGO and consumer activism to target renowned multinationals,[95] which were especially vulnerable to such pressures,[96] as well as specific products and sectors.[97]

A pioneering initiative in the human rights domain, which relied on shareholder activism to leverage corporate behaviour, was the Sullivan Principles. Initiated by anti-apartheid activist Reverent Leon Sullivan in 1977, the Sullivan Principles specified six operating principles relating non-discriminatory labour standards of US corporations conducting business in South Africa. These principles included non-segregation in work facilities, equal and fair employment practices of all employees, equal pay for equal or comparable work and others. Sullivan used his position as a member of General Motors, one of the largest employers of black workers in South Africa at the time, to get companies to publicly endorse and implement the six Sullivan Principles.[98] A new requirement was added in 1984 that business enterprises engage in political activism. It challenged the commonly held view that business enterprises should not interfere in the internal domestic affairs of a host country.[99] This is said to have contributed to the Principles themselves enjoying limited success,[100] although the Sullivan Principles served as a precursor for other initiatives, including the 1984 MacBride Principles relating to the conduct of business enterprises in Northern Ireland.[101]

The CSR movement

Within this context and in response to social pressure,[102] business enterprises started to embrace the concept of CSR[103] in the late 1980s to 1990s. While there was potentially a compelling business case for CSR (e.g. improved market image, employment morale, insurance premiums, consumer confidence, avoiding legal costs, maintaining long-term competitiveness, etc.), it had not been substantiated at the time. Imperatives for CSR were mainly political for this reason.[104] CSR presented a strategic tool for companies to accommodate external NGO and consumer pressures by displaying their commitment to human rights and demonstrating a capacity to self-regulate. Codes of conduct could create positive perceptions of their policies and actions in the eyes of the public affected by their activities.[105] CSR also served as a means to preempt external legal regulation and accountability at the national and international level for which many NGOs advocated.[106] Business enterprises presented private and self-regulation as an alternative and sufficient tool to fill the regulatory void.

Individual codes adopted by companies unilaterally and industry-wide codes undertaken jointly by companies or by an association representing a particular industry[107] figured prominently initially.[108] The uptake and substance of these codes were not uniform across countries. Codes emerged in the US at first, and later in Europe.[109] The national institutional environment in the US is said to have been more conducive to MNEs assuming explicit responsibility through voluntary commitment, programs and strategies as compared to European countries.[110] Industry-wide codes were adopted at the regional and the international level. An early example is the 1975 International Council of Infant Food Industries (ICIFI) code of business ethics. The self-regulatory approaches drew from the scholarly works in business management and found a basis in ethics, corporate citizenship and the triple-bottom line concept.[111]

The CSR agenda then covered only a few of the broad range and diverse aspects of CSR issues that the concept encompasses today. These issues were mainly environmental and social.[112] The social aspect of CSR furthermore was confined to only a limited range of labour issues.[113] This has been explained in relation to the strategic approaches to CSR prevalent in the 1970s to the 1980s, which were reactive. Codes of conduct tended to emerge especially in those industries that sold their products on consumer markets and that for this reason were especially vulnerable to social and consumer pressure. Examples of these industries are apparel, carpets, retail, tourism, electronics and the coffee industry.[114] The codes tended to focus on labour rights, and child labour in particular, because of the relatively high (child) labour intensity of these industries and their global supply chains.[115] Western companies often extended the scope of their codes to cover labour issues that they may be involved in through their suppliers and contracts.[116] The ILO's core labour standards, as codified in the ILO Labor Conventions relating to children, forced labour, freedom of association, collective bargaining and discrimination issues, often served as a reference.[117]

In the 1990s, the integrity of these responsive displays of CSR and self-regulation approaches became increasingly questioned.[118] Perceptions and exposures of actual business malpractices led to accusations of self-regulation amounting to nothing more than 'public relations'[119] and 'green-washing'[120] exercises.[121] This critique was also directed at the proliferation of codes that varied greatly in order to respond to issues and stakeholder concerns, and the fact also that these did not address these concerns in a comprehensive and objective manner. The actual implementation of the codes in the workplace and supply chains was deemed inadequate, hence leaving the substance of codes meaningless in practice.[122] Independent verification and monitoring mechanisms that could expose these shortcomings in performance and encourage compliance were often lacking or insufficient.[123]

In what has been perceived as an attempt to overcome the limitations of self-regulation, as well as those of government regulation,[124] regulatory approaches took a turn to civil regulation and multi-stakeholder initiatives.[125] If business enterprises sought self-regulation, NGOs collaborated with business enterprises in the development of new regulatory arrangements to govern this change of practices in a manner externally perceived as legitimate.[126] Also, multi-stakeholder initiatives were created to improve both the legitimacy and quality of CSR activities. The engagement of a broad range of stakeholder interests other than business in decision-making made these initiatives seem more credible.[127,128] The initiatives were intended to assist business enterprises in improving their CSR policies and practices for a more systematic integration of CSR within corporate structures.[129] They developed standards and systems for monitoring, verification and reporting.[130]

The Kimberley Process, a multi-stakeholder process engaging governments, industry and civil society, was created to control the flow of so-called conflict diamonds that are used by rebels to finance war. The impetus for this initiative was a report by Amnesty International exposing the role of the diamond industry in fuelling bloody armed conflict in Sierra Leone through the purchase of these diamonds.[131] The Fair Labor Association (FLA), another multi-stakeholder initiative in the apparel and footwear industries, was created in response to public discontent about sweatshop practices in the supply chain of key brands involving Nike, Wall-Mart and GAP.[132] Other examples of multi-stakeholder initiatives are the Global Network Initiative (GNI), the Global Reporting Initiative (GRI), accounting schemes (e.g. SA8000) and standard-setting and monitoring schemes (e.g. the Ethical Trading Initiative). Certain multi-stakeholder initiatives were also created to harmonize and standardize a proliferation of standards creating confusion and possibly imposing diverging and conflicting requirements on companies.[133]

The UN Global Compact (the UNGC) was created in 2000 as a network-model organization to promote constructive engagement between powerful business and market leaders and other actors, including NGOs, around best practices based on the UNGC Principles. Business enterprises that voluntarily join the initiative, embrace, support and enact within their sphere of influence a set of ten core principles in the areas of human rights, labour standards, the environment and anti-corruption. The aim of the UNGC was, through social learning and accumulated business experiences, to arrive at a common understanding of these Principles and desired best practices. The initiative sought to induce change in corporate behaviour through such learning and the internalization of the Principles in business enterprises, conforming to best practices.[134]

Multi-stakeholder initiatives involved a cooperative engagement between State and non-State actors, including NGOs, companies, business associations and governmental and intergovernmental organizations.[135] The active participation by certain business enterprises in these initiatives has been explained as having a clear interest in not only averting criticism, but also in leveraging the CSR movement, or even by taking a lead in order to shape the CSR agenda at their convenience.[136] New academic theories signalled the significance of stakeholder engagement and the clear strategic, organizational and economic benefits that can be gained through such proactive engagement.[137] The role of business enterprises alongside NGOs and citizens in 'good governance' was supported by the Commission on Global Governance in its 1995 report,[138] in which it called for 'more inclusive and more participatory mechanisms of global governance that included not only the traditional State-based actors but also NGOs, citizen movements and TNCs'.[139]

While these multi-stakeholder initiatives emerged in part to improve the quality of self-regulation, they came to be perceived as inhibiting similar shortcomings.[140] Multi-stakeholder initiatives reached limited scale in efforts.[141] They engaged only a small portion of the tens of thousands of business enterprises that spanned the globe, and their hundreds of thousands of affiliates and suppliers. They also addressed only those initiatives that decided to join the initiatives on a voluntary basis.[142] Corporate laggards thus fell outside their scope. The companies tended to belong to certain sectors and firm categories particularly sensitive to brand reputation.[143] The adverse impacts of business enterprises operating in other sectors and contexts, and beyond their supply chains were thus left largely unregulated and unaccounted for by these multi-stakeholder initiatives.

Critique about weak standards and procedures for monitoring and verifying compliance also figured prominently.[144] The UNGC lacked such procedures and faced accusations for assisting signatory business enterprises with half-hearted CSR performances in 'blue-washing' their public image by associating themselves with the blue flag of the UN.[145] Other multi-stakeholder initiatives were poorly implemented.[146] This was in part because they were responsive to a wide range of issues. Monitoring actual compliance with all these issues throughout vast corporate structures and complex global supply chains proved highly challenging.[147]

> Given the scale and international reach of TNC activities, the costs involved, and the reliance on commercial auditing techniques and analytical frameworks that often ignore the root causes of non-compliance and fail to obtain reliable information from workers and managers, mainstream monitoring and reporting often simply scratch the surface.[148]

The standards and systems that multi-stakeholder initiatives developed were considered 'relatively superficial'.[149]

There were also concerns that CSR standards and procedures were ineffective and had adverse implications for workers, business enterprises and governments in the Global South.[150] Where the design of multi-stakeholder initiatives reflected the interests and agendas of Northern actors, the standards and measurement were not necessarily relevant or appropriate to the priorities, concerns and problems of southern workers.[151] The institutional and economic conditions in developing countries made for an environment that was hardly conducive to achieving progress on CSR.[152] Where standards and practices are incompatible with domestic laws, or inappropriate to local practices and traditions, this could incite non-compliance. Southern firms have, relative to companies in the North, also lesser capacities to comply.

The challenges of southern firms were amplified by the need to abide by a growing number of standards and processes imposing diverging and contradicting requirements. This risked introducing confusion and enhancing the cost of doing business considerably. Multi-stakeholder initiatives were charged with having protectionist implications by creating non-tariff barriers or obstructing access to global markets for such southern firms.[153] Also more generally, the growing body of multi-stakeholder initiatives was perceived as problematic. This was especially the case because there were significant differences between the substantive CSR standards, approaches and methods and levels of stakeholder involvement of these initiatives.[154] Some initiatives were said to be in competition with other initiatives for influence, authority and business adherence.[155]

Multi-stakeholder initiatives were also considered lacking in legitimacy and democratic governance. Concerns were raised relating to participation, representativeness, and accountability. Stakeholder participation was not perceived as 'genuine'. There were imbalances in the participation of different stakeholders' interests and North/South interests.[156] In certain initiatives, the governance structure, design and implementation processes exhibited a clear business interest.[157] Calls were made for an expansion of stakeholder participation in all stages of verification, monitoring and certification processes, and at all levels. Some argued that both NGOs and business enterprises are unaccountable and not legitimate representatives of the public interest. Multi-stakeholder initiatives were considered as 'largely detached from democratic processes and public policy'.[158] There were also calls for complaint mechanisms to redress corporate malpractices.[159]

The corporate accountability and the business and human rights movement

Concerns resulted in efforts being reframed and redirected towards enhancing corporate accountability, including through law and public policy. The corporate accountability movement has been identified as the main driving force behind this shift. The quest for accountability grew in strength and legitimacy as concerns about the credibility of multi-stakeholder initiatives increased. The rise of the accountability movement marked the beginning of a new phase in which processes were initiated at the national, regional and international level to strengthen the law and enforcement of business responsibilities in relation to human rights, and in which also the legal BHR discourse took flight.

The accountability movement had emerged around the same time as, and had evolved in parallel to, the CSR movement, also in response to similar concerns about the globalization's detrimental effects. It incorporated ideas of the human rights approach to development and 'anti- or alternative globalization',[160] hence it differed from the CSR movement in significant aspects. The ideas of the human rights-based approach, which the accountability movement incorporates and that had gained traction in policies and practice after the end of the Cold War, sets the realization of human rights as the objective of development.[161] It applies the human rights discourse, which has its foundation in law at the national, regional and international levels.[162] Accountability is understood in terms of legal justiciability, however alternative approaches that rely on performance standards and employ monitoring, reporting, public debate, and citizen participation to determine conformity were also relied upon as complementary means to operationalize the rights-based approach.[163]

The BHR discourse,[164] which originated from the works of human rights legal scholars and the activities of human rights advocates, is primarily concerned with the victims and impaired communities. It responds to their quest for corporate accountability for the prevention and mitigation of negative impacts on their human rights, and legal responsibility for actual impacts the company caused or to which it contributed. The responsibilities of business enterprises are articulated by reference to universal human rights principles codified in international human rights instruments. The rationale is that these instruments provide a clear basis for remedies and justice.[165] The BHR discourse furthermore views an important role for businesses, States and NGOs in benchmarking the performance of businesses against 'universally recognized human rights principles embodied in a key set of treaties'.[166]

The accountability movement and those supportive of the BHR discourse were driving legislative and policy action at the national, regional, international and global levels to advance corporate accountability.

In the 1990s, certain NGOs and lawyers advocated for criminal accountability for business enterprises before the International Criminal Court (the ICC).[167] This prompted France to issue a proposal at the 1998 Rome Diplomatic Conference on the establishment of the ICC to include a provision in the Rome Statute that would grant the ICC jurisdiction over juridical persons.[168] This proposal triggered deeply diverging responses. Amongst the opponents were countries whose domestic criminal law did not provide for corporate liability for international crimes. It followed from the concept of complementarity[169] that the ICC would gain jurisdiction automatically if a company would commit a crime in a State's jurisdiction and this country would be unable to carry out the prosecution. The proposal was eventually withdrawn, after it had become clear that no consensus could be reached in the short time span foreseen for the negotiations. The ICC was granted jurisdiction over natural persons only.[170]

The signing of the ICC gave impetus for national jurisdictions to create new avenues for corporate criminal liability for violations of international crimes. In certain jurisdictions, these avenues were created incidentally[171] through the implementation of the Statute of the ICC and the integration of its provisions in national criminal law. Where national criminal laws applied the same standards to individual and legal persons, the incorporation of the ICC Statute in these laws extended responsibility and liability for international crimes to corporations.[172] In other jurisdictions, criminal codes were amended in order to create new causes of action for prosecuting also legal persons for violations of international crimes under national criminal law. These developments enable victims to sue corporations under national law for having committed an international crime that is codified in the Rome Statute. This possibility remains theoretical, however, since no cases have been brought on this basis thus far.[173]

The incorporation of the ICC into national criminal laws has had some influence on the development of national criminal law norms. National judges have turned to the jurisprudence and law of the ICC for guidance when developing concepts for attributing criminal liability to corporations and corporate officers under national criminal laws. National courts have also drawn from the jurisprudence of the Nuremberg Trials in the post WW-II period and the jurisprudence of the ad hoc international criminal tribunals on individual liability that has been developed by the International Criminal Tribunal for the former Yugoslavia, the International Criminal Tribunal for Rwanda and the Special Court for Sierra Leone.[174]

In the late 1990s, NGOs began to rely on civil law avenues in national jurisdictions of Western 'host' States to challenge business conduct. In continental Europe, tort claims alleged 'negligence' of a parent company involving its subsidiary, 'complicity' or vicarious liability based on 'agency' in human rights abuses.[175] In the Americas, hopes were vested on the Alien Tort Claims Act (ATCA), a jurisdictional Statute created in 1789 that allowed foreign nationals to sue foreign nationals for an alleged tort committed in violation of international customary law norms.[176] Unocal, Royal Dutch Shell, Coca Cola, Union Carbide, Drummond and Daimler Chrysler were sued in court and faced allegations of complicity in egregious human rights violations of governments, including torture, extra-judicial killings, kidnapping, murder, battery and assault.[177] The ATCA was rediscovered in the 1980s, after its existence having been unnoticed for over a century.[178] The ATCA's ambiguity in relation to its origins and intended purpose created scope for the ATCA to take on a judicial function in providing a civil law avenue in the aforementioned scenarios. This same ambiguity contributed to the ATCA losing in functional importance later on, however, as judges became more cautious in their interpretation of the ATCA's jurisdictional scope, in order to not overstep their judicial mandate by creating (extraterritorial) legal effects where none may have been intended by the US Congress. Such legal effects could furthermore create frictions in the relation with foreign nations and go against the international comity that the ATCA was allegedly set out to promote.[179]

In *Sosa*, the US Supreme Court affirmed that the ATCA extends jurisdiction only to a small category of egregious human rights abuses falling within the ambit of the law of nations, those 'accepted by the civilized world and defined with specificity comparable to the features of the 18th century paradigms'.[180] Precarious was the landmark decision of *Kiobel v. Royal Dutch Petroleum* in 2013, in which the US Supreme Court ruled that a 'presumption against extraterritoriality' applied to the ATCA, excluding from ATCA's applicable scope those cases that do not sufficiently 'touch and concern' the US. Most cases have been dismissed or ended in a settlement. Also in light of the significant hurdles that victims face, which are jurisdictional, substantive, procedural and practical, the relevance of the ATCA in providing access to remedies for victims has been depicted as merely existential.[181]

Reform efforts at the national level also attempted at bridging the accountability gap through domestic laws that legally enforced CSR practices. 'Softer' approaches to legalizing corporate responsibilities were adopted. New laws, regulations and judicial practice emerged to legally encourage, permit or oblige business enterprises to discharge social responsibilities.[182] Examples include an interpretation of directors' duties of loyalty and care in company law that permit or require directors to consider social interests in managing their business enterprise;[183] the integration of social concerns into public procurement legislation;[184] the creation of public reporting and disclosure obligations for companies relating to social issues;[185] and legislation on unfair business practices that subjects business enterprises to liability risks for false or misleading statements in their CSR reports.[186] Such soft forms of regulations have been referred to as 'responsive regulation'[187] and 'regulated self-regulation'.[188] States advanced indirect regulation and internal corporate control systems as an adequate substitute to direct command-control regulation. 'According to this logic, the social responsibility of business may be best ensured through persuasion, education and the development of non-state voluntary codes and social standards by "civil society" organizations'.[189]

The 2000s: the business and human rights movement and the UN Norms

The UN Norms

Within the UN, concerns about the influence of business enterprises operating globally propelled interest in codifying legally binding international human rights standards for business enterprises. The Sub-Commission on the Promotion and Protection of Human Rights, a subsidiary body of the former Commission on Human Rights, created a five-member sessional Working Group in 1998 with a mandate to examine the working methods and activities of business enterprises.[190] Initially created for a three-year period, this mandate was extended in 2001 for an additional three years. The Working Group was officially tasked to compile and contribute to drafting relevant human rights norms.[191] This led to the UN Norms.[192] The UN Norms were presented as a restatement of existing international norms[193] and applying the principle that business enterprises

> within their respective spheres of activity and influence [...] have the obligation to promote, secure the fulfilment of, respect, ensure respect of and protect human rights recognized in international as well as national law, including the rights and interests of indigenous peoples and other vulnerable groups.[194]

The Sub-Commission on the Promotion and Protection of Human Rights approved the UN Norms in its Resolution 2003/16, 13 August 2003. In the same Resolution, it transmitted the text to the former Commission on Human Rights for its 'consideration and adoption' and recommended the Commission to invite interested parties to submit comments on the draft text.[195] The latter distanced itself from the initiative, noting that the UN Norms 'contain useful elements and ideas', but 'had not been requested by the Commission and, as a draft proposal, has no legal standing'.[196]

The UN Norms were controversial and unsuccessful in obtaining the backing from the Members of the former UN Commission on Human Rights. States articulated objections on the basis of various considerations. There were concerns among developing states that the UN Norms might de facto transfer the authority for the implementation of human rights standards from States to companies.[197] The UN Norms could undermine their economic interests as host States in case the extension of foreign direct liability would cause divestment and companies to disengage from their country.[198] Developed countries emphasized the State's role as the primary legal actor responsible for the implementation of human rights standards, and regulating the conduct of companies under domestic law. Some objected to the fact that the UN Norms may oblige transnational enterprises to adhere to treaties that did not apply or were not enforced in the countries where they operated.[199]

Certain States were sceptical about the enforcement mechanisms proposed by the UN Norms, and expressed their preference for voluntary initiatives creating awareness. The OECD Guidelines and the ILO Tripartite Declaration were mentioned as successful examples in this regard.[200] The US challenged the legal status of the UN Norms, noting that they 'have no status – legal or otherwise'. It also challenged the democratic nature of the UN Norms, emphasizing how their development fell outside the mandate of the Sub-Commission, and how it 'was undertaken wholly without consideration for the views of the States'.[201] This position was reflected in the Commission's Resolution stating that the UN Norms 'had not been requested by the Commission'.[202]

The rejection by UN Commission of the UN Norms was to a large extent due to the business community's firm opposition to this initiative. Several objections by businesses related to the so-called 'privatisation of human rights', which was explained as the separation of the activities of private business from the duties of the State, the real duty-holder according to business.[203] If the UN Norms were to be given effect as international law, it was argued, business enterprises would be required to assume tasks that should be incumbent on States, for instance balancing decisions, protecting human rights,[204] and exercising the power to determine the substance of the vaguely formulated obligation of conduct.[205] Businesses also noted that the UN Norms' artificial definition of human rights, and its vague provisions 'turn human rights into highly subjective, politicized claims – and this will undermine the credibility of international human rights law that so many people have worked so hard to achieve'.[206] Some argue that these arguments obscured the real intent of business enterprises behind objecting to the UN Norms, i.e. to evade regulation creating corporate legal accountability for human rights.[207]

Civil society made public statements to express their support for the UN Norms, in an attempt to preempt the Commission from acting against this initiative, which they argued 'to be detrimental to the notion of corporate accountability'. NGOs commended the UN Norms as a 'major step forward' in arriving at a common global framework on business and human rights. The contribution of the UN Norms was not to create new legal obligations, they argued, but to add coherence to existing standards. 'The Norms do not create new legal obligations, but simply codify and distil existing obligations under international law as they apply to companies.'[208] NGOs iterated that the UN Norms clearly referred to States as the primary duty bearers for human rights obligations.[209] They restated the nature and scope of the responsibilities of business enterprises as defined in the UN Norms and the potential contribution of the UN Norms to creating favourable environments for business:

> [i]ndeed the entire thrust of the Norms is to encourage the development of stable environments for investment and business, regulated by the rule of law, in which contracts are honored, corruption reduced, and where business enterprises, both foreign and domestic, have clearly defined rights and responsibilities.[210]

The outcome was discouraging for those supportive of the accountability movement. As civil society began to rely on the document as an authoritative interpretation of international human rights law,[211] the Commission distanced itself from it. The latter noted that the UN Norms 'contain useful elements and ideas', but 'had not been requested by the Commission and, as a draft proposal, has no legal standing'.[212] The UN Norms thus never received formal legal authority.[213] The Commission requested the Office of the High Commissioner of Human Rights (OHCHR) to issue a report on human rights and corporations, which was published in February 2005.[214] As the controversies had not been resolved the following year, the Commission requested the creation of the mandate of the SRSG.[215] On 25 July 2005, former UN Secretary-General Kofi Annan appointed Harvard Professor and former UN Assistant Secretary-General for Strategic Planning John Ruggie to the position.[216]

Conclusion

This chapter provided insights into the legalization of business responsibilities for human rights in the CSR and BHR field during the previous decades. It reflected on the first initiatives to regulate the conduct of business enterprises. These originated in the 1970s and emerged out of the quest of developing countries to consolidate their control over the activities of large western companies in their territory and their autonomy to pursue domestic socioeconomic development objectives free from external interference. These countries asserted themselves in intergovernmental fora to create international non-legally binding codes of conducts. Attempts at developing issue-specific agreements were mostly successful and resulted in the adoption of, *inter alia*, the ILO Tripartite Declaration and the OECD Guidelines for MNEs.

The 1980s witnessed a shift towards neoliberalist-inspired reforms of deregulation and privatization across countries at different stages of development. Legal instruments developed that were supportive of trade liberalization, investment and production at the international level. These initiatives contributed to environments conducive for business enterprises to grow in size, geographical spread, economic power and influence. Business enterprises came to be perceived more favourably as engines of growth and prosperity that, as sources of jobs, capital, technology and investment, could make valuable contributions to the realization of a wide range of human rights. This was not automatic, however. These governance gaps became more apparent as NGOs brought to light the involvement of corporations with high public profiles in egregious human rights abuses, exposing the true impacts of globalization on human rights.

Business enterprises started to self-impose CSR responsibilities on a voluntary basis and integrate human rights demands through non-binding individual or industry-wide codes of conduct. These were supplemented by multi-stakeholder initiatives. The UNGC and the Kimberley Process Certification Scheme are two examples of a great diversity[217] of CSR instruments[218,219] that emerged, ranging from corporate codes of conduct and multi-stakeholder initiatives to certification and labelling, model codes, sectorial initiatives, international frameworks and socially responsible investment.[220] These initiatives were driven by the CSR movement, which had gained in strength as a business response to public condemnation of these irresponsible practices and as an attempt to avert legal regulation and accountability by demonstrating a capacity to self-regulate.

The 1990s also witnessed attempts at strengthening corporate accountability for negative impacts on human rights through laws and policies at national and international level. Prominent examples are the reinvigoration of the ATCA for the purpose of corporate civil liability, and the French proposal for the ICC's jurisdiction to extend to legal persons. The accountability movement and the BHR movement were important driving forces behind these initiatives. The BHR movement is more narrowly focused on the quest for corporate accountability for negative human rights impacts through binding laws and access to remedies and justice for victims or impacted communities.[221]

The chapter also reflected on the initiative of the UN Norms, which was an attempt at developing an international soft law document. The drafters of this instrument adhered to a traditional top-down approach to international law making. The UN Norms were an application of a broad selection of international human rights obligations directly to companies, with the aim of binding these companies to human rights and achieve consistency in the international human rights system. This initiative was never accepted by the UN Commission on Human Rights. John Ruggie, who was appointed to SRSG in 2005, distanced himself from the UN Norms and decided not to build further on this initiative. As the next chapter will demonstrate, the SRSG was supportive of a different approach to legalization, one that takes account of the wider (polycentric) governance context and a changing role of business for human rights in a global economy.

Notes

1 A. Ramasastry, *Closing the Governance Gap in the Business and Human Rights Area: Lessons from the Anti-Corruption Movement*, *in* Human Rights Obligations of Business: Beyond the Corporate Responsibility to Respect? (Surya Deva & David Bilchitz eds., Cambridge University Press 2013).
2 Werner J. Feld, Multinational Corporations and UN Politics: The Quest for Codes of Conduct, 5 (Pergamon Press 1980).
3 Some argue that, as a catalyst of economic progress in both home and host countries, companies and their activities could equalize living standards and narrow the economic and social gap. Centre of Transnational Corporations, *International Action on the Problem of Corrupt Practices*, 1 The CTC Reporter, 19 (1977).
4 Sten Niklasson, *The OECD Guidelines for MNEs and the UN Draft Code of Conduct: Some Political Considerations*, *in* Studies in Transnational Economic Law (Horn ed. 1980).
5 Feld, *supra* note 2, at 29.
6 In what has been referred to as social dumping, 'social oppression' was used to depress costs below a 'natural level', facilitating unfair pricing strategies against foreign competitors. Bob Hepple, *A Race to the Top? International Investment Guidelines and Corporate Codes of Conduct (1999)*, 20 Comparative Labor Law & Policy Journal, 347 (1999).
7 Centre of Transnational Corporations, *supra* note 3, at 17.
8 Ramasastry, *supra* note 1, at 165.
9 Declaration on the Establishment of a New International Economic Order, G.A. Res. 3201 (S-VI), U.N. Doc. A/RES/S-6/3201 (1 May 1974).
10 The Declaration stated the following principle with regards to MNCs; 'Regulation and supervision of the activities of transnational corporations by taking measures in the interest of the national economies of the countries where such transnational corporations operate on the basis of the full sovereignty of those countries.' *Id.* Principle 4(g).
11 Charter of Economic Rights and Duties of States, Article 1, G.A. Res. 3281 (XXIX), U.N. Doc. A/RES/29/3281 (12 Dec. 1974).
12 *Id.* art. 2.
13 Draft International Code of Conduct on the Transfer of Technology, U.N. G.A. 40/184. U.N. Doc. Res. A/RES/40/184 (17 Dec. 1985).
14 Restrictive Business Practices, U.N. GA Res. 35/63 U.N. Doc. A/RES/35/63 (5 Dec. 1980).
15 Jeffrey J. Dunoff, et al., International Law: Norms, Actors, Process: A Problem Oriented Approach, 220 (Aspen Publishers 2006).
16 Helen Keller, *Corporate Codes of Conduct and Their Implementation: The Question of Legitimacy*, 9, www.yale.edu/macmillan/Heken_Keller_Paper.pdf.
17 UN Department of Economic and Social Affairs, Multinational corporations in world development (United Nations 1973).
18 Report of the Secretary-General: The Impact of Multinational Corporations on Development and International Relations, UN Economic and Social Council, U.N. Doc. E/5500/Rev.1 ST/ESA/6 (14 June 1974).
19 ECOSOC resolution 1913 (LVII) of 5 December 1974.
20 UN ECOSOC, *Transnational Corporations: Code of Conduct; Formulations by the Chairman*, *in* Horn, 493 (Norbert Horn ed. 1979).
21 Proposed Text of the Draft Code of Conduct on Transnational Corporations, UN ECOSOC, 2d Sess., Annex, U.N. Doc. E/1990/94 (1990).
22 J. Ruggie, Business and Human Rights: The Evolving International Agenda, 2 (John F. Kennedy School of Government, *Corporate Social Responsibility Initiative Working Paper No. 31*, 2007).

23 Ramasastry, *supra* note 1, at 241. Karin Buhmann, *The Development of the 'UN Framework': A Pragmatic Process towards a Pragmatic Output*, *in* The UN Guiding Principles on Business and Human Rights: Foundations and Implementation, 87 (R. Mares ed. 2012).
24 The following three paragraphs originate from: Bijlmakers, et al., Report on Tracking CSR Responses FRAME Deliverable 7.4 (Nov. 2015, 2014), www.fp7-frame.eu/wp-content/uploads/2016/09/Deliverable-7.4.pdf.
25 ILO, *Tripartite Declaration of Principles Concerning Multinational Enterprises and Social Policy*, ILO (2006), www.ilo.org/wcmsp5/groups/public/-ed_emp/-emp_ent/-multi/documents/publication/wcms_094386.pdf.
26 *Id.* ¶ 2.
27 *Id.*
28 *Id.* ¶ 1.
29 *Id.* ¶ 10.
30 *Id.* ¶ 12.
31 The MNE Declaration was amended in 2000, 2006 and 2017. An addendum was added in 2000, recognizing that MNEs should 'fully take into account' the objectives of the 1998 ILO Declaration on Fundamental Principles and Rights at Work. *Id.* Addendum II.
32 Theo W. Vogelaar, *The OECD Guidelines: Their Philosophy, History, Negotiation, Form, Legal Nature, Follow-up Procedures and Review*, *in* Legal Problems of Codes of Conduct for Multinational Enterprises, 130–131 (Norbert Horn ed. 1980).
33 Norbert Horn, Legal Problems of Codes of Conduct for Multinational Enterprises, 4 (Kluwer 1980). Since 1979, the OECD Guidelines for Multinational Enterprises were revised, in 1984, 1991, 2000 and 2011. OECD, Preface, *in* OECD Guidelines for Multinational Enterprises, ¶ 1 (OECD Publishing 2011), http://dx.doi.org/10.1787/9789264115415-en.
34 Vogelaar, *supra* note 32, at 134.
35 *Declaration on International Investment and Multinational Enterprises (21 June 1976)*, *in* Legal Problems of Codes of Conduct for Multinational Enterprises, 452 (Horn ed. 1980).
36 OECD, Preface, OECD Guidelines for Multinational Enterprises, ¶ 5 (OECD Publishing 2011), http://dx.doi.org/10.1787/9789264115415-en.
37 *Id.* at 135.
38 *Id.* preface, ¶ 6.
39 Roger Blanpain, *The OECD Guidelines and Labour Relations: Badger and Beyond*, *in* Legal Problems of Codes of Conduct for Multinational Enterprises, 145, 148 (Kluwer ed. 1980).
40 Decision of the Council on Inter-Governmental Consultation Procedures on the Guidelines for Multinational Enterprises, *in* Legal Problems of Codes of Conduct for Multinational Enterprises, 462 (Horn ed. 1980).
41 John Ruggie & Tamaryn Nelson, *Human Rights and the OECD Guidelines for Multinational Enterprises: Normative Innovations and Implementation Challenges* (John F. Kennedy School of Government, Corporate Social Responsibility Initiative Working Paper No. 66, 2015).
42 Martin Holland, *The EEC Code for South Africa: A Reassessment*, 41 The World Today, at 12 (1985).
43 Hans W. Baade, *Codes of Conduct for Multinational Enterprises: An Introductory Survey*, *in* Legal Problems of Codes of Conduct for Multinational Enterprises, 429 (Kluwer ed. 1980).
44 Kathyn Sikkink, *Codes of Conduct for Transnational Corporations: The Case of the WHO/UNICEF Code*, 40 International Organization, 182 (1986).
45 *Id.*
46 Ramasastry, *supra* note 1, at 241.

47 According to Baade, these instruments share four major specificities: they are the attempt 'to regulate non-state actors; express reservations as to the legal nature of the instruments adopted; firm multilateral governmental pronouncements on an important subject of transnational legal relations; and last but hardly least, follow-up devises involving State action'. Hans W. Baade, *The Legal Effects of Codes of Conduct for MNEs: Commentary, in* Legal Problems of Codes of Conduct for Multinational Enterprises, 7 (Horn ed. 1980).
48 The OECD, whose membership consisted mainly of developed States, presented a forum more congenial to Western interest than the UN with its universal membership. Baade, *supra* note 43, at 416.
49 Jonathan I. Charney, *Transnational Corporations and Developing Public International Law*, Duke Law Journal 748, 750–751, 765 (1983).
50 David Levy & Rami Kaplan, *Corporate Social Responsibility and Theories of Global Governance: Strategic Contestation in Global Issue Arenas in* The Oxford Handbook of Corporate Social Responsibility, 2 (A. Crane, et al. eds. 2008).
51 Keller, *supra* note 16, at 12.
52 Baade, *supra* note 47, at 354.
53 Peter Utting, *Regulating Business Via Multistakeholder Initiatives: A Preliminary Assessment* (UNRISD project on Business Responsibility for Sustainable Development, Technology, Business and Society, 2001), www.unrisd.org/80256B3C005BCCF9/(httpAuxPages)/35F2BD0379CB6647C1256CE6002B70AA/$file/uttngls.pdf.
54 Privatization entails 'the introduction of contracting into public arenas and the delegation of a range of activities (from waste disposal to the running of prisons) to service providers'. Sol Picciotto, Regulating Global Corporate Capitalism, 9 (Cambridge University Press 2011).
55 Peter Utting, *Rethinking Business Regulation: From Self-Regulation to Social Control*, 1 (UNRISD Programme Papers on Technology, Business and Society, Paper No. 15, Sept. 2005), www.unrisd.org/80256B3C005BCCF9/(httpAuxPages)/F02AC3DB0ED406E0C12570A10029BEC8/$file/utting.pdf.
56 Richard Snyder, *After Neoliberalism: The Politics of Reregulation in Mexico*, 51 World Politics (1999). Utting, *id.* at 1.
57 Single European Act, 28 Feb. 1986, O.J. (L 169), Treaty on European Union (Maastricht Treaty), 7 Feb. 1992, O.J. (C 191).
58 Utting, *supra* note 55, at 19.
59 *Id.* at 1.
60 Michael Kerr, et al., Corporate Social Responsibility: A Legal Analysis, 35 (LexisNexis 2009).
61 Stiglitz, Globalization and Its Discontents (W.W. Norton & Company 2003).
62 *Id.* at 74. Joseph Stiglitz, Making Globalization Work (W.W. Norton & Company 2006).
63 J. Ruggie, *International Regimes, Transactions, and Change: Embedded Liberalism in the Postwar Economic Order*, 36 International Regimes, 383 (1982).
64 Picciotto, *supra* note 54, at 261.
65 UNCTAD, Bilateral Investment Treaties 1995–2006: Trends in Investment Rule-making, at 17, UNCTAD/ITE/IIA/2006/5 (2007).
66 Daniele Archibugi & Andrea Filippetti, *The Globalisation of Intellectual Property Rights: Four Learned Lessons and Four Theses*, 1 Global Policy (2010).
67 Kerr, et al., *supra* note 60, at 3.
68 J.A. Zerk, Multinationals and Corporate Social Responsibility: Limitations and Opportunities in International Law (Cambridge University Press 2006).
69 *Id.*
70 This growth does not apply to all business enterprises. Indeed, the landscape of business enterprises is highly diverse, in terms of organizational structure, nature of activities, and clearly, globalization has not affected all business enterprises equally.

The growth of business enterprises relative to that of States is said to have been overestimated. For a critical note, *see* Paul de Grauwe & Filip Camerman, *Are Multinationals Really Bigger Than Nations?*, 4 World Economics (2003).

71 *Id.* at 4.

72 Robert McCorquodale & Richard Fairbrother, *Globalization and Human Rights*, 21 Human Rights Quarterly, 743 (1999).

73 Business enterprises can increase tax revenues, promote a more efficient division of labour, and their investments can contribute to improving 'the balance of payments through import substitution, export generation or efficiency-seeking investment' and further the competitiveness of countries. De Grauwe & Camerman, *supra* note 70, at 173.

74 Utting, *supra* note 55, at 19.

75 As stipulated in the 1996 Human Development Report, examples of unwelcome forms of economic growth are:

> jobless growth, which does not increase employment opportunities; ruthless growth, which is accompanied by rising inequality; voiceless growth, which denies the participation of the most vulnerable communities; rootless growth, which uses inappropriate models transplanted from elsewhere; and futureless growth, which is based on unbridled exploitation of environmental resources.
>
> UNDP, *Human Development Report 2013: The Rise of the South: Human Progress in a Diverse World*, 65 (2013)

76 J. Ruggie, *Taking Embedded Liberalism Global: The Corporate Connection*, at 2 (2002), www.cid.harvard.edu/events/papers/LSE-final.pdf.

77 Liesbeth F. Enneking, Foreign Direct Liability and Beyond: Exploring the Role of Tort Law in Promoting International Corporate Social Responsibility and Accountability (Eleven International Publishing 2012).

78 Cees van Dam, *Tort Law and Human Rights: Brothers in Arms on the Role of Tort Law in the Area of Business and Human Rights*, 3 Journal of European Tort Law, 223 (2011).

79 '[S]tates acting individually are to a growing extent lacking the necessary steering capacity to effectively channel the various processes of globalisation to the benefit of their citizens and in pursuance of the promotion of global public goods'. K. Nowrot, Global Governance and International Law, 14 (Inst. für Wirtschaftsrecht 2004).

80 As noted by Stiglitz, critical perspectives on globalization have pointed to five concerns: the unfair nature of the rules that govern globalization that work in favour of advanced industrial countries and at the expense of poorest countries; the advancement of material values over public interest concerns like the environment; the erosion of developing countries sovereignty and decision-making capacity as a result of the way globalization has been managed; evidence showing that globalization does not benefit all; and the imposition of an Americanization or economic policy or culture on developing countries. Stiglitz, *supra* note 62, at 9.

81 Regulatory autonomy implies the extent to which a State is able to formulate and pursue goals of a public nature.

82 Larry Catá Backer, *On the Evolution of the United Nations 'Protect-Respect-Remedy' Project: The State, the Corporation and Human Rights in a Global Governance Context*, 9 Santa Clara Journal of International Law, 41 (2011).

83 Archibugi & Filippetti, *supra* note 66, at 1.

84 The race to the bottom is condemned widely, even in the FDI community. *See* for example, NAFTA, art. 1114(2);

> The Parties recognize that it is inappropriate to encourage investment by relaxing domestic health, safety or environmental measures. Accordingly, a Party should not waive or otherwise derogate from, or offer to waive or otherwise derogate

from, such measures as an encouragement for the establishment, acquisition, expansion or retention in its territory of an investment of an investor.

NAFTA, 32 International Legal Materials 289 and 605 (1993)

85 Karl P. Sauvant, *The Rise of International Investment Agreements and Investment Disputes*, *in* Appeals Mechanism in International Investment Disputes, 3, 7 (Karl P. Sauvant ed. 2008).
86 For instance, the Multilateral Agreement on Investment (MAI), developed under the auspices of the OECD, was abandoned in 1996. This was after civil society organizations had protested against it out of concern for its adverse effects on human rights, as well as on the capacity of States to satisfy their human rights obligations to ensure economic, social and cultural rights. There was also concern about it creating unequal advantages between a privileged minority and disenfranchised majority. Report of the Subcommission on Prevention of Discrimination and Protection of Minorities on its 50th Sess., 3–28 Aug. 1998, U.N. Doc E/CN.4/1999/4, E/CN.4/Sub.2/1998/45 (30 Sept. 1998).
87 Jeswald W. Salacuse, *The Emerging Global Regime for Investment*, 51 Harvard International Law Journal, 433–434 (2010).
88 *Id.*
89 Jeff Waincymer, *Balancing Property Rights and Human Rights in Expropriation*, *in* Human Rights in International Investment Law and Arbitration (Pierre-Marie Dupuy, et al. eds. 2010). While the right of a country to regulate in the interest of human rights may be recognized in IIAs, concerns partly emanate from perceived structural biases inherent to IIAs that make arbitration awards most likely to be ruled in favour of the investor.
90 Kerr, et al., *supra* note 60, at 37.
91 *See*, David P. Baron, The Industrial Organization of Private Politics (Stanford University 2011).
92 For an extensive database on business and human rights reports covering NGO activities, *see* the Business and Human Rights Documentation (B-HRD) database: www.bhrd.org/fe/keysearch.php?cx=005946333796321323341%3Ayyspjuq2fiy&cof=FORID%3A10&ie=UTF-8&q=campaign&x=0&y=0.
93 *See*, Baron, *supra* note 91, at 13. Also *see* David P. Baron, Private Politics and Private Policy: The Theory of Boycotts (Stanford Graduate School of Business ed. 2002).
94 *Id.* at 828.
95 Levy & Kaplan, *supra* note 50, at 2.
96 Sikkink, *supra* note 44, at 40.
97 Peter Utting & Kate Ives, *The Politics of Corporate Responsibility and the Oil Industry*, 2 Stair, 23 (2006).
98 The Sullivan Principles were originally signed by the following 12 companies: 'American Cyanamid, Burroughs Corporation, Caltex Petroleum Corporation, Citicorp, Ford Motor Company, General Motors Corporation, IBM Corporation, International Harvester Company, Minnesota Mining & Manufacturing Company, Mobil Corporation, Otis Elevator, and Union Carbide Corporation'. S. Prakash Sethi & Oliver F. Williams, *Creating and Implementing Global Codes of Conduct: An Assessment of the Sullivan Principles as a Role Model for Developing International Codes of Conduct – Lessons Learned and Unlearned*, 105 Business and Society Review, 170–171 (2000).
99 S. Prakash & Oliver F. Williams, Economic Imperatives and Ethical Values in Global Business: The South African Experience and International Codes Today, 186 (Kluwer Academic Publisher 2000).
100 This can be explained, as Hepple argues, by the fact that if business enterprises operating in South Africa complied with the Sullivan Principles, this would mean

that they would have to act in breach of apartheid laws. The Sullivan Principles lost credibility because business enterprises were not willing to do so, which resulted in company divestment rather than engagement in the mid-1980s. Hepple, *supra* note 6, at 361. For an analysis of the success of the Sullivan Principles, *see* S. Prakash Sethi, Setting Global Standards: Guidelines for Creating Codes of Conduct in Multinational Corporations (Wiley 2003).

101 The original Sullivan Principles were amended several times before the ending of the programme in 1994. They were re-launched in 1999 as the Global Sullivan Principles of Social Responsibility. They served as a catalyst for other labour-oriented codes of conduct, for instance the 1984 MacBride Principles, the Slepak Principles, the Miller Principles and the Maquiladora Standards of Conduct. Keller, *supra* note 16, at 7–8. Ramasastry, *supra* note 1, at 240.

102 Shamir Rohen, *The De-Radicalization of Corporate Social Responsibility*, 30 Critical Sociology, 671 (2004).

103 Kerr, et al., *supra* note 60, at 35.

104 Levy & Kaplan, *supra* note 50.

105 M. C. Suchman, *Managing Legitimacy: Strategic and institutional Approaches*, 20 Academy of Management Review (1995). M. Rahim, *Raising Corporate Social Responsibility – The 'Legitimacy Approach'*, 9 Macquarie Journal of Business Law, 72 (2012).

106 Rohen, *supra* note 102, at 671.

107 Keller, *supra* note 16, at 17.

108 Shamir Rohen, *Capitalism, Governance and Authority: The Case of Corporate Social Responsibility*, Annual Review of Law and Social Science, 539 (2010).

109 Catherine Langlois & Bodo B. Schlegelmilch, *Do Corporate Codes of Ethics Reflect National Character? Evidence from Europe and the United States*, Fourth Quarter Journal of International Business Studies (1990).

110 Dirk Matten & Jeremy Moon, *'Implicit' and 'Explicit' CSR: A Conceptual Framework for a Comparative Understanding of Corporate Social Responsibility*, 33 Academy of Management Review 2, 404–424 (2008).

111 *See* John Elkington, Cannibals with Forks: The Triple Bottom Line of 21st Century Business (Capstone 2002).

112 The environmental prong of CSR can be linked to the 1992 Earth Summit in Rio de Janeiro and the Agenda 21 that had recognized a role for business and industry in achieving sustainable development. Kerr, et al., *supra* note 60, at 18.

113 Keller, *supra* note 16, at 20.

114 Ans Kolk & Rob Tulder, *Setting New Global Rules? TNCs and Codes of conduct*, 14 Transnational Corporations, 7 (2005).

115 *Id.*

116 Next to labour issues, codes often addressed environmental standards, bribery and corruption and consumer protection. Keller, *supra* note 16, at 18.

117 First codified in ILO Convention No. 138, 182, 29, 87, 98, 100 and 111. In 1998, these labour standards were incorporated in a single normative framework, the ILO Declaration on Fundamental Principles and Rights at Work. *Id.* at 20.

118 Utting, *supra* note 53, at 5–7.

119 For instance, accounting research indicates that corporate representation through formalistic reporting amounts to mere 'public relations' to leverage societal perceptions that the company acts responsibly, i.e. 'to manage public perceptions, to respond to public pressure, or to react to perceived public opinion', without actual improvements in performance. Laufer W., *Social Accountability and Corporate Greenwashing*, 43 Journal of Business Ethics, 255 (2003).

120 The Oxford Dictionary defined the term 'greenwash' as: 'disinformation disseminated by an organization so as to present an environmentally responsible image'. Utting, *supra* note 53, at 539.

121 Rohen, *supra* note 108, at 539.
122 Utting, *supra* note 53, at 6–7.
123 Utting, *supra* note 55, at 2.
124 Utting, *supra* note 53, at 4.
125 *Id.*
126 Baron, *supra* note 91.
127 Keller, *supra* note 16, at 14.
128 The engagement of one or more actors in their design and implementation of codes of conduct has been referred to as 'co-regulation'. If multi-stakeholder initiatives viewed an active or leading role for NGOs and civil society organizations, they were said to involve 'civil regulation'. Utting, *supra* note 53, at 4. Vogel defines 'global civil regulation' as: 'voluntary, private, non-state industry and cross-industry codes that specify the responsibilities of global firms for addressing labor practices, environmental performance, and human rights policies'. David Vogel, *The Private Regulation of Global Corporate Conduct: Achievements and Limitations*, 49 Business Society 68, 68 (2010).
129 Kerr, et al., *supra* note 60, at 15.
130 Utting, *supra* note 55, at 9.
131 Ramasastry, *supra* note 1, at 242.
132 *Id.*
133 Utting, *supra* note 53, at 14.
134 J. Ruggie, *The Global Compact as Learning Network*, 7 Global Governance 4, 371–378 (2001).
135 Utting, *supra* note 55, at 2.
136 *Id.*
137 Utting, *supra* note 53, at 5.
138 *Id.* at 6.
139 *Id.*
140 *Id.* at 22.
141 *Id.* at 12.
142 *Id.* at 12.
143 *Id.* at 12.
144 *Id.* at 18.
145 *Id.* at 16. Oshionebo, *The U.N. Global Compact and Accountability of Transnational Corporations: Separating Myth From Realities*, 19 Florida Journal of International Law 1, 1–38 (2007). Berliner & Prakash, *From Norms to Programs: The United Nations Global Compact and Global Governance*, 6 Regulation & Governance 2, 149–166 (2012).
146 Utting, *supra* note 55, at 8.
147 *Id.* at 8.
148 *Id.* at 9.
149 *Id.* at 7.
150 Utting, *supra* note 53.
151 *Id.* at 20.
152 *Id.* at 20–21.
153 *Id.* at 21.
154 *Id.* at 23–25.
155 L. Fransen, *Why Do Private Governance Organizations Not Converge? A Political-Institutional Analysis of Transnational Labor Standards Regulation*, 24 Governance: An International Journal of Policy, Administration, and Institutions (2011).
156 Utting, *supra* note 55, at 21.
157 Utting, *supra* note 153, at 19.
158 Utting, *supra* note 55, at 9.

159 *Id.* at 7.
160 *Id.* at 18.

> Those calling for a more fundamental reshaping or rolling-back of globalization emphasized the need to reassert social control over corporations via civil society, social movements, national policy and regulations, and international rules designed and implemented by democratic institutions; the downsizing or break-up of corporations; halting altogether certain economic activities that have perverse social and environmental impacts; redirecting state resources and creating a policy environment conducive to local development and small enterprises; subsidiarity; and collective property rights.
>
> Broad cited in: *id*. at 18

161 *Id.* at 18. Overseas Development Institute, *What Can We Do with a Rights-based Approach to Development?*, 1 (Briefing Paper 3, Sept. 1999), *available at* www.odi.org/sites/odi.org.uk/files/odi-assets/publications-opinion-files/2614.pdf.
162 Overseas Development Institute, *id.* at 1.
163 *Id.* at 4.
164 Ramasastry notes that the BHR movement at its inception was 'not a true "movement" but more a set of emerging crises where companies and governments scrambled to respond once their connections to human rights abuses were made public'. Ramasastry, *supra* note 1, at 242.
165 *Id.* at 238.
166 *Id.* at 238.
167 Utting, *supra* note 55, at 6.
168 'Juridical persons' was defined as

> a corporation whose concrete, real or dominant objective is seeking private profit or benefit, and not a State or other public body in exercise of State authority, a public international body or organization registered, and acting under the national law of a State as a non-profit organization.
>
> A. Clapham, Human Rights Obligations of Non-State Actors, 245 (Oxford University Press 2006)

State and public corporations were thus excluded from its scope. Criminal liability was furthermore linked to the criminal liability of a natural person, and more specifically,

> the individual criminal responsibility of a leading member of a corporation who was in a position of control and committed the crimes, acting on behalf of and with the explicit consent of the corporation in the course of its activities.
>
> International Commission of Jurists, Corporate Complicity and Legal Accountability, Volume 2: Criminal Law and International Crimes, 56 (2008), http://icj.wpengine.netdna-cdn.com/wp-content/uploads/2012/06/Vol.2-Corporate-legal-accountability-thematic-report-2008.pdf

169 The Preamble of the ICC Statute states that 'the International Criminal Court established under this Statute shall be complementary to national criminal jurisdictions'. Art. 17.1 (a) stipulates that

> the Court shall determine that a case is inadmissible where: (a) The case is being investigated or prosecuted by a State [that] has jurisdiction over it, unless the State is unwilling or unable genuinely to carry out the investigation or prosecution.
>
> Rome Statute of the International Criminal Court, 17 July 1998

170 *Id.* art 25(1).
171 Foley Hoag LLP, UNEP FI, Banks and Human Rights: A Legal Analysis (2015), www.unepfi.org/fileadmin/documents/BanksandHumanRights.pdf.

172 *Id.* 4. *See* J. Ruggie, *Remarks by Ruggie at Business & Human Rights Seminar Old Billingsgate*, London (8 Dec. 2005), http://business-humanrights.org/en/doc-remarks-by-john-g-ruggie-business-human-rights-seminar-old-billingsgate-london-december-8–2005.

173 Foley Hoag LLP, UNEP FI, *supra* note 171.

174 *Id.*

175 Enneking, *supra* note 77, at 45. Special Representative on the Issue of Human Rights and Transnational Corporations and Other Business Enterprises, Business and human rights: further steps towards the operationalization of the 'protect, respect and remedy' framework, A/HRC/14/27, 20 (9 Apr. 2010) (by John Ruggie).

176 Cees van Dam, *supra* note 78, at 232.

177 As Enneking explains, NGOs resorted to the active pursuit and encouragement of foreign direct liability cases in Western home country tort systems to promote international CSR and accountability. This has been referred to as a trend towards 'transnational human rights litigation'. These strategies had several purposes: to establish corporate accountability for victims of adverse human rights impacts by business enterprises; to incite home states to take political or legislative action to facilitates foreign direct liability cases; and to elicit action by host countries that are unwilling or unable to effectively regulate business activities. Enneking, *supra* note 77, at 495–497.

178 *See* for example, *Doe v. Unocal Corp.*, 110 F. Supp. 2d 1294 (C.D. Cal. 2000), *Sosa v. Alvarez Machain et al.*, 542 US 692 (Sup. Ct. 2004), *Wiwa v. Royal Dutch Petroleum Co*, 226 F 3d 88 (2nd Cir 2000).

179 *Kiobel v. Royal Dutch Petroleum*, 621 F.3d 111 (2d Cir. 2010), at 38.

180 Moreover, as was held in *Sosa*, only a norm that has obtained sufficient 'content and acceptance among civilized nations' can support a cause of action under US federal common law. *Id.*

181 Ruggie notes that 'the mere fact of providing a remedy for certain human rights abuses companies may have committed abroad has made a difference to corporate human rights practices'. *See* J. Ruggie, *Remarks by Ruggie at Business & Human Rights Seminar Old Billingsgate*, London, 186 (8 Dec. 2005), http://business-humanrights.org/en/doc-remarks-by-john-g-ruggie-business-human-rights-seminar-old-billingsgate-london-december-8–2005.

182 Kerr, et al., *supra* note 60.

183 J. Lowry, *The Duty of Loyalty of Company Directors: Bridging the Accountability Gap Through Efficient Disclosure*, 68 The Cambridge Law Journal 3, 607–622 (2009).

184 Sauvant, *supra* note 85, at 3, 7.

185 Tineke Elisabeth Lambooij & N Van Vliet, *Transparency on Corporate Social Responsibility in Annual Reports*, 5 European Company Law (2008).

186 De Tienne & Lewis, *The Pragmatic and Ethical Barriers to Corporate Social Responsibility Disclosure: The Nike Case*, 60 Journal of Business Ethics (2005).

187 Ayres & Braithwaite, Responsive Regulation: Transcending the Deregulation Debate (Oxford University Press 1995).

188 C. Parker, *Meta-regulation: Legal Accountability for Corporate Social Responsibility?*, *in* The New Corporate Accountability: Corporate Social Responsibility and the Law (Doreen McBarnet, et al. eds. 2007). Mares, for instance, has pointed to the so-called approach of 'regulated self-regulation', meaning the application of procedural-type regulation that guides a company's discretion, without regulating CSR directly. Three main practical methods of regulating companies can be identified that fit this approach; the creation of laws that aim for sound internal management systems, social disclosure by companies and obtaining an enabling environment by supporting actors externally to companies. R. Mares, *Global Corporate Social Responsibility, Human Rights and Law: An Interactive Regulatory Perspective on the Voluntary-Mandatory Dichotomy*, 1 Transnational Legal Theory, 240 (2010).

189 Rohen, *supra* note 102, at 678.

190 Report of the Subcommission on Prevention of Discrimination and Protection of Minorities on its 50th Sess., 3–28 Aug. 1998, U.N. Doc E/CN.4/1999/4, E/CN.4/Sub.2/1998/45 (30 Sept. 1998).

191 The Working Group was authorized to compile a list of human rights instruments and norms, to contribute to the drafting of relevant human rights norms, and to '[a]nalyse the possibility of establishing a monitoring mechanism in order to apply sanctions and obtain compensation for infringements committed and damage caused by transnational corporations, and contribute to the drafting of binding norms for that purpose'. U.N. Sub-Commission on the Promotion and Protection of Human Rights Res. 2001/3, The effects of the working methods and activities of transnational corporations on the enjoyment of human rights, U.N. Doc E/CN.4/Sub.2/2001/40 (2001).

192 Sub-Commission on the Promotion and Protection of Human Rights, *Norms on the Responsibilities of Transnational Corporations and Other Business Enterprises with Regard To Human Rights*, E/CN.4/Sub.2/2003/12/Rev.2, approved by U.N. Sub-Commission on the Promotion and Protection of Human Rights by resolution 2003/16, U.N. Doc. E/CN.4/Sub.2/2003/L.11 at 52 (13 Aug. 2003).

193 David Weissbrodt & Muria Kruger, *Norms on the Responsibilities of Transnational Corporations and Other Business Enterprises with Regard to Human Rights*, 97 The American Journal of International Law 901, 912 (2003).

194 Sub-Commission on the promotion and protection of human rights Res. 2003/16, Responsibilities of transnational corporations and other business enterprises with regard to human rights, U.N. Doc. E/CN.4/Sub.2/2003/L.11 (13 Apr. 2003).

195 *Id.*

196 Commission on Human Rights Res. 2004/116: Responsibilities of transnational corporations and related business enterprises with regard to human rights, 56th meeting, E/2004/23 – E/CN.4/2004/127 (20 Apr. 2004).

197 Pini Pavel Miretski & Sasha-Dominik Bachmann, *The UN 'Norms on the Responsibility of Transnational Corporations and Other Business Enterprises with Regard to Human Rights': A Requiem*, 17 Deakin Law Review Volume (2012).

198 *Id.*

199 Facsimile message from the Australian Mission to the United Nations, to OHCHR, *Comments by Australia in Respect of the Report Requested from the Office of the High Commissioner for Human Rights by the Commission on Human Rights in its Decision 2004/116 of 20 April 2004 on Existing Initiatives and Standards Relating to the Responsibility of Transnational Corporations and Related Business Enterprises With Regard to Human Rights* (8 Sept. 2004).

200 Australia argued that the addition of a new monitoring system, as envisaged by the UN Norms, to a treaty body system that already overstretched its capacity. Inadequate enforcement would not only undermine the effectiveness of the UN Norms, but also risks undermining the legitimacy and role of the former Commission on Human Rights, it was argued. *Id.* Letter from The Norwegian Ministry of Foreign Affairs, to OHCHR, *Decision 2004/116 – Responsibilities of transnational corporations and related business enterprises with regard to human rights* (4 Nov. 2004), *available at* www2.ohchr.org/english/issues/globalization/business/docs/norway.pdf.

201 Cited in: Miretski & Bachmann, *supra* note 197.

202 Commission on Human Rights Res. 2004/116: Responsibilities of transnational corporations and related business enterprises with regard to human rights, 56th meeting, E/2004/23 – E/CN.4/2004/127 (20 Apr. 2004).

203 IOE & ICC, *Joint views of the IOE and ICC on the draft 'Norms on the responsibilities of transnational corporations and other business enterprises with regard to human rights'* (2003), www.reports-and-materials.org/sites/default/files/reports-and-materials/IOE-ICC-views-UN-norms-March-2004.doc.

204 *Id.* at 4.
205 *Id.* at 22.
206 *Id.* at 2.
207 David Kinley & Rachel Chambers, *The UN Human Rights Norms for Corporations: The Private Implications of Public International Law*, 45 Human Rights Law Review (2006).
208 *Id.*
209 The UN Norms also makes clear that the privatization of human rights would not diminish a State's obligations. *See* ¶ 19 of the UN Norms;

> Nothing in these Norms shall be construed as diminishing, restricting, or adversely affecting the human rights obligations of States under national and international law, nor shall they be construed as diminishing, restricting, or adversely affecting more protective human rights norms, nor shall they be construed as diminishing, restricting, or adversely affecting other obligations or responsibilities of transnational corporations and other business enterprises in fields other than human rights.
>
> Sub-Commission on the Promotion and Protection of Human Rights, *supra* note 192

210 Civil Society, Statement of Support for the UN Human Rights Norms for Business: To be delivered at the 60th Session of the Commission on Human Rights (15 Mar.–23 Apr. 2004), http://business-humanrights.org/en/nearly-200-ngos-join-in-oral-statement-to-un-commission-on-human-rights-supporting-the-un-norms-on-business-human-rights-0#c39763.
211 *See* ESCR-Net, Corporate Accountability Working Group Part I: The Mandate of the Special Representative Advocacy Guide on Business and Human Rights (2009), https://docs.escr-net.org/usr_doc/ESCRNet_BHRGuideI_Updated_Oct2009_eng_FINAL.pdf.
212 Commission on Human Rights Res. 2004/116: Responsibilities of transnational corporations and related business enterprises with regard to human rights, 56th meeting, E/2004/23 – E/CN.4/2004/127 (20 Apr. 2004).
213 Indeed, the Sub-Commission lacked the legal mandate or authority to create new international human rights obligations. If the UN Norms were to have obtained any form of authoritativeness, it would have had to derive from their acceptance by the former UN Commission on Human Rights, a subsidiary body to the ECOSOC then.
214 Report of the United Nations High Commissioner on Human Rights on the responsibilities of transnational corporations and related business enterprises with regard to human rights, U.N. Doc. E/CN.4/2005/91 (2005).
215 *See* Commission on Human Rights Res. 2005/69: Human Rights and Transnational Corporations and Other Business Enterprises, 59th meeting, E/CN.4/RES/2005/69 (20 Apr. 2005).
216 Prof. Ruggie is the Berthold Beitz Professor in Human Rights and International Affairs at the Kennedy School of Government and an Affiliated Professor in International Legal Studies at Harvard Law School. Previous to his mandate, he served as UN Assistant Secretary-General for Strategic Planning and as Special Advisor of the UN Secretary-General on the UNGC, of which he also was one of the main architects. For details on the bibliography of Prof. Ruggie, *see* www.hks.harvard.edu/m-rcbg/johnruggie/bio.html.
217 Diversity was reflected in the areas covered, origins and objectives of the different instruments. OECD, *Annual Report* 2008, 237 (2008), www.oecd.org/newsroom/40556222.pdf.
218 Deborah Leipziger, The Corporate Social Responsibility Code Book (Greenleaf Publishing 2003).

219 Michael R. Macleod, *Emerging Investor Networks and the Construction of Corporate Social Responsibility*, The Journal of Corporate Citizenship (2009).

220 Classifications and typologies vary. This classification has been provided in the OECD 2008 Annual report. Diversity was reflected in the areas covered, origins and objectives of the different instruments. OECD, *supra* note 217, at 238–239.

221 *Id.* at 238.

2 The UN Guiding Principles on business and human rights

Principled pragmatism and polycentric governance

Introduction

This chapter examines the work of the SRSG in developing the UNGPs, in order to advance towards a more effective global regime for the prevention of, and remedy for, business-related human rights harm, including specific legal measures. This chapter rests on the assumption that in order to understand why and how the UNGPs came about and its potential for fostering change, we should take into account the broader intellectual and global governance context. Since it is the SRSG who developed the UNGPs, it is important to understand the SRSG's views and intentions. The objectives of the UNGPs can only be properly ascertained by reference to the SRSG's approach of 'principled pragmatism' and understanding of CSR as a key component of 'polycentric' governance. The SRSG situates the UNGPs in terms of 'polycentric' global governance and characterizes the UNGPs, too, as polycentric governance. These elements are part of a multifaceted narrative of human rights in the global economy,[1] which furthermore fosters new perspectives to 'legalizing' business responsibilities in relation to human rights.

The SRSG's project and its theoretical foundations

The SRSG links the key problem in the field of business and human rights to globalization, and in particular its economic aspect. Globalization and the expanding power of economic forces and actors have come to pose regulatory challenges to global governance. With operations and relations encompassing the entire globe, business can create both risks and opportunities for the realization of human rights.[2] All companies can affect all human rights, in virtually any type of operational context.[3] Transnational entities, which the SRSG refers to as 'globalisation's most visible embodiment', have an important role to play, not only because of their expanding power, but also because their operating models make the effective governing of these entities and their operations a complex task.[4]

The expanding power of transnational corporations is well documented. The accumulated wealth of these entities, which may exceed that of some States, is illustrative of their international scale and importance.[5] The same holds true for their sheer increase in number,[6] engagement in cross-border activities and share in the movement of capital and technology.[7] Some corporations have adopted so-called 'network-operating models', which involve multiple corporate entities operating within and across different countries in the form of transnational corporate networks.[8] For the purpose of the law, each entity has a separate legal personality. The separate legal personality and the principle of limited liability shield a parent company from legal liability in case a subsidiary entity in the group causes harm to people. The transnational corporate group or network as a whole is not effectively governed by international law.[9]

The *problematique* in the domain of business and human rights thus results from these economic forces and business enterprises, whose activities impact the daily lives of people across different countries, not being embedded in an adequate regulatory framework at the global level. This domain is, according to the SRSG, implicated by gaps in governance:

> The root cause of the business and human rights predicament today lies in the governance gaps created by globalization – between the scope and impact of economic forces and actors, and the capacity of societies to manage their adverse consequences. These governance gaps provide the permissive environment for wrongful acts by companies of all kinds without adequate sanctioning or reparation. How to narrow and ultimately bridge the gaps in relation to human rights is our fundamental challenge.[10]

The SRSG recognized the urgency of addressing these governance gaps. These gaps risked creating social instability and globalization to be unsustainable and ineffective in the long term.[11] The SRSG warns against the tendency of so-called ugly 'isms' of the post-Cold War era, 'protectionism, populism, nationalism, ethnic chauvinism, fanaticism and terrorism', to resurface, unless these regulatory problems are attended to.[12] These nationalist and fundamentalist sympathies and political agendas may revamp as economically disadvantaged but powerful segments of society demand social protection.[13] The SRSG notes how 'embedding global markets in shared values and institutional practices is a far better alternative; contributing to that outcome is the broadest macro objective of this mandate'.[14]

The challenge thus relates to filling the gaps and the institutional misalignments in the regulatory ecosystem for business and human rights. This includes building the interactions between, the capacities of and the incentives structure for States and business enterprises to undertake activities that affect and coordinate the regulation of business conduct in relation to human rights. Some States lack the willingness and/or capacity to effectively regulate business conduct. This is prevalent in areas affected by conflict in which the worst corporate-related human rights abuses take place.[15] These governance gaps not only result from the deficient capabilities of States to take effective regulatory action, but also collective action problems at the international level.[16]

These governance gaps and institutional misalignments cannot be fully appreciated and addressed without taking into consideration the global institutionalized context in which the actors that govern business conduct operate. States are no longer the sole actors that govern in the area of business and human rights, however. In his earlier writings on the 'global public domain',[17] Ruggie explains how a broader institutionalized arena is emerging at the global level in which, apart from States, also non-state actors perform public functions, e.g. IOs, civil society organization and business enterprises. The activities of these State and non-state entities have transforming effects on world policy. The SRSG refers to this process as

> the reconstitution of the global public domain – away from one that equated the 'public' in international politics with states and interstate realm to one in which the very system of states is becoming embedded in a broader, albeit still thin and partial, institutionalized arena concerned with the production of global public goods.[18]

Business enterprises are amongst the 'new' actors and systems that have taken on social roles in this global domain. Their governing activities consist of articulating and enacting CSR expectations through 'private' governance arrangements.[19] Ruggie notes the emergence of a 'new transnational world of transaction flows' as businesses 'have developed and instituted novel management systems for themselves and for relations with their subsidiaries, suppliers, and distributors that they deem necessary given the scope, pace, and complexity of operating in those transactional spaces'.[20] This governance by businesses is 'new' in that it gives business enterprises prominence as governing entities which they did not enjoy previously, and creates new sites from which these businesses and other non-state actors can exercise and expand their global public role.[21]

The SRSG, in application of the notion of 'polycentric' governance, recognizes that business conduct at the global level is shaped by three governance systems:

> The first is the traditional system of public law and governance, domestic and international. Important as it is, by itself it has been unable to do all the heavy lifting on this and many other global policy challenges, ranging from poverty eradication to combating climate change. Indeed, formal state-based multilateralism has become harder, not easier in the past decade or so. The second is a system of civil governance involving stakeholders affected by business enterprises and employing various social compliance mechanisms, such as advocacy campaigns, law suits and other forms of pressure, but also partnering with companies to induce positive change. The third is governance by business enterprises of their own affairs, which internalizes elements of the other two. In the case of multinational corporations, corporate governance so conceived is a distinct transnational law-making system in its own right – the private law of contracts, with direct consequences that can equal and in many

> cases surpass the scale and effectiveness of public governance in particular issue areas.[22]

The SRSG noted that the business and human rights field is 'a microcosm of a larger crisis in contemporary governance'.[23] It is therefore not surprising that the SRSG in constructing the UNGPs took into account global governance's polycentric characteristics. As elaborated below, the SRSG situates the UNGPs in terms of 'polycentric' global governance and characterizes the UNGPs, too, as polycentric governance. The SRSG envisioned that, if the UNGPs were embedded in the business and human rights regulatory ecosystem, 'a new regulatory dynamic' would emerge that would strengthen the positive interactions between the governance systems referred to above. These public and private governance systems would be strengthened under this regulatory dynamic, become better aligned and create positive cumulative effects and change.[24] Such regulatory dynamic was required for each of these governance systems 'to add distinct value for one another's weaknesses, and play mutually reinforcing roles-out of which a more comprehensive and effective global regime might evolve, including specific legal measures'.[25]

Principled pragmatism

The SRSG's approach of principled pragmatism and human rights

The SRSG opted for the approach of 'principled pragmatism', which he defined as an

> unflinching commitment to the principle of strengthening the promotion and protection of human rights as it relates to business, coupled with a pragmatic attachment to what works best in creating change where it matters most in the daily lives of people.[26]

This formulation reflects its dual character: 'principled pragmatism' is both value-based and pragmatic. The promotion and protection of human rights as they relate to business was the SRSG's normative concern and his primary focus of attention went to the pursuit of this long-term aspiration. This pursuit was pragmatic in nature, however; action should be determined by practical circumstances and goals. The SRSG described his main strategic goal as 'achieving the maximum reduction in corporate-related human rights harm in the shortest possible period of time'.[27]

The SRSG did not favour one particular ideological or governance approach to accomplishing this strategic objective. The SRSG did not opt for the legalistic approach that seeks to coerce compliance by business enterprises with minimum human rights standards. Illustrative is the SRSG's rejection of the UN Norms that, as elaborated in the previous chapter, adhered to such a top-down legal approach by seeking to impose a limited range of human rights obligations directly on companies. Nor did the SRSG choose to advance 'corporate voluntarism'. Instead, the SRSG steered a middle course and, drawing from the perspective of polycentric governance, decided to give consideration to all the ways and means that may be relevant for enhancing the realization of human rights by making possible contributions to the reduction of corporate-related harm to human rights.

The SRSG thus concentrated on practical measures that 'provide the best mix of effectiveness and feasibility'.[28] The SRSG elaborated in a letter issued in 2006:

> My mandate, as I read it, is not to devise new ways or grounds for regulating transnational corporations per se; rather, it is to strengthen the promotion and protection of human rights as they relate to transnational corporations and other business enterprises by identifying and advocating the adoption of *whatever* measures work best in creating change where it matters most: in the daily lives of people. This is the 'principled pragmatism' of which I wrote in my report. It has guided me from the moment I accepted this important assignment, and I shall abide by it through to the mandate's end.[29]

It is important to note the SRSG's understanding of human rights, which has been inspired by the writings of Amartya Sen. Sen views human rights as primarily articulations of significant ethical demands, the substantive content of which reflects (and assert the importance of) freedoms of human beings.[30] The recognition of these ethical demands translates into ethical requirements or 'imperfect obligations' on the part of anyone that is in a plausible position to contribute to the realization of these freedoms to be willing to consider seriously doing just that what is reasonably expected of them to do, taking into account the parameters of the cases involved.[31]

The SRSG deliberately opted for a conception of human rights that differs from the one adhered to by the law-centric approach, viewing human rights as legal demands or 'laws in waiting'.[32] This broader conception serves to capture how human rights can be publicly recognized through instruments other than the law. He notes:[33]

> [B]esides, in Amartya Sen's felicitous words, viewing human rights solely as 'parents' or 'progeny' of law would 'unduly constrict' – Sen even uses the term incarcerate – the social logics and processes other than law that drive enduring public recognition of human rights. Human rights are better seen more broadly: as mediators of social relations, especially relations that involve significant power asymmetries, in which hard law is but one part of a larger ecosystem of instruments.

The SRSG's 'principled pragmatism' may be understood as a deliberate attempt to transcend classical legality with a focus on promoting the effectiveness of human rights through practical measures. As elaborated above, global governance is no longer reserved to governments alone. Business enterprises and non-state actors have come to participate in the formulation and enactment of new expectations regarding CSR. The SRSG relied on the notion of 'poly-centric governance' to advance towards business respect for human rights within the global economy.[34] According to Ruggie:

> The idea that business enterprises might have human rights responsibilities independent of legal requirements in their countries of operation is relatively new, in large part a byproduct of the most recent wave of globalization.
>
> The successful expansion of the international human rights regime to encompass business enterprises must activate and mobilize the full array of rationales and institutional means that affect corporate conduct. That is what the United Nations Guiding Principles on Business and Human Rights seek to do.[35]

The SRSG's mandate and principled pragmatism

Principled pragmatism guided the SRSG throughout his mandate. Various facets of the process of developing the PPR Framework and the UNGPs give expression to this approach. At an early stage, the SRSG decided to not recommend the negotiation of a treaty placing binding obligations on business enterprises. The SRSG emphasized the importance of short-term practical measures to address immediate challenges and to provide immediate relief for human rights abuses.[36] The view of the SRSG was that a treaty-making process could take (too) long and risked 'undermining effective shorter-term measures'. The SRSG reasoned that it was in the interest of victims of human rights that results were delivered sooner rather than later, noting that '[e]ven if we were to go down the treaty route, we still need immediate solutions to the escalating challenge of corporate human rights abuses'. The former UN High Commissioner for Human Rights remarked that absent such immediate solutions, 'much damage [to victims] could be done in the meantime'.[37]

The SRSG constructed a knowledge base and forged a consensus around the PRR Framework and the UNGPs through an extensive programme of systemic research and multi-stakeholder consultations.[38] The extensive research was aimed at informing the debate, moderating excessive claims and providing a knowledge foundation that was shared across different stakeholder groups.[39] The UNGPs reflect this knowledge foundation and derive substantive legitimacy[40] from its factual underpinnings. Future debates and collaboration on business and human rights can build on and draw legitimacy from this knowledge foundation.[41]

Another feature of principled pragmatism is the inclusive multi-stakeholder consultative process that the SRSG organized throughout his mandate. The process was open to all stakeholders and highly participatory, engaging participants from the various stakeholders groups, including business enterprises, at all stages of the mandate.[42] According to the SRSG, the UNGPs furthermore were developed through the means of polycentric governance.[43] This approach was a method of garnering legitimacy[44] and support for both the development process and the UNGPs across these stakeholder groups more generally.[45] Appending the influence of business lobbying on derailing the negotiations on the UN Norms,[46] the SRSG attached considerable importance to business involvement.[47] The degree of engagement by business organizations in the process was remarkable[48] and, according to the SRSG, imperative to ensure the buy-in of business enterprises and to secure their commitment to the implementation of the UNGPs.[49]

The multi-stakeholder approach was also aimed at achieving a so-called 'thick stakeholder consensus'.[50] Pauwelyn, Wessel and Wouters describe how a normatively superior benchmark of 'thick stakeholder consensus' is emerging as a 'code of good practice' in new cooperation.[51,52] The concept of 'thick stakeholder consensus' has been contrasted with 'thin state consent', which refers to the State consent that is often viewed as sufficient to justify international law.[53] The underlying presumption is that non-binding instruments and informal modes of cooperation can be constraining in a similar way as traditional international law. These instruments should therefore meet certain essential substantive requirements in order to ensure ex ante and ex post legitimacy and generate legal effects.[54]

And indeed, the SRSG was successful in leveraging the stakeholder consensus into the unanimous endorsement of the UNGPs by the HRC on 16 June 2011. States, civil society and business enterprises seemed aligned and expressed their support for the UNGPs. This act of endorsement by the HRC was unique in that, the SRSG notes, 'it marked the first time that either body "endorsed" a normative text on any subject that governments did not negotiate themselves'.[55] This endorsement furthermore had the positive effect of adding to the authoritativeness of the UNGPs, 'helping to achieve their uptake by other international standard-setting bodies, and embedding them in the global regulatory ecosystem for business and human rights'.[56]

The UNGPs and principled pragmatism

The PRR Framework and the UNGPs integrate the SRSG's view on principled pragmatism. The first section of the UNGP, entitled 'General Principles' reflects this. It provides guidance on how the sections of the UNGP should be interpreted and applied generally.

> These Guiding Principles are grounded in recognition of:
>
> (a) States' existing obligations to respect, protect and fulfil human rights and fundamental freedoms;
> (b) The role of business enterprises as specialized organs of society performing specialized functions, and required to comply with all applicable laws and to respect human rights;
> (c) The need for rights and obligations to be matched to appropriate and effective remedies when breached.

This section suggests that the corporate responsibility to respect human rights should be read in recognition of the foundational structure of the UNGPs which integrates the perspectives of 'principled pragmatism' and polycentric governance.

The role of business enterprises, which is an essential component of this structure, is hierarchically inferior to the role of States, which are recognized as primarily responsible for the realization of human rights and fundamental freedoms.[57] The source and scope of States' obligations are determined by international human rights law. The social role and responsibilities of businesses differ from those of States and reflect their nature as specialized organs of society. These responsibilities reflect the specialized functions businesses perform in society and are of a dual character: (i) to comply with all applicable laws and (ii) to respect human rights. The need for appropriate and effective remedies is cast as a necessary consequence of a breach of human rights or obligations resulting from corporate-related activities.

The General Principles furthermore note that the UNGPs 'should be understood as a coherent whole and should be read, individually and collectively, in terms of their objective'. The UNGPs thereby specify that the UNGPs, and the corporate responsibility to respect human rights, should be interpreted to conform to the circumstances and conditions that the UNGPs specify. They should furthermore be read in light of the UNGPs as a whole and their strategic objective, which the UNGPs define as the pursuit of 'of enhancing standards and practices with regard to business and human rights so as to achieve tangible results for affected individuals and communities, and thereby also contributing to a socially sustainable globalization'.

The General Principles note that: 'Nothing in these Guiding Principles should be read as creating new international obligations, or as limiting or undermining any legal obligations a State may have undertaken or be subject to under international law with regard to human rights.'[58] This provision reflects the understanding that the UNGPs in and by themselves do not create any new international obligations or alter the obligations that States have under international human rights law. The UNGPs instead reflect an interpretation of standards and practices of States and business enterprises as they exist, rather than as they should be, and elaborate on their meaning and implications.[59,60]

The General Principles also indicate that the UNGPs apply generally 'to all States and all business enterprises, both transnational and other, regardless of their size, sector, location, ownership and structure'.

The General Principles furthermore note that:

> These Guiding Principles should be implemented in a non-discriminatory manner, with particular attention to the rights and needs of, as well as the challenges faced by, individuals from groups or populations that may be at heightened risk of becoming vulnerable or marginalized, and with due regard to the different risks that may be faced by women and men.

The UNGPs thereby stipulate the principle of non-discrimination under international human rights law, which entails that human rights are subject to enjoyment without distinction of any kind.[61] The General Principles specify that the UNGPs should be implemented with particular regard to the rights, needs and challenges faced by individuals who belong to groups at heightened risk of becoming vulnerable or marginalized, and that thereby due regard should be had of gender-related risks.

The objectives of the UNGPs

The UNGPs' objectives go well beyond classical legal obligations. They integrate the understanding that there are no 'silver bullets', which a resort to positivist law would be, and that measures should be pragmatic and progress gradual. The UNGPs are presented as a set of 'universally applicable and yet practical Guiding Principles on the effective prevention of, and remedy for, business-related human rights harm'.[62] The UNGPs note:

> The Guiding Principles' normative contribution lies not in the creation of new international law obligations but in elaborating the implications of existing standards and practices for States and businesses; integrating them within a single, logically coherent and comprehensive template; and identifying where the current regime falls short and how it should be improved. Each Principle is accompanied by a commentary further clarifying its meaning and implications.[63]

The PRR Framework and the UNGPs serve several aims. A principle aim is to achieve clarity and convergence among existing and newly emerging standards with regards to business and human rights.[64,65] The scope of this effort is not limited to the identification of existing legal standards and practices in the State-law system. The UNGPs also provide interpretations of emerging norms that State and non-state actors have recognized and accepted through their respective governance systems. The SRSG distilled these interpretations from intense research and stakeholder engagement through multi-stakeholder consultations.[66] The UNGPs thus in and by themselves do not create new standards.

Apart from providing clarity, the UNGPs present a framework for the interaction and reorganization of the expected contributions of key State and non-state actors and their respective governance systems. These contributions take the form of preventative and remedial measures. The PRR Framework organizes these contributions in a template with the view to coordinate the actions of these actors and their respective governance systems. The PRR Framework thus reflects a holistic and coherent template for a better functioning system of preventative and remedial measures. This system not only affects the behaviour of business enterprises, but also the preventative and remedial measures by which this behaviour is governed.

The structure of the PRR Framework rests on three foundational pillars, which the SRSG described as follows:

> The Framework rests on three pillars: the State duty to protect against human rights abuses by third parties, including business; through appropriate policies, regulation, and adjudication; the corporate responsibility to respect human rights, which means to act with due diligence to avoid infringing on the rights of others and to address adverse impacts that occur; and greater access for victims to effective remedy, judicial and non-judicial.

The three pillars thus reflect the different components of a dynamic system of preventative and remedial measures. The pillars are *differentiated* in that each component reflects on the different social role that an actor – State and business enterprises – and their respective governance systems play in regulating business conduct. The duties and responsibilities of States and business enterprises as defined under each pillar correlate with these actors' differing social roles and exist independently of, and do not jeopardize, one another. Moreover, these pillars draw from, but do not change, the rationales and discourses existing within the governance systems of these respective actors.[67] They are also *complementary*: the pillars are connected, interrelated and each is essential in supporting this system.[68] The PRR Framework reflects an international consensus around this regulatory framework and serve as 'an authoritative focal point around which the expectations and actions of relevant stakeholders could converge'.[69]

The UNGPs provide 'concrete and practical recommendations' that actors can rely on for implementing the PRR Framework, and thus serve as a focal point for the *operationalization* on this framework.[70] The UNGPs elaborate on the meaning and implications of these principles for law, policy and practice.[71] They are designed as a platform on which cumulative action can be built. The effective implementation of the UNGPs is expected to foster greater alignment in the interactions between social institutions and actions that cohere and generate reinforcing effects that will cumulate into progress over time.[72] The expectation is that once the actions by States and business enterprises reach a sufficient scale, they may compound into systemic change and, eventually, lead to the institutionalization of a new harmonized global business and human rights regime.[73,74,75]

An institutionalization approach

An important aspect of the SRSG's project was the pursuit of institutionalization of the governance systems affecting business conduct, within a global context. Institutionalization can be characterized by the following elements:

Multifaceted: The UNGPs take into account, and to some extent reflect, the characteristics of the 'global public domain'.[76,77] It is based on a conception of a broader global institutionalized context and States and non-state actors operating within this context performing social roles in governing business conduct.[78] The UNGPs address and reflect these social roles and responsibilities. The UNGPs appreciate these actors and governance systems in all their facets and they are set out to leverage the plurality of institutions, processes and actions affecting and coordinating the regulation of business behaviour, to the extent relevant to achieving progress.

Polycentric: The UNGPs reflect a polycentric governance system. It is organized around the three polycentric systems that govern business conduct and, furthermore, seek to foster greater alignment between these systems and human rights. The UNGPs do not alter but reflect different discourses and rationales of these governance systems and their social roles in regulating business conduct.[79,80] While the UNGPs affirm and seek to reinforce State adherence to their duty to protect, the polycentric governance outlook is not centred on the State and the public-law system. Also part of the polycentric governance mix is the civil governance system and stakeholders affecting business conduct through social compliance mechanisms. The UNGPs also reflect the social role of business enterprises and the understanding that business conduct is shaped by the private law of contract created by companies, which, the SRSG notes, can 'surpass the scale and effectiveness of public governance in particular issue areas'.[81]

Regulatory dynamic: The UNGPs provide an authoritative framework that, once embedded in policy and practise, should foster a regulatory dynamic under which the public and private governance systems (public, civil and corporate) become better aligned and perform mutually reinforcing roles in relation to business and human rights. This regulatory dynamic draws from a 'smart mix of measures' adopted by stakeholders in the pursuit of the common goals of reducing harm caused by corporate-related activities. It does not depend only on the State and the law/policy system to effectuate change in business conduct, but builds on the actions of all key stakeholders and the three governance systems that affect business conduct. These actions are founded on different and interlinking sources of obligation (legal, social, moral),[82] and are drawn from different types of hard and soft laws that serve as a basis to apply norms. They are interrelated and mutually reinforcing, reflecting a 'smart mix of measures – national and international, mandatory and voluntary'.[83]

The regulatory dynamic and the mix of measures from which it draws, individually and in combination, potentially affect and coordinate the regulation of business conduct. It leverages the variables or factors that explain such adherence by these actors to their duties and responsibilities (e.g. incentives, capacities and engagement) in a changing global context. As a consequence of this regulatory dynamic, business enterprises should be exposed in an evolutionary manner to legal or normative constraints that bind business enterprises to meeting their responsibilities for human rights.[84] The UNGPs confirm that 'both voluntarism and law have relevant and reinforcing roles to play in governing business behavior'.[85] The PPR and the GPs have been described as 'a platform of guidelines by which stakeholders may define mechanisms using either compelling regulatory mechanisms or indeed voluntary initiatives'.[86]

Flexibility: The UNGPs allow for flexibility of facts and circumstances in the application of the duties and responsibilities to States and business enterprises. The PRR Framework and the UNGPs point to various incentives and opportunities that businesses have to respect human rights in practice. These incentives relate to the factual circumstances and characteristics of the company. The UNGPs allow flexibility for companies to exercise their responsibilities to respect human rights by adopting measures that are appropriate and proportionate to their circumstances.[87] Also, States have discretion to adopt measures that are commensurate to their capabilities and appropriate to their country context.

The 'smart mix' of methods that States and non-state actors employ to discharge their roles and responsibilities can be of instrumental importance in fostering business respect for human rights by leveraging the aforementioned variables or factors. The UNGPs advance the understanding that the business and human rights domain is complex; there is not one single formula to achieving more effective prevention and remedy for corporate-related human rights harm. The SRSG notes:

> The Guiding Principles are not a tool kit, simply to be taken off the shelf and plugged in. While the principles themselves are universally applicable, the means by which they are realized will reflect the fact that we live in a world of 192 United Nations Member States, 80,000 transnational enterprises, ten times as many subsidiaries and countless millions of national firms, most of which are small and medium-sized enterprises. When it comes to means for implementation, therefore, one size does not fit all.[88]

Participatory: Stakeholder engagement is embedded in all three pillars of the UNGPs.[89] This suggests that the UNGPs promote stakeholder engagement in a systemic fashion. The effective implementation of the UNGPs thus could contribute to more systemic practices of stakeholder engagement. This depends on how stakeholder engagement is operationalized in practice and the extent to which stakeholders seize the opportunities to partake in these processes. Stakeholder engagement has intrinsic and instrumental importance, as well as a constructive role in the process towards enhanced standards and practices.[90] Its effective operationalization in practice could also serve as a democratizing force that renders the polycentric governance system more responsive to the public.[91]

Conclusion

This chapter sought to ascertain, based on the SRSG's academic writings, the objectives of the UNGPs. It also examined the SRSG's approach to 'principled pragmatism', which is more complicated for law and practice, because it defies the option of 'single bullets' such as, presumably, a resort alone to positivist law would be. It presumes that measures should be pragmatic and progress should be gradual. The chapter shed light on the SRSG's understanding of the 'global public domain', the new actors and regulatory processes that have come to occupy the public sphere and the social roles of these actors in creating CSR and BHR standards and expectations. It also reflected on the SRSG's perspective of poly-centric governance and the notion that three governance systems (law, civil, corporate), in which the aforementioned actors participate, shape business behaviour.

The SRSG situates the UNGPs in terms of 'polycentric' global governance and characterizes the UNGPs, too, as polycentric governance. The UNGPs provide clarity on existing standards and practices related to business and human rights. They also reflect a reorganization of the expected contributions of the actors and their respective governance systems in a holistic and coherent template for a better functioning system. The main structure and features of this template, which the PRR Framework presents and the UNGPs further elaborate on, allow for the UNGPs to function as a platform for action in support of enhanced standards and practice of both States and business enterprises. Their effective implementation is expected to have an impact on coherence between actions and to generate reinforcing effects that will cumulate in progress. The expectation is that once the UNGPs are embedded in the business and human rights regulatory ecosystems, and actions reach a sufficient scale, they may in time compound into systemic change and lead to the institutionalization of a new harmonized global business and human rights regime.[92]

The UNGPs provide a template for an emerging global business and human rights regime. They advance an *institutional* approach and focus attention on the institutional misalignments that exist within and between the three governance systems in the business and human rights domain. The approach is *systemic* in that the strategic objective is to address all aspects that contribute to the problem of misalignments. This includes addressing the institutional incapabilities of the key stakeholders and the misaligned incentive structures that are supportive of this problem. These misalignments call for systemic changes in the way that States and business enterprises operate. The solution lies in a process through which effective connectivity within and between governance systems is enhanced.[93]

The PRR Framework and the UNGPs promote an *integrative* approach that appreciates the existence and working of the three governance systems in the regulation of business conduct and seeks to strengthen their positive interactions. The approach is *multifaceted* by acknowledging and simultaneously pursuing all institutions, processes and outcomes within the three governance systems, to the extent that these are of instrumental importance to achieving progress. The approach is *interactive* by drawing attention to the connections within and between the governance systems and to fostering these in order for actions to cohere and have mutually reinforcing effects. The UNGPs furthermore promote a *regulatory dynamic* that is aimed at fostering compliance by States and business enterprises through a smart mix of measures. The approach is *flexible* in that discretion is left for the adoption of measures that are appropriate to facts and circumstances. The approach is *participatory* by promoting stakeholder engagement that empowers individuals to give direction to the decision-making that affects them and to foster action that is appropriate from a rights-holder perspective.

Notes

1 Radu Mares, A *Rejoinder to* G. *Skinner's Rethinking Limited Liability of Parent Corporations for Foreign Subsidiaries' Violations of International Human Rights Law*, 73 Washington and Lee Law Review Online 117, at 73 (2016).

2 The SRSG notes that

> [b]usiness is the major source of investment and job creation, and markets can be highly efficient means for allocating scarce resources, capable of generating economic growth, reducing poverty, and increasing demand for the rule of law, thereby contributing to the realization of a broad spectrum of human rights.
>
> Report of the Special Representative on the Issue of Human Rights and Transnational Corporations and Other Business Enterprises, *Draft: Guiding Principles For The Implementation Of The United Nations 'Protect, Respect and Remedy' Framework* (2010) [hereinafter *Draft UNGPs*]

3 *Id.*

4 J. Ruggie, *Business and Human Rights: The Evolving International Agenda* (John F. Kennedy School of Government, Corporate Social Responsibility Initiative Working Paper No. 31, 2007).

5 Joel Slawotsky, *The Global Corporation as International law Actor*, 52 Virginia Journal of International Law, 83 (2012).

6 Also the sheer increase in their number illustrates their expanding scope, the SRSG notes, which is estimated at 'some 70,000 transnational firms, together with roughly 700,000 subsidiaries and millions of suppliers'. *Interim Report of the Special Representative of the Secretary-General on the Issue of Human Rights and Transnational Corporations and Other Business Enterprises*, ¶ 11, U.N. Doc. E/CN.4/2006/97 (Feb. 2006) [hereinafter *2006 Interim Report*] (by John Ruggie).

7 Slawotsky, *supra* note 5, at 84.

8 Ruggie, *supra* note 4, at 7.

9 *Id.*

10 Report of the Special Representative on the Issue of Human Rights and Transnational Corporations and Other Business Enterprises, *Protect, Respect and Remedy: A Framework for Business and Human Rights*, ¶ 3, U.N. doc. A/HRC/8/5 (7 Apr. 2008) [hereinafter Ruggie, *2008 Report*] (by John Ruggie).

11 *2006 Interim Report*, *supra* note 6, ¶ 18.

12 J. Ruggie, *Taking Embedded Liberalism Global: The Corporate Connection*, 3 (2002), www.cid.harvard.edu/events/papers/LSE-final.pdf.

13 *2006 Interim Report*, *supra* note 6, ¶ 18.

14 *Id.* ¶ 18.

15 *Draft UNGPs*, *supra* note 2.

16 J. Ruggie, *The Social Construction of the UN Guiding Principles on Business and Human Rights* (Corporate Responsibility Initiative, Working Paper No. 67, 2017).

17 The SRSG describes the global public domain as

> an increasingly institutionalized transnational arena of discourse, contestation and action concerning the production of global public goods, involving private as well as public actors. It does not by itself determine global governance outcomes

> any more than its counterpart does at the domestic level. But it introduces opportunities for and constraints upon both global and national governance that did not exist in the past.
>
> Ruggie, *supra* note 22

18 *Id.* at 500.
19 *Id.* at 500.
20 *Id.* at 503.
21 The creation of these governance systems provides

> a historically progressive platform by creating a more inclusive institutional arena in which, and sites from which other social actors, including CSOs, international organizations and even states can graft their pursuit of broader social agendas onto the global reach and capacity of TNCs.
>
> *Id.* 503

22 Ruggie, *Life in the Global Public Domain: Response to Commentaries on the UN Guiding Principles and the Proposed Treaty on Business and Human Rights* (23 Jan. 2015), available at http://papers.ssrn.com/sol3/papers.cfm?abstract_id=2554726. *See* J. Ruggie, Regulating Multinationals: The UN Guiding Principles, Civil Society, and International Legalization, 2 (Regulatory Policy Program, Working Paper RPP-2015–04, 2015).
23 J. Ruggie, *Global Governance and 'New Governance Theory': Lessons from Business and Human Rights*, 20 Global Governance, 6 (2014).
24 John Ruggie, *Opinion: Business and Human Rights – The Next Chapter* (7 Mar. 2013).
25 John Gerard Ruggie, Just Business Multinational Corporations and Human Rights, 78 (W.W. Norton & Company 2013).
26 *2006 Interim Report, supra* note 6, ¶ 81.
27 John Ruggie, Address at the Royal Society for the Encouragement of Arts, Manufacturers and Commerce, Sir Geoffrey Chandler Speaker Series (11 Jan. 2011).
28 Backer, *supra* note 40, at 82.
29 John G. Ruggie, Letter from John G. Ruggie, Special Representative of the UN Secretary-General for Business and Human Rights, to Olivier De Schutter, Secretary-General and Antoine Bernard, Executive Director, FIDH (20 Mar. 2006).
30 Freedom is explained as 'descriptive characteristics of the conditions of persons'. There are two aspects to freedom; 'opportunity' and 'process'. The 'opportunity' aspect of freedom is understood from a capability perspective as the actual opportunities an individual has to achieve valuable combinations of human functionings: 'what a person is able to do or be'. Sen notes that '[c]apabilities and the opportunity aspect of freedom, important as they are, have to be supplemented by considerations of fair processes and the lack of violation of the individual's right to invoke and utilize them'. Amarthya Sen, *Elements of a Theory of Human Rights*, 32 Philosophy & Public Affairs 315, 328–338 (2004).
31 *Id.* 340–341.
32 Sen notes that

> [a]n ethical understanding of human rights goes not only against seeing [human rights] as legal demands [...], but also differs from a law-centered approach to human rights that sees them as if they are basically grounds for law, almost 'laws in waithing'.
>
> *Id.* at 315, 326

33 Ruggie, *supra* note 16, at 15.
34 Mares, *supra* note 1.
35 Ruggie, *supra* note 24. To be noted is that the SRSG found inspiration in the work of Amartya Sen:

> Sen insists that human rights are much more than law's antecedents or progeny. Indeed, he states, such a view threatens to 'incarnate' the social logics and processes other than law that drive public recognition of rights. My work, including the Guiding Principles, has sought to contribute to the freeing of human rights discourse and practice from these conceptual shackles, by drawing on the interests, capacities and engagement of states, market actors, civil society, and the intrinsic power of ideational and normative factors.
>
> Ruggie, *supra* note 22

36 Ruggie, *supra* note 25, at 57.
37 *Id.*
38 *UNGPs*, *supra* note 75, ¶ 4.
39 Ruggie, *supra* note 27.
40 Larry Catá Backer, *From Institutional Misalignments to Socially Sustainable Governance: The Guiding Principles for the Implementation of the United Nations Protect, Respect and Remedy and the Construction of Inter-Systemic Global Governance*, 25 Global Business & Development Law Journal, 96 (2012).
41 *UNGPs*, *supra* note 75, at 4.
42 Stakeholder engagement was part of the SRSG's mandate as set out in resolution 2005/69, which requested the SRSG to consult 'on an ongoing basis with all stakeholders'. The Commission on Human Rights provided a non-exhaustive list of relevant stakeholders, *see* Commission on Human Rights Res. 2005/69: Human Rights and Transnational Corporations and Other Business Enterprises, 59th meeting, E/CN.4/RES/2005/69 (20 Apr. 2005).
43 *See* Ruggie, *supra* note 23, at 10.
44 The approach to the stakeholder consultations by striving for the fullest and equal participation of all stakeholders created (democratic) legitimacy for the process (and the UNGPs). Stéphanie Bijlmakers, *Business and Human Rights Governance and Democratic Legitimacy: The UN 'Protect, Respect and Remedy' Framework*, 26 Innovation: The European Journal of Social Sciences 288 (2013).
45 The participation of stakeholder individuals, groups and institutions that had contributed to the mandate had come to constitute 'a global movement of sorts in support of a successful mandate'. *UNGPs*, *supra* note 75, Introduction.
46 For an analysis of value of an expansion of business participation in international law making from the perspective of public international legal theory, as well from pragmatic political and procedural points of view, *see* Jonathan I Charney, *Transnational Corporations and Developing Public International Law*, Duke Law Journal 748, 750–751, 776–777 (1983).
47 The draft history of the resolution informed the SRSG's stakeholder approach, and in particular the previous experiences in the development of the UN Norms, which had been criticized for being opaque and insufficiently consultative. David Kinley & Rachel Chambers, *The UN Human Rights Norms for Corporations: The Private Implications of Public International Law*, 6 Human Rights Law Review (2006). But also *see*, contra, David Kinley & Junko Tadaki, *From Talk to Walk: The Emergence of Human Rights Responsibilities for Corporations at International Law*, 44 Virginia Journal of International Law 16, 959 (2004). Surya Deva, *Multinationals, Human Rights and International Law: Time to Move beyond the 'State-Centric' Conception*, *in* Human Rights and Business: Direct Corporate Accountability and Human Rights 27, 37, fn 45 (Jernej Letnar Černič & Tara Van Ho eds. 2015).
48 Karin Buhmann, *Navigating from 'Train Wreck' to Being 'Welcomed': Negotiation Strategies and Argumentative Patterns in the Development of the UN Framework*, *in* Human Rights Obligations of Business: Beyond the Corporate Responsibility to Respect? 29, 30 (Surya Deva & David Bilchitz eds. 2013); K Buhmann, *Regulating Corporate Social and Human Rights Responsibilities at the UN Plane: Institutionalising*

New Forms of Law and Law-making Approaches?, 78 Nordic Journal of International Law (2009).

49 Ruggie, *supra* note 27.

50 Ruggie, *supra* note 22.

51 The authors uphold the normative threshold that 'any exercise of public authority must be kept accountable'. The authors adhere to the explanation of 'exercise of public authority' by Bogdandy and Goldmann as 'any kind of governance activity ... [which] determines individuals; private associations; enterprises; states; or other public institutions'. Joost Pauwelyn, et al., *When Structures Become Shackles: Stagnation and Dynamics in International Law Making*, 25 The European Journal of International Law, 745 (2014).

52 The assumption is that non-legally binding instruments like the UNGPs and informal modes of cooperation that can affect public policymaking and individual freedom should be subject to requirements of legal justification like any other form of coercion. Despite not being 'legally binding' in the strict legal sense, they can generate compliance in a way that traditional international law can and be as constraining, potentially becoming 'shackles'. *Id.* at 746.

53 *Id.* at 748.

54 These criteria relate to the source (and authority) and the procedural and substantive quality of a norm. More specifically, the substantive requirements of the 'thick consensus' benchmark are: '(i) the source and authority of the norm-creating body, (ii) transparency, openness, and neutrality in the norm's procedural elaboration, and (iii) the substantive quality; consistency, and overall acceptance (consensus) of the norm'. *Id.* at 761.

55 Ruggie, *supra* note 22(b), at 1.

56 Ruggie, *supra* note 22.

57 Backer, *supra* note 40, at 86.

58 *Id.* at 106.

59 *UNGPs*, *supra* note 75, ¶ 14.

60 This does not automatically exclude the UNGPs from having any legal effects. The UNGPs, as will be elaborated below, can be viewed as soft law that can affect the course of legal development in the future through their potential normative affects on the behaviour of States and business enterprises.

61 This principle is contained in Art. 2 of the UDHR and a number of principle international human rights treaties. Also *see* for instance, Art. 14 ECHR and Art. 1 of Protocol No. 12 to the ECHR. Oliver de Schutter, et al., *Commentary to the Maastricht Principles on Extraterritorial Obligations of States in the Areas of Economic, Social and Cultural Rights*, 34 Human Rights Quarterly, 1087 (2012).

62 *UNGPs*, *supra* note 75, ¶ 16.

63 *Id.* ¶ 14.

64 Backer, *supra* note 40, at 81.

65 The SRSG noted,

> insofar as the overall global context itself is in transition, standards in many instances do not simply 'exist' out there waiting to be recorded and implemented but are in the process of being socially constructed. Indeed, the mandate itself inevitably is a modest intervention in that larger process.
>
> *2006 Interim Report*, *supra* note 6, ¶ 54

66 Addo, *supra* note 80, at 135.

67 The SRSG notes that:

> To foster that alignment, the GPs draw on the different discourses and rationales that reflect the different social roles these governance systems play in regulating corporate conduct. Thus, for states the emphasis is on the legal obligations they have under the international human rights regime to protect against human

> rights abuses by third parties, including business, as well as policy rationales that are consistent with, and supportive of, meeting those obligations. For businesses, beyond compliance with legal obligations, the GPs focus on the need to manage the risk of involvement in human rights abuses, which requires that companies act with due diligence to avoid infringing on the rights of others and address harm where it does occur. For affected individuals and communities, the GPs stipulate ways for their further empowerment to realize a right to remedy. I described this approach as principled pragmatism.
>
> Ruggie, *supra* note 22(b), at 3

68 The UNGPs indicate that

> [e]ach pillar is an essential component in an inter-related and dynamic system of preventive and remedial measures: the State duty to protect because it lies at the very core of the international human rights regime; the corporate responsibility to respect because it is the basic expectation society has of business in relation to human rights; and access to remedy because even the most concerted efforts cannot prevent all abuse.
>
> *UNGPs*, *supra* note 75, ¶ 6

69 *Id.* Introduction, at 3.
70 *Draft UNGPs*, *supra* note 2, ¶ 12; Backer, *supra* note 40, at 93.
71 Ruggie, *supra* note 22.
72 'Lacking was an authoritative basis whereby these governance systems become better aligned in relation to business and human rights, compensate for one another's weaknesses, and play mutually reinforcing roles – out of which cumulative change can evolve over time'. Ruggie, *supra* note 22, at 2.
73 Ruggie, *2008 Report*, supra note 10, ¶ 6.
74 *Id.*
75 Special Representative on the Issue of Human Rights and Transnational Corporations and Other Business Enterprises, *Guiding Principles on Business and Human Rights: Implementing the United Nations "Protect, Respect and Remedy" Framework*. U.N.Doc. A/HRC/17/31, Introduction (March 21, 2011) [hereinafter UNGPs] (by John Ruggie).
76 It is not surprising that the 'global public domain' finds expression in the UNGPs in light of the SRSG's observation that the *problematique* in the domain of business and human rights is 'a microcosm of a larger crisis in contemporary governance'. Ruggie, *supra* note 10, at 6.
77 *Id.* at 6.
78 The UNGPs, for instance, indicate that NGOs are a credible, independent expert resource that business enterprises should consider consulting when undertaking human rights impact assessments in situations where consultations with potentially affected stakeholders themselves are not possible (Commentary to GP 18). Business enterprises are also advised to draw on the expertise of NGOs when assessing how to respect the principles of internationally recognized human rights when operating in complex country and local contexts. The UNGPs also expressly addresses the roles of NHRI (Commentary to GP 23, GP27 and GP 2), multilateral institutions (GP 10) and multi-stakeholder initiatives (GP 30). *UNGPs*, *supra* note 75, Commentary to GP 18.
79 Ruggie, *supra* note 22.
80 As such, the States remain the main subject of public-law systems of governance (national and international). Michael K. Addo, *The Reality of the United Nations Guiding Principles on Business and Human Rights*, 14 Human Rights Law Review, 146 (2014).
81 Ruggie, *supra* note 22.
82 Backer, *supra* note 40, at 96.
83 Ruggie, *supra* note 22(b), at 3.
84 Backer, *supra* note 40, at 91.

85 Mark B. Taylor, *The Ruggie Framework: Polycentric Regulation and the Implications for Corporate Social Responsibility*, 5 Etikk i praksis – Nordic Journal of Applied Ethics 1, 20 (2011).
86 Addo, *supra* note 80, at 83.
87 *UNGPs*, *supra* note 75, GP 17.
88 *Draft UNGPs*, *supra* note 2, ¶ 14.
89 ICCPR, Article 25.
90 *See*, Amartya Sen, Development as Freedom, 152–159 (Oxford University Press, 1999).
91 Carnegie Council on Ethics and International Affairs, *The Impact of Corporations on Global Governance* (2004).
92 Ruggie, *2008 Report*, *supra* note 10, ¶ 6.
93 The SRSG elaborates on effective connectivity, noting the need for 'more robust horizontal linkages' within States (e.g. across governmental departments), within business enterprises (e.g. across business functions), between States and businesses (e.g. smart regulation), and between businesses and their external stakeholders (e.g. stakeholder engagement and grievance mechanisms). Ruggie, *supra* note 27.

3 The evolution of the corporate responsibility to respect human rights

From a soft into a hard obligation for companies under national and international law?

Introduction

This chapter sets out a scenario for the 'legalization' of the corporate responsibility to respect human rights, in a global governance context. It examines the legal status of the UNGPs as a soft law document, and of the SRSG's conception of the corporate responsibility to respect human rights, as a responsibility that is differentiated yet complementary to the duty of States, and furthermore embedded in a global policy context. As elaborated in the previous chapter, the UNGPs aim at starting a process of advancing towards the emergence of a new governance system, one in which stakeholders and their respective existing governance systems become aligned in the pursuit of 'the effective prevention of, and remedy for, business-related human rights harm'. This process is ongoing and meant to promote a gradual improvement in standards and practices, as States and business enterprises actively implement their rights and duties under the UNGPs. The UNGPs thus are set out to advance a regulatory dynamic that encourages transformative change and a continuous and progressive evolution of the corporate responsibility to respect human rights.

This chapter notes how this regulatory dynamic potentially affects and coordinates the regulation of business conduct. It sees that compliance (i.e. factual adherence) by business enterprises to the corporate responsibility to respect human rights is possibly motivated by a number of variables or factors in a changing global context. It argues that if the UNGPs are effectively embedded in the regulatory ecosystem of business and human rights, the corporate responsibility to respect human rights, as it is currently conceived, should further evolve. Consequently, while the corporate responsibility to respect human rights may not be legally binding in its inception, this responsibility is expected to acquire: (i) normative force, through its recognition and acceptance by State and non-State actors; and (ii) effectiveness, through the actual implementation of the UNGPs. It sets out the scenario of this norm acquiring binding-ness and normative force, including the (selective) translation of such responsibility into 'hard' (legally binding) norms at the national, regional and international level.

The legal status of the UN Guiding Principles on business and human rights as soft law

An analysis of the legal status of the corporate responsibility to respect human rights requires first an assessment of the legal status of the UNGPs within which this norm was adopted. The text of the UNGPs does not address this point. However, in the words of the SRSG, '[t]hey are a soft-law instrument that prescribes minimum standards of conduct for all states and all business enterprises in relation to all human rights'.[1] It seems that the SRSG adheres to a broad definition of soft law that resembles more recent soft law definitions.

More recent conceptions of soft law which have been commonly applied in legal scholarship define 'soft law' as 'voluntary' by its very nature, and by its intrinsically international and public character. Zerk defines soft law as 'principles and policies which have been negotiated and agreed upon between States, or promulgated by international institutions, yet which are not mandated by law or subject to any formal enforcement mechanisms'.[2] This definition characterizes instruments as soft law by reference to their non-legally binding and non-enforceable nature, from a strict legal perspective, and the legal authority of States. According to this definition, soft law depends on State action for its existence, and such action finds expression in the acceptance by States between themselves or through international organizations.

According to Shelton, soft law entails 'any international instrument other than a treaty that contains principles, norms, standards, or other statement of expected behaviour'.[3] It is not clear what gives a soft law instrument its 'international' character, whether this is the State's consent to the instrument or the State's involvement in the process of its development. The definition seems to attach greater importance to content, rather than the formality by which the instrument has been developed and adopted. The characterization of an instrument as soft law thus seems to depend, in part, on the instrument's functionality in articulating statements of expected behaviour.

Chinkin provides a broader definition of soft law, and, more precisely, one which encompasses within its scope also statements by non-State actors that have not been negotiated or formally adopted by States, but which articulate international principles:

> Soft law instruments range from treaties, but which include only soft obligations ('legal soft law'), to non-binding or voluntary resolutions and codes of conduct formulated and accepted by international and regional organisations ('non-legal soft law'), to statements prepared by individuals in a non-governmental capacity, but which purport to lay down international principles.[4]

According to this definition, an instrument depends on its content for its existence as soft law, which should reflect an attempt 'to lay down international principles'. The form of the initiative, or the formality of the process by which it has been developed or adopted seems not to be of the essence. This definition also characterizes as soft law initiatives that have been developed at a micro-level,[5] hence bringing within its scope a diversity and range of CSR mechanisms (e.g. codes of conduct, private-hybrid, self or multi-stakeholder governance initiatives).

It seems that the SRSG adheres to a definition of soft law that is similarly broad in scope. The SRSG characterizes CSR mechanisms as soft law by virtue of their non-binding nature in a strict legal sense and their reflection of norms and social expectations that derive normative force from their recognition by States and other key actors.[6] Instruments do not depend on any formal procedures for their development or acceptance in order to exist as soft law. A mechanism can be designated as soft law simply because the initiative carries within its content the potential to bind. The UNGPs may thus be characterized as soft law on various grounds.

First, they have an 'international' character by reason of having been developed at the international level and having obtained the 'endorsement' of the HRC. While not having been negotiated by States,[7] the UNGPs have obtained the anonymous 'endorsement' by the HRC, which testifies to State support for the UNGPs. However, the exact legal implications of such an act of 'endorsement' (as opposed to the 'acceptance') of the UNGPs are far from clear.

Second, the UNGPs can be characterized as soft law even more clearly by their content. The UNGPs recognize, clarify and elaborate existing and newly emerging standards and practices of States and business enterprises regarding the prevention and remediation of businesses' harm to human rights. The UNGPs thus constitute soft law by reason of their ability to bind addressees to these international principles.

The choice of soft law v. hard law

The previous section established that the UNGPs can be characterized as soft law. This section reflects on the SRSG's choice for soft law over hard law. It seems that the SRSG opted for the adoption of the UNGPs as soft law because this constituted an effective method of progress towards the ultimate goal of achieving full respect for human rights by all enterprises. As set out in detail in the previous chapter, the realization of this goal depends on the actions of key stakeholders to meet their obligations and responsibilities under the UNGPs. The UNGPs are the starting point for an ongoing process of enhancing standards and practices that contributes to a regulatory dynamic and global system that binds business enterprises to respect for human rights. The underlying assumption appears to be that such a system would generate similar effects as hard law does in terms of achieving business compliance with human rights.

This section reflects on the SRSG's rationale to propose the PRR Framework and the UNGPs as an alternative to starting negotiations of an overarching international treaty placing binding obligations on business enterprises under international law. The SRSG elaborated on some of these arguments in an essay published in *Ethical Corporation*, entitled 'treaty road not travelled'.[8] Therein the SRSG expressed the following three reservations against the treaty route:

> First, treaty-making can be painfully slow, while the challenges of business and human rights are immediate and urgent. Second, and worse, a treaty-making process now risks undermining effective shorter-term measures to raise business standards on human rights. And third, even if treaty obligations were imposed on companies, serious questions remain about how they would be enforced.

The SRSG elaborated on some of these arguments in more recent debates on the negotiation of a UN business and human rights treaty.[9]

This section builds on the literature on the legal relevance of soft law.[10] The next sections thus consider the SRSG's choice of soft law in the light of this literature and concludes that this choice has been partially informed by expectations of compliance. The normative potential of the UNGPs to generate compliance by business enterprises with the corporate responsibility to respect human rights will be examined in this section.

The reflections that follow shed light on the SRSG's rationale for creating the UNGPs as a soft law instrument, as well as the SRSG's soft law approach to the corporate responsibility to respect human rights, which draws upon social expectations and moral obligations as a basis for the application of responsibilities to business enterprises. As noted by Nolan, 'soft law has played a prominent role in the development of the SRSG's concept of why and how a corporation might be responsible for human rights'.[11]

One of the main rationales for the SRSG not to recommend treaty negotiations was a need for 'immediate solutions to the escalating challenge of corporate human rights abuses'.[12] The process of negotiating a treaty would be lengthy and complicated, in part because of the complexity of the subject of business and human rights. According to the SRSG, this complexity would be reflected in the many facets that would need to be considered when negotiating a comprehensive treaty, especially the broad range of issues that such a treaty would need to encompass.[13] The SRSG elaborated on this point, in an issues-brief, as follows:

> It includes complex clusters of different bodies of national and international law – for starters, Human Rights law, Labour law, Anti-Discrimination law, Humanitarian law, Investment law, Trade law, Consumer Protection law, as well as Corporate law and Securities regulation. The point is not that these are unrelated, but that they embody such extensive problem diversity, institutional variations, and conflicting interests across and within States that any attempt to aggregate them into a general business and human rights treaty would have to be pitched at such a high level of abstraction that it is hard to imagine it providing a basis for meaningful legal action.

The subject of business and human rights is thus complex because of the variety of bodies of law, the extensive problem diversity, the institutional variations and the conflicting interests of the various actors that the subject engages within and across States. This complexity poses significant obstacles to negotiating a treaty, the SRSG argued: 'The crux of the challenges is that business and human rights is not so discrete an issue-area as to lend itself to a single set of detailed treaty obligations.'[14]

In addition, the SRSG was of the view that negotiating an all-encompassing treaty would be inappropriate when the duration of such negotiations would be too long. This was the case for a comprehensive international human rights treaty. '[T]he broader the scope and the more controversial the subject, the longer the duration', he noted.[15] This consideration became particularly applicable to a treaty on the subject of business and human rights.[16,17]

The SRSG went one step further and argued that a treaty-making process could risk 'undermining effective shorter-term measures'. In the light of the previously noted complexity, deriving from the subject of business and human rights and political dynamics, the SRSG was sceptical about pursuing at the same time both an all-encompassing treaty and practical measures for more urgent relief. A dual approach would be counterproductive, he argued, because States could derive justification from a treaty-making process not to act to raise standards on business and human rights in the meantime. The SRSG thus noted that '[States] may invoke the fact of treaty negotiation as a pretext for not taking other significant steps, including changing national laws – arguing that they would not want to "preempt" the ultimate outcome'.[18] Moreover, a treaty-making process is resource intensive and can detract valuable attention and resources from stakeholders, resources which could be spent elsewhere, for instance on interim-innovations, the SRSG argued. By opting for soft-measures, the resources that would have been spent on lengthy negotiations could thus be redirected towards initiatives which could potentially deliver more immediate relief to victims of human rights abuses.

Where treaties can take decades to negotiate, and soft law can deliver quicker results, the choice for soft law thus seems like a better alternative.[19] Soft law may have the advantage of a less complex negotiation process than a legally binding international standard, simply because soft law is 'not constrained by a legal straight jacket'.[20] Due to its non-legally binding nature, a soft instrument can recognize and apply norms facing less resistance because these norms do not generate immediate legal effects, in and of themselves. Consequently, by turning to soft law, the time frame for setting standards and implementation procedures can be reduced. Soft norms can obtain the support by States and business enterprises with greater ease, due to their non-legally binding nature. Soft law can be used to respond to the need for more immediate measures to address corporate-related human rights breaches and achieve practical results, thereby reducing the number of incidents of harm caused and hence deliver short-term benefits to victims.[21]

The choice of soft over hard law can be explained by the political dynamics in the former Commission on Human Rights and the lack of agreement on an effective response. By the time the SRSG's mandate was launched, there was no consensus among States on the existence of direct legal obligations for companies, or, for that matter, on the necessity or desirability of such obligations. According to the SRSG, there was no shared knowledge base to build on, nor agreement on desirable international responses.[22] Consensus did not go far beyond a 'we need to consider doing something about the problem' approach.[23] An agreement on the existence or creation of human rights duties having hard law effects did not seem forthcoming.

The reminiscence of previous failed attempts to create a UN document on business and human rights played a part as well, especially the previous UN Norms, which did not obtain the backing of States. The political dynamics within the Commission on Human Rights (which was replaced by the HRC in 2006), which operated on a consensus basis, seemed hardly conducive to States negotiating, let alone signing and ratifying a treaty creating direct human rights obligations for companies.[24,25] The political dynamics signalled constraints on the aspirations for an international legally binding treaty and the importance of proceeding with caution in a difficult political climate.[26] The SRSG also noted that 'greater shared understanding and consensus needed to be built from the bottom up'.[27]

It seems that the use of soft law, precisely because of its non-binding nature, allowed the SRSG to reach a consensus among States within the HRC on the corporate responsibility to respect human rights where no such consensus would have been recognized in relation to hard law. More progressive rules on the corporate responsibility to respect human rights were thus adopted rather than those which were more likely to be possible had hard law been chosen.[28,29] Moreover, the SRSG cautioned that treaty making could restrict innovation and experimentation[30] and risked resulting in legal standards reflecting the lowest-common denominator. Treaty making could be counterproductive to raising human rights standards if it were to cement a lower standard in international law than the standards set by existing voluntary initiatives. The discretion of companies to adhere to the lower standard prescribed by international law risked undermining the social leverage of stakeholders pressuring companies to do better, the SRSG argued.

The SRSG also raised the argument that a treaty may not alleviate the problem of inadequate enforcement. First, were States prepared to give their political consent to a treaty in the first place, such a treaty would trigger few consequences for business enterprises if the treaty were to be left unimplemented and un-enforced. A treaty would have too limited an effect in constraining corporations by law or in impressing upon companies the possibility or prospect of legal liability. In the view of the SRSG, much of the treaty's legitimacy and effectiveness would thus be lost.

Second, the SRSG dismissed the enforcement of treaty obligations by host States as 'redundant or irrelevant'.[31] According to the SRSG, it also seemed unlikely that States previously reluctant to take on new human rights obligations would ratify a new treaty on business and human rights in the future. It would also not be self-evident that those States previously unwilling or unable to discharge their obligations under human rights treaties would enforce a future treaty, he argued, although a State may feel more inclined to do so where a treaty resolves collective action problems.[32]

Third, the SRSG further discarded the option of extraterritorial enforcement of an international treaty by States other than the host State. While international law permits States to take action to regulate the human rights breaches of their corporations abroad, he argued, few have been willing to do so. Both States and business enterprises are concerned that extraterritorial jurisdiction may compromise the competitive position of companies. Developing States, on the other hand, feared extraterritorial jurisdiction impinging on their national sovereignty. In the absence of State support for new treaty obligations on extraterritorial enforcement, starting such an initiative 'could backfire and reduce the scope of existing possibilities', reasoned the SRSG.

Fourth, the SRSG discarded the possibility of establishing an international court for companies any time soon as 'unrealistic'.[33] An alternative option was to establish a new treaty body to monitor corporate compliance. However, the SRSG was of the view that this would pose insurmountable difficulties in practice. Designing selection criteria and handling cases for millions of companies, in relation to all human rights of all persons adversely affected by business enterprises and their activities, would be a daunting task, the SRSG argued.[34]

These arguments are consistent with the idea that compliance might often make soft law preferable to hard law. According to Shelton, the choice may fall on soft law in case a reasonable possibility exists that States will be unable or unwilling to comply with hard-law obligations and, therefore, unwilling to agree to an instrument creating such obligations.[35] Concerns about the possibility of non-compliance can be triggered by a number of factors, including 'domestic political opposition, lack of ability or capacity to comply, uncertainty about whether compliance can be measured, or disagreement with aspects of the proposed norms'.[36] The SRSG refers to almost all of these factors in support of his argument that a treaty would not constitute the most effective path to address the problem of inadequate enforcement in the business and human rights context.

Another argument supporting the choice of soft over hard law relates to the opportunities that soft law creates for non-State actors to participate in the law-making processes.[37] As set out in more detail above, the multi-stakeholder consultative approach was of essential importance to the development of the UNGPs. The participation of stakeholders in this process can be viewed as intrinsically important, but also had an instrumental value to ensure both the normative quality of the UNGPs and support for their effective implementation. As highlighted by Nolan, the SRSG may have opted for the development of the corporate responsibility to respect through a soft law approach because 'the informal nature of soft law allows for a broader group of participants (including non-State actors) in both its development and enforcement'.[38,39] The 'thick stakeholder consensus' that the SRSG strived for in the process of developing the UNGPs supports the claim that resorting to such a soft law approach is not necessarily undesirable from the perspective of accountability or legitimacy, and may furthermore enhance the flexibility and quality of the resulting standards.[40]

The SRSG's decision not to recommend recourse to a classic international treaty reflected the expectation that adopting such a treaty would be difficult.[41] The SRSG examined in detail the likelihood that States would reach an agreement on an overarching treaty that would be enforceable and effective in providing an immediate response to pressing business and human rights challenges. The SRSG pointed to a variety of factors, which, at the time, supported the choice of soft law over an overarching treaty on business and human rights. Most important among these factors were the complexity of the area of business and human rights and need for an immediate response, and the likely possibility of non-acceptance and/or non-enforcement of an international treaty and securing the acceptance of (and commitment to), by non-State actors, the implementation of the UNGPs. The political dynamics at the international level, including within the HRC, did not seem conducive to a successful negotiation of such an international treaty. It should be noted that these factors are primarily of a political and practical, rather than of a legal nature.

The SRSG's choice also relates to the normative and strategic objectives that the SRSG set for his mandate and constituted an exercise of retrospective principled pragmatism. The creation of an authoritative framework was cast as an alternative to the treaty route and the best hope to starting a process of enhancing standards and practices and the constitution of a system that will affect business behaviour in practice. The fact that the UNGPs were conceived as soft law enabled an approach of principled pragmatism. The extensive multi-stakeholder processes involving State and non-State actors that characterized the adoption of the UNGPs, for example, might have not been possible in the framework of treaty negotiations. The choice of soft law may also reflect the expectation that soft law would be a more suitable method for the operation of the governance system that the UNGPs intended to advance. It may be precisely because of the UNGP's nature as soft law and, thus, without direct legal effect, that the UNGPs may be applied and interpreted as a (self-referential) framework across governance systems without directly affecting or being affected by existing law and authority structures.[42]

In conclusion, the resort to soft law by the SRSG appears to have been informed by considerations of compliance. The assumption underpinning the UNGPs is thus that soft law can be a method that is as useful as hard law in generating legal effects in terms of fostering compliance by business enterprises and the effective application of human rights. The section will reflect on the normative potential of the UNGPs to generate compliance and affect the evolution of the corporate responsibility to respect human rights, which may acquire normative force or binding effect through the exposure to and restatement in, of the UNGPs, soft and hard-law provisions. The underlying assumption is, in short, that the dynamic interaction between soft and hard-law obligations in the emerging governance system and their cumulative binding effects will foster business efforts to respect human rights.

A soft law approach to the corporate responsibility to respect human rights and expectations of compliance

This section reflects on the UNGP's soft law approach to formulating the duty of corporate respect for human rights and the expectation that the UNGPs will affect compliance (i.e. actual adherence) by business enterprises to the rules the UNGPs contain. The UNGPs recognize that business enterprises have a responsibility to respect human rights. This responsibility is a social/moral norm founded in global social expectations rather than a legal obligation founded in international human rights obligations. Consequently, the corporate responsibility to respect human rights, as soft law, does not generate, in and of itself, legally binding effects. Such responsibility nonetheless includes within its normative scope the capability to affect the behaviour of business enterprises by virtue of its potential acceptance and recognition by State and non-State actors alike.[43]

The section draws from the literature on the social relevance of soft law more generally, in order to explore the variables or factors that motivate businesses to comply with the corporate responsibility to respect human rights in practice. The potential normative force or binding effect of the corporate responsibility to respect human rights and potential effect on business compliance can be explained by the following three factors: (i) context; (ii) content and (iii) institutional setting.[44]

The assumption is that the UNGPs intend to promote a system that affects and coordinates the regulation of the corporate responsibility to respect human rights through the variables or factors that motivate business enterprises to comply with this norm in practice in a changing global context. The aim of the following sections is to consider these variables or factors that explain business compliance in certain detail.

Context

The legal relevance of the corporate responsibility to respect human rights as soft law may first be appraised by reference to its context. This context relates to the mandate of the SRSG and the HRC, within which the UNGPs were developed and adopted.[45] The normative force of such responsibility can be assessed in relation to the authoritativeness of the UNGPs within which the responsibility has been recognized. This authoritativeness, which may be related to the norm's perceived legitimacy,[46] can result from the SRSG's official UN mandate, its independent nature, and the SRSG's stature as a renowned expert in the field of business and human rights.[47] Also, the consensus that exists around the UNGPs and their formal endorsement by the HRC can affect the normative potential of the UNGPs. Finally, the multi-stakeholder approach to the UNGPs development process is a relevant factor that potentially motivates compliance by business enterprises and therefore ought to be taken into consideration.

The normative force of the corporate responsibility to respect human rights can also be appreciated in terms of the broader context, that is the newly emerging global business and human rights regime, and the combination and dynamic interplay between hard and soft norms within this regime.[48,49] Attention may be paid to soft and hard-law instruments that create corresponding norms of different types of obligations, which complement and interact with one another in a joint effort to advance towards the overall goal of a reduction of business harm to human rights.

Shelton has noted how 'soft law rarely stands in isolation; instead; it is used most frequently either as a precursor to hard law or as a supplement to hard-law instruments'.[50] The SRSG's recourse to a soft law approach to the corporate responsibility to respect human rights, as was indicated in certain detail above, can be viewed as a method to address gaps and generate normative effects where the adoption of hard law was difficult. States were unlikely to reach a consensus on the existence or need to create hard-law international legal obligations for companies. The soft law approach was thus preferred as a timely alternative that was more likely to receive approval from States.

The SRSG casts the corporate responsibility to respect as a soft norm having its sources in social expectations rather than international law and being founded on social/moral, rather than legal obligation. As a consequence of the SRSG's avoidance of hard law, Nolan argues, the responsibility was decoupled from binding law, in terms of both its source of obligation and enforcement mechanisms, which had the effect of 'reducing its normative value and making it softer and more inchoate than might be required'.[51] As a consequence, the corporate responsibility to respect human rights primarily derives normative force from the expectation that companies may be exposed to the 'court of public opinion' and 'occasionally to charges in actual courts'.[52]

The binding force and normative effects of a rule of soft law are not static, however, but can change and fluctuate over time. The rule can thus acquire or lose in normative force. The corporate responsibility to respect human rights may take on a more binding force for example, when exposed to enforcement processes, restated into soft law rules of another type and, ultimately, when transposed into 'hard' law.[53] As will be set out in detail below, it is reasonable to assume that the governance system that the UNGPs are set out to promote, while not of a legally binding nature, may affect the evolution of the corporate responsibility to respect human rights into more binding norms under various hard and soft law sources at a variety of levels. To be noted is that the prospect that the corporate responsibility to respect human rights might or will harden into a binding obligation at the national and/or international level in time, in and of itself, may be relevant also for understanding compliance by business enterprises.[54]

Content of the norm

The content of the corporate responsibility to respect human rights can also affect compliance by business enterprises. The level of detail with which the corporate responsibility to respect human rights is formulated thus becomes of significance. The normative force and binding effects of a rule of soft law become greater where the rule is articulated in more precise language. There is a degree of open-endedness in the corporate responsibility to respect human rights, which leaves discretion to companies on how to exercise it. This flexibility may be viewed negatively as reducing the responsibility's normative potential by allowing 'for too much wiggle room [and including] too many "should" in place of "shalls"'.[55] According to Nolan, 'looseness of the language is perhaps more likely to invite inaction and a business-as-usual approach from companies that remain hesitant about their responsibility to act'.[56]

Others view the flexibility of the said responsibility as having a positive impact and increasing its normative potential by allowing room for responses tailored to the concrete circumstances of the company. Compliance with substantive requirements may require measures of a different complexity and scale. A degree of flexibility is built into the human rights due diligence concept, which allows companies to meet their responsibility by adopting measures that are appropriate to their circumstances. From this point of view, it could be argued that flexibility fosters greater compliance because the required standard is commensurate to the context and capabilities of the company.

The content of the corporate responsibility to respect human rights may have a variety of implications for companies, depending on a number of different variables or factors in an ever-changing global context. These variables relate to the factual circumstances of the company, and include awareness (e.g. the company's understanding of the UNGPs), the company's capabilities (e.g. the resources the company has at its disposal), and country-specific conditions creating an environment conducive to respect for human rights. Other variables relate to the characteristics of the company and include its size (e.g. small or large) and ownership/nature (e.g. public or private). These variables or factors relate to the opportunity and incentives of business enterprises to respect human rights. The importance of individual variables for understanding compliance may differ depending on the factual circumstances or type of business enterprises.[57] Furthermore, the combination of, and interaction between, these variables is important for understanding actual business compliance.[58] A brief analysis of factors follows.

Non-compliance by individual companies may reflect a lack of *awareness* of the company about the UNGPs and/or the corporate responsibility to respect, or a lack of understanding by the company of this responsibility, the manner in which this responsibility applies to the company and the consequences of the effective implementation of this responsibility for the company. The assumption is that, the more the company has engaged with the work of the SRSG and is familiar with the UNGPs, the greater the degree of compliance will be. Greater compliance is expected, for example, from companies that have an understanding about how to acquire knowledge about their potential and actual impacts,[59] the extent of human rights due diligence that is required from companies in relation to these impacts[60] and how to engage with stakeholders.

Consideration should also be paid to the commercial rationales that create incentives for companies to comply, also referred to as the *business case*. Such rationales may range from 'it is the right thing to do' to 'human rights are part of effective risks management', and 'commitment to human rights is in our code of conduct', 'our employees expect it of us', 'it gives us a competitive advantage' and 'engagement with civil society organizations'.[61,62] The corporate responsibility to respect varies in the impact it is likely to have on the business case of a company. It is reasonable to assume that the norm will acquire enhanced normative force if consistent with the commercial incentives of the company.

Compliance furthermore depends on the *capacity* of a company, meaning the capabilities of a company to engage in the desired behaviour and the opportunity to use these capabilities for implementing its responsibility. The perceived costs of compliance are therefore a relevant variable. The corporate responsibility to respect human rights varies in the costs that it is expected to impose on companies. Where capacity is an issue, the opportunities for companies to comply may expand as the company obtains access to resources and credible information[63] and frameworks or methodologies in order to understand the company's human rights impacts,[64] and to good practice case studies and public guidance on how to implement the UNGPs.[65,66]

The *form* of a company, i.e. the organizational and ownership-related characteristics of the company (e.g. whether it is structured as a corporation, partnership, joint venture, etc.) is relevant to expectations of compliance. The corporate responsibility to respect human rights varies in its implications for companies of different legal natures. The opportunities to comply may be affected by the business model (e.g. cooperative and partnerships), or whether a business enterprise is a publicly listed company or a private company.[67] For private enterprises that do not face similar constraints, other variables may motivate compliance, e.g. business opportunities or legal constraints.[68]

The *size* of the company is also a relevant variable. Research suggests that the awareness,[69] the priorities,[70] capabilities,[71] and opportunities to use its capabilities,[72] as well as the commercial incentives[73] to implement the UNGPs, may differ between companies depending on their sizes.

There are also *country*-specific factors, i.e. the conditions in the company's country of origin[74] and the country in which the company operates, that should be considered. The corporate responsibility to respect human rights varies in its implications for companies that operate in different country contexts. Compliance may be understood by the extent to which conditions in these countries favour such compliance. For instance, compliance may be greater for companies that operate in contexts where local laws are enforced and multi-stakeholder initiatives are in place[75] or whose country of origin enforces mandatory reporting requirements on companies in high-risk countries and imposes legal requirements to conduct human rights due diligence.[76]

Sector-specific factors are also relevant. The challenges that the corporate responsibility to respect human rights pose may vary between companies that belong to different sectors.[77]

The institutional setting

Compliance may be understood not only by reference to the substantive content of this norm, but also the institutions that, through their standards and practices, bind business enterprises to implementing this responsibility. The SRSG distinguishes five types of such standards and practices: (i) the 'State duty to Protect'; (ii) 'Corporate responsibility and accountability for international crimes'; (iii) 'Corporate responsibility for other human rights violations under international law'; (iv) 'Soft law mechanisms'; and (v) 'self-regulation'.[78] The assumption holds that States and business enterprises will enhance their standards and practices in order to actively implement their rights and duties under the UNGPs. The corporate responsibility to respect is expected to take ground as a result of the restatement and enactment of the UNGPs through soft and hard-law instruments that affect and coordinate the regulation of business conduct.

It should be noted that compliance by business enterprises can be understood not only by reference to legislation, regulation, judicial and non-judicial redress mechanisms, emanating from the public governance (national and international) system, but also to other governance systems that shape business conduct (i.e. the corporate governance system and the civil governance system). The corporate responsibility to respect human rights may thus derive normative force, for example, from the standard-setting activities of international multilateral institutions, the authoritative opinions of treaty monitoring bodies that help to clarify expectations regarding businesses' responsibility, the exposure of corporations to the monitoring activities of NGOs, the integration of the corporate responsibility to respect human rights into self-regulatory practices of business enterprises, etc.

Norms and ideational factors

The presumption is that the UNGPs are set out to promote a global system for business and human rights that can affect and coordinate the regulation of compliance by business enterprises with the corporate responsibility to respect human rights in practice. Compliance by business enterprises can be understood also in relation to the internalization of business respect for human rights within corporate culture and practises.[79] Melish and Meidinger suggest that the SRSG's thought-process can be traced back to his earlier writings on social constructivism and argue that the SRSG found inspiration in the theoretical perspective of 'idealist institutionalism'.[80] This perspective premises on the understanding that social norms emerge and crystallize, and that change in behaviour occurs through processes of socialization and acculturation. Change in behaviour is effectuated through ideational factors, i.e. 'intersubjective beliefs' that are 'widely shared across world cultures', and acculturation processes. According to this theoretical perspective, normative, institutional and behavioural change cannot be attributed to the material self-interests of actors alone, or coercion and persuasion through formal legal regulations.

The compliance by business enterprises, Melish and Meidinger point out, thus relates to the socialization processes and the internalization of shared norms in corporate cultures and State practices. According to the authors, the UNGPs can be perceived as a global script for human rights compliance systems. Once this script is widely accepted by relevant parties and diffuses globally, the authors argue, a new set of constitutive rules can emerge that define and pre-structure socially acceptable corporate conduct. Such constitutive rules can emerge once the norms contained in the UNGPs have passed through stages of 'persuasion, socialization and ultimately internationalization' and have assumed a '[t]aken-for-granted quality'.[81]

Preliminary considerations

The UNGPs are thus an attempt at intervening in the regulatory ecosystem of business and human rights, and promoting an institutional approach to creating a global system for business and human rights that affects and coordinates the regulation of business conduct in relation to human rights. The variables/factors that affect this change in business conduct to comply with their responsibility to respect human rights relate to 'the interests, capacities and engagement of states, market actors, civil society, and the intrinsic power of ideational and normative factors'.[82] With regards to context, the UNGPs are set out to promote a regulatory dynamic within this global system that can progressively bind business enterprises to respect for human rights. This dynamic can potentially affect the evolution of this responsibility from a soft into a 'harder' norm.

The content of the corporate responsibility to respect human rights provides flexibility for companies to meet a minimum human rights due diligence standard by adopting measures that are commensurate to their capabilities and appropriate to their circumstances. The UNGPs furthermore promote a better organization of the regulatory contributions of different institutional actors and their governance systems in a systematic and comprehensive manner. The UNGPs, as a result of their embedding in the regulatory ecosystem, can induce changes in conduct, by reconstructing interests and identities and bringing these into alignment with human rights. To the extent that business enterprises, as a result of socialization and institutionalization, have a deeper commitment to adhere to the corporate responsibility to respect, then this norm has already taken on binding-ness and normative force.

Arguably, the UNGPs thus advance a system for the further crystallization of the corporate responsibility to respect human rights into norms of different types of obligation, and their potential transition into 'hard norms' under national, sub-international (i.e. EU), and international law. The corporate responsibility to respect should take on normative force if the duties and responsibilities of States and business enterprises are given full effect to the normative objective of ensuring human rights and fundamental freedoms. The realization of this objective affects and is affected by the extent to which the corporate responsibility to respect human rights is regulated through the public system.

A scenario for an emerging regulatory regime on business and human rights

The previous section reflects on the normative potential of the UNGPs to foster compliance by business enterprises with the corporate responsibility to respect human rights. This section focuses on the presumption that the UNGPs are expected to affect the evolution of the corporate responsibility to respect human rights from a soft law norm into a more binding norm, and their potential transposition into a hard-law norm at the national, sub-international (i.e. the EU), and international level.

The UNGPs in and of themselves may affect compliance by recognizing that the corporate responsibility to respect human rights exists as a consensus-based global standard of conduct for companies, and by clarifying and elaborating on the content of this norm and its implications. The UNGPs furthermore serve as a platform from which a global system for business and human rights can be created, one that features a regulatory dynamic through which this social norm may acquire additional binding-ness and normative force.[83] Compliance by business enterprises in practice can be understood in relation to the 'socialization' and 'acculturation' processes that abound, contributing to the internalization of the respect for human rights within corporate cultures and practices.

The UNGPs, while by themselves non-legally binding, however, may thus serve as a platform for the operationalization of a global system that is meant to serve as a crystallization point for the corporate responsibility to respect human rights to evolve and eventually be transposed into hard law at the national, sub-International (e.g. EU) or international level.[84] The presumption is that the corporate responsibility to respect can and should acquire additional normative force as existing duties and responsibilities of States and business enterprises, as defined in the UNGPs, are given full effect to the normative objective of ensuring human rights and fundamental freedoms.

The UNGPs recognize that the corporate responsibility to respect human rights exists as a norm in and by itself independent from legal liability and enforcement.[85] This does not mean that the norm exists independent of the law. Compliance with all applicable laws wherever companies operate is an integral part of the corporate responsibility to respect human rights.[86] The standard does not operate in 'a law-free zone'.[87] The corporate responsibility to respect human rights can take on hardening effects where States expect compliance and codify the corporate responsibility to respect human rights into legally binding norms.

States thus can harden the corporate responsibility to respect by transposing the norm into regulation at the domestic level.[88] Certain elements of the corporate responsibility for human rights, as the SRSG has pointed out, can be an object of legal regulation under domestic law and create legal duties for corporations.[89,90] The SRSG is said to have clearly envisioned a process through which the norm of human rights due diligence would make such a transition.[91]

The UNGPs expressly recommend that States consider regulatory measures as part of a smart mix to promote business respect for human rights in practice.[92] In doing so, the UNGPs recognize that States can and should rely on such regulatory measures to discharge their State duty to protect as appropriate. The UNGPs provide that where States have laws in place that are intended or have the effect of requiring businesses to respect human rights, these laws should be enforced effectively, their adequacy assessed periodically, and any gaps should be addressed.[93] This entails that States must establish new laws and/or enforce existing laws that set out such requirements, including in the area of corporate law, and subject these laws to a review in order to ensure their adequacy to foster businesses' respect for human rights in practice. States furthermore should provide effective guidance and, where appropriate, require communication from business enterprises on their respect for human rights.[94]

The interaction between Pillar 1 and 2 of UNGPs suggests that conditions may require that States adopt such regulatory measures as appropriate. The State duty to protect human rights is founded on international human rights law. States can, and where appropriate should, regulate the corporate responsibility to respect human rights, or human rights due diligence elements, under domestic law. As will be addressed below, States already have obligations under international human rights law to protect against human rights violations by regulating business respect for human rights, and in requiring human rights due diligence in certain conditions, e.g. contexts of heightened risks to human rights.

The State duty to protect thus requires States to legally enforce the corporate responsibility to respect, or relevant aspects of the human rights due diligence process where necessary and appropriate in order to ensure business respect for human rights in practice. Such reading also corresponds with the object and purpose of the UNGPs that elaborate on the State duty to protect, which the UNGPs define as 'enhancing standards and practices with regard to business and human rights so as to achieve tangible results for affected individuals and communities, and thereby also contributing to a socially sustainable globalization'.[95]

The concept of the corporate responsibility to respect has some unique qualities that lends itself for usage as a regulatory concept in different areas of law. As will be elaborated at a later point, there are a number of characteristics relating to their design that explain this. First, the corporate responsibility to respect human rights is universally applicable and formulated in open-ended language.[96] Second, the concept has legal pedigree in legal systems across the world.[97] Third, the conduct of business enterprises is benchmarked against international human rights standards. And lastly, the corporate responsibility to respect human rights is central to the emerging global business and human rights regime.

The due diligence concept on which the corporate responsibility to respect human rights is anchored has legal pedigree in national laws in various areas. One study shows that the due diligence concept is widely used across legal systems in States around the world to ensure that businesses respect established standards.[98] While these standards often do not explicitly reference human rights, their use provides evidence that due diligence 'is not a foreign legal or regulatory concept in most countries' and that there is scope for States to 'make far greater use of legal tools to ensure business respects human rights in general, and that companies implement due diligence for human rights in particular'.[99] The same study illustrates that the human rights due diligence concept is suitable for enactment and enforcement in national laws should States decide to adopt measures to this effect.[100]

International human rights law provides the benchmark that business enterprises and relevant stakeholders should assess corporate conduct against. As noted previously, the corporate responsibility to respect human rights is divorced from hard law in terms of its source of obligation and consequences. The norm derives its obligation from social expectations, rather than international law, and primarily depends for its enforcement on civil society. The content of the corporate responsibility to respect human rights, and the due diligence standard that applies to companies, however, directly relates to international human rights law. The corporate responsibility to respect human rights requires that companies abide by their legal obligations, including national and international human rights obligations. Beyond compliance with the law, companies are required to be proactive by undertaking human rights due diligence in order to meet their responsibility. The nature and extent of human rights due diligence that is required from companies should be evaluated on the basis of principles of international human rights law.[101]

It could be stated in this regard that the corporate responsibility to respect human rights derives normative authority and content from international human rights law, though it depends for its effectiveness on its enactment and enforcement through existing governance systems. The link with international human rights law furthermore seems to ensure that the corporate responsibility to respect is applied to companies in a manner that empowers victims and enables access to remedies. As indicated by Ramasastry, it is important that conduct is benchmarked against 'universally recognized human rights principles embodied in a key set of treaties', because this allows right-holders to articulate their concerns in terms of international human rights law and provides a basis for remedies and justice.[102] The human rights due diligence concept thus enables the assessment of business conduct against international human rights standards by victims of human rights abuse and civil society.

The corporate responsibility to respect human rights requires that business enterprises are proactive and conduct a human rights due diligence process in order to 'identify, prevent, mitigate and account for how they address their impacts on human rights'. This responsibility and its human rights due diligence component may be viewed in two different manners. It may be viewed as a forward-looking management process that aims for the prevention of adverse impacts to human rights. Another way to view the human rights due diligence requirement is as a standard of conduct that is expected from business enterprises in order to 'know and show that they respect human rights'.[103] In terms of the latter usage, companies would be expected to abide by this human rights due diligence standard, a breach of which runs counter to their responsibility.

The SRSG appears to support the view that the human rights due diligence concept can be used in both the former and latter sense. The 2009 report of the SRSG notes the following:

> Due diligence is commonly defined as 'diligence reasonably expected from, and ordinarily exercised by, a person who seeks to satisfy a legal requirement or to discharge an obligation'. Some have viewed this in strictly transactional terms what an investor or buyer does to assess a target asset or venture. The Special Representative uses this term in its broader sense: a comprehensive, proactive attempt to uncover human rights risks, actual and potential, over the entire life cycle of a project or business activity, with the aim of avoiding and mitigating those risks.

According to this paragraph, human rights due diligence may be understood as a business practice aimed at identifying human rights risks that may be attached to a project or business activity in order to avoid or mitigate this risk. It may be used by business enterprises as a method to identify and avoid risks of acting in breach of national laws. Due diligence may also be a requirement or obligation under existing law, however. In this context, abiding by the human rights due diligence standard is a matter of legal compliance for companies.

Currently, the human rights due diligence standard in and by itself is not a legal standard of performance.[104] Due to this norm having its source of obligation in social expectations, a breach of this norm will expose a company to condemnation by societal forces and, occasionally, to charges in court. As noted by the SRSG:

> [V]iolations of this social norm are routinely brought to public attention globally through mobilized local communities, networks of civil society, the media including blogs, complaints procedures such as the OECD NCPs, and if they involve alleged violations of the law, then possibly through the courts. This transnational normative regime reaches not only Western multinationals, which have long experienced its effects, but also emerging economy companies operating abroad, and even large national firms.[105]

The SRSG indicates that the norm 'exists independently of State duties and variations in national law'.[106] It is not inconceivable that in time States will restate and integrate the human rights due diligence standard into national laws, including corporate or civil law. In this regard, the relevance of human rights due diligence as a standard of conduct may vary according to whether this concept has been restated as a legal requirement or obligation under public laws (national and international).

The human rights due diligence concept may be applied to assess business conduct in a way that is similar to how the legal due diligence standard is used under national laws and international human rights law. It entails a judgement and a test whether the company has exercised due diligence as appropriate. In this regard, the human rights due diligence requirement reflects a typical due diligence test, 'which asks whether "a more active and more efficient course of procedure might have been pursued" to avoid a particular type of harm'.[107] It could be argued that the human rights due diligence concept can be used in a functionally similar way as international law and national law have used due diligence as a standard of behaviour.[108] While thus distinct in character and source of obligation, the due diligence standard resembles existing due diligence principles. It thus could potentially serve as a blue print for a future legal standard at national and international level, though more exacting language of its content is necessary before conduct can be assessed against this standard.

The UNGPs promote the further evolution of the corporate responsibility to respect human rights and its normative force or binding-ness by placing the concept at the heart of the emerging business and human rights regime. As outlined above, while in itself a soft norm with limited normative force, the corporate responsibility to respect human rights may take on normative force and be 'hardened' through the emerging governance system. 'Soft law increases in power: it is formally non-existent, yet can become a powerful and effective force of substantive behavioural regulation.'[109] These assumptions are part of the SRSG's overall project and relevant for understanding the scenario for future legal developments that the UNGPs set out and the role that the concept of the corporate responsibility to respect human rights has in it.

The SRSG has noted that the UNGPs reflect an attempt at articulating 'a more precise and commonly accepted definition of the corporate responsibility to respect human rights, what specific measures it entails, and how it can be linked more effectively with the public-law construction of internationally recognized rights'.[110] This definition furthermore reflects a responsibility on the part of the company to abide by the requirements that are imposed on a company by the two external governance systems that the company is subject to. These systems are 'the system of public law and authority, and a non-state-based social and civil system grounded in the relations between corporations and their external stakeholders'.[111] The requirements that originate from these systems may apply to companies in varying degrees, depending on circumstances.

The definition of the corporate responsibility to respect human rights is placed at the centre of policies and practices within the different governance systems. Taylor notes the following:

> The Ruggie Framework brings together social expectations and law into an emerging regulatory framework for business and government that in effect defines the nature of business compliance with human rights standards. In so doing, the Framework lays the foundation for the further development of business responsibility, as a coherent area of policy and regulation in its own right. As an arena of activity and debate, CSR has contributed to this regulatory dynamic. The challenge for the field of CSR will be to adapt to an emerging reality in which business responsibility for 'the social' is increasingly a question of both compliance and beyond.

The UNGPs by promoting a new regulatory dynamic in the emerging business and human rights regime thus potentially affects the evolution of the corporate responsibility to respect human rights as a soft norm. The implementation of the UNGPs should result in actions that contribute to the further clarification, shaping and crystallization of the corporate responsibility to respect human rights through hard law and soft law. The normative force of the corporate respect for human rights is expanded by their increased recognition and acceptance by States and other non-state actors through their respective governance systems. Progress can be evaluated in terms of greater acceptance and recognition of the norm by relevant actors. Effectiveness can be assessed by the operational impact on the ground (i.e. the behaviour of business enterprises that reflect actual acceptance and compliance) and their uptake by other initiatives (i.e. inspiration to and recognition by other initiatives).[112]

The integration of the corporate responsibility to respect human rights in national laws and regulations could add legal clarity to this standard in a particular country context. The interpretations by judicial bodies could contribute to the further development of the concept through national jurisprudence.[113] The consistent integration of human rights due diligence may contribute to the re-configuration of the laws themselves. The concept may be understood as reformatory potential that can drive conceptual changes within existing laws in order to resolve tensions. The simultaneous integration of the human rights due diligence concept across different areas of law and policy could have the effect of strengthening the connections between these different areas of law and drive greater convergence between them.

The state duty to protect and regulatory action to ensure business respect for human rights

As has been elaborated above and the UNGPs affirm, States have a positive duty to ensure that the human rights of individuals within their territory and/or jurisdiction are protected against infringements by business enterprises. The duty to protect imposes on States a positive obligation to take appropriate measures or exercise human rights due diligence 'to prevent, investigate, punish or redress' such abuses. A State may incur responsibility if it has failed to take the appropriate due diligence measures to prevent or respond to human rights abuse resulting from corporate activity. Non-compliance with this duty can arise by act or omission. International human rights law thus imposes a due diligence standard of performance on the State. However, there exists no exact definition of the conduct that is expected of States to meet this due diligence standard with regards to the activities of business enterprises. The nature and scope of this standard is amendable to facts and circumstances, hence it 'can be restrictively or expansively interpreted, as the particular facts and circumstances require'.[114,115] The standard's indeterminacy means that a breach by a State of its due diligence obligation cannot be assessed easily.[116] Conditions will determine whether a State's act or omission amounts to a breach of the States' due diligence obligations in the context of business and human rights. The standard of due diligence furthermore relates to the object and purpose of the international treaties giving rise to this duty of human rights due diligence.

UN treaty monitoring bodies through recent authoritative interpretations of the human rights treaty they supervise have shed further clarity on the due diligence standard of performance for States in the context of corporate-related activities. Of particular relevance are two documents, one statement by the UN Committee on Economic, Social and Cultural Rights (the CtESCR), adopted in May 2011, and the other is the General Comment No. 16 of the UN Committee on the Rights of the Child (the CtRC), adopted in 2013.[117] These interpretations articulate the State duty to protect human rights in more exacting language than the UNGPs, affirming that international human rights law has evolved and imposes a more demanding duty on States than before. More specifically, the interpretations support the view that States may act in breach of their due diligence obligations under international human rights law if they fail to ensure that the human rights of individuals are adequately protected from infringements by corporate activity by adopting regulatory measures that require, as appropriate, business enterprises to respect human rights, including by requiring human rights due diligence in certain operational contexts that pose heightened risks to human rights.

The following three developments can be identified.

First, the interpretations recognize that companies have a responsibility to respect human rights and to undertake human rights due diligence. Second, the State duty to exercise due diligence is framed in terms of an obligation to adopt regulatory measures where 'necessary, appropriate and reasonable' to ensure compliance by companies with this societal norm in order to prevent infringements of human rights by corporate activity. Third, the standard of due diligence is adaptable to circumstances and the adoption of mandatory and prescriptive requirements for companies to exercise human rights due diligence is appropriate in contexts that pose heightened risks to human rights, which may be combined with other means that encourage and support business enterprises to respect human rights. A brief analysis of these authoritative interpretations follows.

The 2011 statement by the Committee on Economic, Social and Cultural Rights

The CtESCR, in a statement adopted in May 2011, clarifies the State's obligations under the International Covenant on Economic, Social and Cultural Rights (the ICESCR) in the context of the corporate activities.[118] The Statement affirms the primary obligation of States under Article 2(1) of the ICESCR to respect, protect and fulfil the rights of all persons under their jurisdiction in this context. The CtESCR interprets the State duty to respect as placing a duty on States to ensure that the laws and policies regarding corporate activities conform with the rights set forth under the ICESCR, thus ensuring that companies 'demonstrate due diligence to make certain that they do not impede the enjoyment of the Covenant rights by those who depend on or are negatively affected by their activities'.[119] This interpretation affirms the societal expectation that companies exercise due diligence in order to manage their negative impacts on human rights and frames the obligation of States to respect human rights in terms of ensuring that companies demonstrate their compliance with this societal standard of behaviour.

The statement furthermore articulates a positive duty for States to take adequate measures or 'due diligence' to ensure that rights holders are effectively safeguarded against infringements of their economic, social and cultural rights by corporate actors. States should discharge this duty by establishing regulatory measures, more specifically 'appropriate law and regulations, together with monitoring, investigation and accountability procedures to set and enforce standards for the performance of corporations'. This State duty extends extraterritorially by imposing on States an obligation to take steps to prevent human rights violations abroad by companies that have their main offices under their jurisdiction 'without infringing the sovereignty or diminishing the obligations of the host States under the Covenant'.[120] The scope of this duty is partly defined in relation to the ability of States to influence the company by legal or political means, in accordance with the UN Charter and applicable international law. The duty to protect furthermore entails that States should 'ensure access to effective remedies to victims of corporate abuses of economic, social, and cultural rights through judicial, administrative, legislative or other appropriate means'.[121]

The CtESCR furthermore recognizes an obligation on the part of the States to fulfil human rights by undertaking to obtain the corporate sector's support for the realization of the ESCR. This entails that the home States shall encourage companies to assist host states 'as appropriate, including in situations of armed conflict and natural disaster, [...] in building the capacities needed to address the corporate responsibility for the observance of [ESCR]'.[122]

The statement of the ICESCR affirms that international human rights law imposes a positive duty on States to undertake 'due diligence' by adopting appropriate regulatory measures to protect against, and to ensure access to effective remedies for, infringements of the rights set out under the ICESCR by corporate-related activity. This duty has an extraterritorial dimension and imposes on States to adopt 'adequate' measures to regulate the conduct of companies in order to prevent adverse human rights impacts abroad. The CtESCR also recognizes that business enterprises have a responsibility to respect and an obligation of States to ensure that they do. The CtESCR does not define the substantive content of the corporate responsibility to respect human rights or indicate that this responsibility should be construed in line with the expectations set out in the UNGPs. Nevertheless, the CtESCR affirms the relevance to the General Comment of the UNGPs and the ILO Tripartite Declaration and indicates that other instruments, *inter alia* the OECD Guidelines, the UNGC, the UN Study on Violence against Children and the Children's Rights and Business Principles served as useful references for the Committee.

General Comment No. 16 of the Committee on the Rights of the Child

The CtRC adopted General Comment No. 16 in 2013, titled 'State obligations regarding the impact of the business sector on children's rights'.[123] In this General Comment, the CtRC clarifies the obligation of States in relation to the impact of business activities and operations on children's rights under the Convention on the Rights of the Child (CRC) and the Operational Protocols thereto.[124] The CtRC recognizes that 'it is necessary for States to have adequate legal and institutional frameworks to respect, protect and fulfil children's rights, and to provide remedies in case of violations in the context of business activities and operations'.[125] The CtRC recognizes that States should:

- a Ensure that the activities and operations of business enterprises do not adversely impact on children's rights;
- b Create an enabling and supportive environment for business enterprises to respect children's rights, including across any business relationships linked to their operations, products or services and across their global operations;
- c Ensure access to effective remedy for children whose rights have been infringed by a business enterprise acting as a private party or as a State agent.[126]

The CtRC expressly refers to the PRR Framework and the UNGPs, the ILO Tripartite Declaration of Principles, the OECD Guidelines for Multinational Enterprises and the Children's Rights and Business Principles as relevant to the General Comment, amongst other 'existing and evolving national and international norms, standards and policy guidance on business and human rights'.[127] The CtRC recognizes that the responsibilities to respect the rights of 'children extend in practice beyond the State and State-controlled services and institutions and apply to private actors and business enterprises [...] therefore, all business enterprises must meet their responsibilities regarding children's rights and States must ensure that they do'.[128] The General Comment thus frames the State's obligations with regards to children's rights and the business sector in terms of ensuring that business enterprises meet their responsibility to respect human rights.

The CtRC reaffirm the obligation of States under Article 4 of the CRC:

> States Parties shall undertake all appropriate legislative, administrative, and other measures for the implementation of the rights recognized in the present Convention. With regard to economic, social and cultural rights, States Parties shall undertake such measures to the maximum extent of their available resources and, where needed, within the framework of international co-operation.

The provision gives rise to an obligation for State Parties to respect, protect and fulfil children's rights in relation to business activities and operations that impact children's rights. The CtRC interprets the State duty to respect as imposing an obligation on States to 'not directly or indirectly facilitate, aid and abet any infringement of children's rights' and 'ensure that all actors respect children's rights, including in the context of business activities and operations'. This entails that a State should 'not engage in, support or condone abuses of children's rights when it has a business role itself or conducts business with private enterprises'.[129]

The CtRC notes that States have an obligation to protect the rights of each child subject to the States' jurisdiction from infringements by third parties. This duty extends to infringements caused by or contributed to by companies. A State can incur responsibility for such infringements if the State failed to take 'necessary, appropriate and reasonable measures to prevent and remedy such infringements or otherwise collaborated with or tolerated the infringements'.[130] Appropriate measures can take the form of 'the passing of law and regulation, their monitoring and enforcement, and policy adoption that frame how business enterprises can impact on children's rights'.[131] The CtRC notes that it is appropriate to require business enterprises operating in conflict areas or other contexts that pose a heightened risk of rights abuses 'to undertake stringent child-rights due diligence tailored to their size and activities'.[132] Additionally, home States should inform businesses that are operating or planning to operate in such areas about the local children's rights context, emphasizing that companies have 'identical responsibilities to respect children's rights in such setting as they do elsewhere'.[133]

The State duty to protect children's rights extends extraterritorially to all children subject to the State's jurisdiction. Home States have extraterritorial obligations to ensure children's rights in the context of businesses' extraterritorial activities and operations, including by enabling access to remedies for children whose rights have been violated by such extraterritorial activities, provided there is 'a reasonable link between the State and the conduct concerned'.[134] The Optional Protocol on the sale of children, child prostitution and child pornography requires that State Parties establish liability for business enterprises for these offences (criminal, civil or administrative), no matter where such offences are committed. The CtRC affirms the duty of States to engage in international cooperation for the realization of children's rights beyond their territorial boundaries,[135] including through their membership in international organizations (e.g. international development, finance and trade institutions).[136]

The CtRC furthermore interprets the duty of States to fulfil children's rights as a positive obligation to implement 'legislative, administrative, budgetary, judicial, promotional and other measures' in order to 'facilitate, promote and provide for the enjoyment of children's rights'.[137] The duty to fulfil imposes an obligation on States to provide 'stable and predictable legal and regulatory environments which enable business enterprises to respect children's rights, [which] includes clear and well-enforced laws and standards on labour, employment, health and safety, environment, anti-corruption, land use and taxation'.[138]

The CtRC affirms the obligation of States to provide effective remedies and reparations for violations of the rights of the child by business enterprises. This obligation entails 'having in place child-sensitive mechanisms – criminal, civil and administrative – that are known by children and their representatives, that are prompt, genuinely available and accessible and that provide adequate reparation for harm suffered'.[139]

The interpretation of the treaty monitoring bodies affirm that international human rights law imposes obligations on States to establish, implement and enforce appropriate legislative and regulatory measures to ensure that companies abide by their responsibility to respect human rights and exercise due diligence, including when operating abroad. States can incur responsibility if they fail to regulate and enforce this responsibility as appropriate, including by requiring human rights due diligence where the operating context poses heightened risks to human rights. Further clarification of the application of this duty to protect human rights by exercising due diligence in requiring business enterprises to abide by their responsibility to respect human rights in order to ensure that their activities do not have adverse human rights impacts at home or abroad is desirable.

The 2016 recommendation by the Committee of Ministers of the Council of Europe on human rights and business

The Committee of Ministers of the Council of Europe adopted a Recommendation on human rights and business on 2 March 2016.[140] The Recommendation is addressed to Member States of the Council of Europe ('Member States'). In it the Committee of Member States ('Committee') expresses 'its commitment to contribute to the effective implementation of the UN Guiding Principles on Business and Human Rights at the European level'.[141] The Recommendation is not a legally binding document, and thus in and of itself, does not alter or create new legal obligations. The instruments that the Member States of the Council of Europe have ratified determine the extent to which Members are bound.[142] The Committee recommends Member States, *inter alia*, to 'review their national legislation and practice to ensure that they comply with the recommendations, principles and further guidance set out in the appendix'.[143]

An Appendix[144] has been attached to the Recommendation, which clarifies the implications of the State duty to protect human rights (Pillar 1 and 3 of the UNGPs) in the European context. The European Convention of Human Rights (ECHR) as interpreted and applied by the European Court of Human Rights (ECtHR) and the European Social Charter (revised), and corresponding conclusions and decisions by the European Committee on Social Rights, are referred to as of particular relevance.[145] While recognizing that all three pillars of the UNGPs are of 'equal value and importance',[146] the Recommendation addresses the second pillar of the UNGPs indirectly, by making recommendations about the measures that Members should implement to enable corporate respect for human rights.[147]

The Recommendation specifies that the State duty to protect entails that (own emphasis added):

13. Member States should:

- apply such measures *as may be necessary* to require business enterprises operating within their territorial jurisdiction to respect human rights;
- apply such measures *as may be necessary* to require, *as appropriate*, business enterprises domiciled in their jurisdiction to respect human rights throughout their operations abroad;
- encourage and support these business enterprises by other means so that they respect human rights throughout their operations.

This paragraph specifies the duty of States to protect human rights against infringements by business enterprises by taking prescriptive or mandatory measures to require business enterprises as may be necessary. The paragraph distinguishes between two scenarios. The first bullet point concerns the regulation of business enterprises that operate in the territory of the State, but that may have their domicile[148] elsewhere. States should adopt regulatory measures as may be necessary to require these business enterprises to respect human rights. The second bullet point concerns the regulation of business enterprises that have their domicile in a Member State but operate outside of Europe. States should adopt regulatory measures as may be necessary to require these business enterprises 'as appropriate' (e.g. to the size, nature or context of the operations) to respect human rights throughout its operations abroad. According to the third bullet point, States furthermore should encourage or support business enterprises to respect human rights through other means (e.g. incentive measures),[149] which seems applicable to both aforementioned scenarios.

The Recommendation furthermore indicates 'that everyone within their jurisdiction may easily have access to information about existing human rights in the context of corporate responsibility in a language which they can understand'.[150] As the commentary explains, this paragraph places emphasis on the right of individuals to have access to information. The underlying reason is that 'persons cannot claim their rights if they do not know about them'.[151]

The Recommendation further specifies the actions that State should take to enable corporate responsibility to respect human rights:

20. Member States should apply such measures as may be necessary to encourage or, where appropriate, require that:

- business enterprises domiciled within their jurisdiction apply human rights due diligence throughout their operations;
- business enterprises conducting substantial activities within their jurisdiction carry out human rights due diligence in respect of such activities;
- including project-specific human rights impact assessments, as appropriate to the size of the business enterprise and the nature and context of the operation.

This paragraph indicates that States should apply regulatory measures as may be necessary, where appropriate, to require that business enterprises apply human rights due diligence, including human rights impact assessments as appropriate to the size of the business enterprise and the nature and context of the operation. The Commentary notes that introducing requirements would seem appropriate, for instance, where

> the nature and context of a business enterprises relate to sectors with particular human rights risks, instances in which the human rights impacts of business activities can be severe, where companies operate in conflict-affected or high-risk areas or other contexts which pose significant risks to human rights.[152]

The application of such requirements differs depending on whether the company is domiciled in the jurisdiction of a Member State, or whether the business merely conducts substantial activities within this jurisdiction. In case of the former, the requirements should apply throughout the operations of the company. In case of the latter, the requirements only should apply in relation to activities within its jurisdiction.[153]

Important to note is the caveat in the Commentary indicating that the Recommendation

> neither seeks to define human rights due diligence, nor does it specify whether, in the event that member States take legislative measures to require human rights due diligence under certain circumstances, such measures should be specifically developed or integrated into corporate or civil law.[154]

This provision most likely reflects the fact that the corporate responsibility to respect human rights, and the human rights due diligence concept has not been recognized as a legally binding concept at the international level. The Recommendation further stipulates that States should 'encourage, and where appropriate, require business enterprises referred to in paragraph 20 to display greater transparency' and 'to provide regularly, or as needed, information on their efforts on corporate responsibility to respect human rights'.[155]

The Recommendation indicates that additional measures are required from Member States when a particular business nexus exists. As noted by the Commentary, the fact that States have more means at their disposal to ensure respect for human rights in the presence of such a State-nexus may in and of itself be a sufficient justification for such additional measures.[156] 'States should apply additional measures to require business enterprises to respect human rights, including, where appropriate, by carrying out human rights due diligence.'[157] The Recommendation identifies in which situations a business nexus exists: 'own or control business enterprises'; 'grant substantial support or deliver services through agencies'; 'grant export licenses to business enterprises'; 'conduct commercial transactions with business enterprises, including through the conclusion of public procurement contracts'; 'privatize the delivery of services'.[158] The measures that a State has taken must be evaluated and findings must be met with a response, *inter alia*, consequences for non-compliance with respect for human rights (e.g. the termination of a public procurement contract).[159]

The Recommendation thus specifies that the State should adopt legislative measures where necessary and appropriate to require business enterprises to apply human rights due diligence. The applicability of such requirements to companies may differ depending on whether the business enterprise is domiciled within the jurisdiction of the Member State, or only conducts substantial activities within this jurisdiction. More may be expected of States in the presence of a business nexus. There is discretion for Member States to define human rights due diligence and there is no obligation for Member States to develop or integrate human rights due diligence into corporate or civil law.[160]

Conclusion

This chapter examined the legal status of the UNGPs as soft law. No direct legal consequences flow from the UNGPs. Nevertheless, the UNGPs in and by themselves can foster compliance by recognizing the existence of a global standard of conduct for companies to respect human rights and by clarifying and elaborating on the content of this standard and its implications. The corporate responsibility to respect human rights is a soft/moral norm founded in global social expectations, hence it is non-legally binding in a strict legal sense. The corporate responsibility to respect carries within its normative content the force to pull compliance. The UNGPs furthermore serve as a platform for further actions through which this social norm potentially acquires additional normative force. The expectation is that this norm can and should acquire additional normative force as existing duties and responsibilities of States and business enterprises as set out in the UNGPs are given full effect to the normative objective of ensuring human rights and fundamental freedoms. An expansion of such normative force can result from the increased recognition and clarification of this norm by States and non-state actors through collaborative engagement within the different governance systems. Progress can be assessed in relation to enhanced standards and practices on business and human rights reflecting such increased recognition.

The corporate responsibility to respect human rights as a soft/moral norm lies at the heart of the emerging global regime on business and human rights. Its nature and legal relevance should be understood within this context. The UNGPs, by recognizing and clarifying this responsibility and by providing a platform of action, have the potential to affect the evolution of this concept from a soft norm into a harder obligation. The design of the corporate responsibility to respect is key in this respect, allowing for its transposition into legal form at the national level and usage across different areas of law. That this transposition is feasible is evidenced by the due diligence concept already having been incorporated into certain national laws as an applicable standard. It is not inconceivable that the SRSG chose the concept of human rights due diligence in order to enable the incorporation of a generally applicable standard of conduct into different areas of national and international law.

Recent interpretations by treaty monitoring bodies have articulated the State duty to conduct human rights due diligence not only in more exacting language, but have also framed this duty in terms of ensuring that business enterprises abide by their responsibility to respect human rights. These interpretations support the view that the duty of States to conduct due diligence in order to ensure the protection of human rights from infringements by business enterprises requires that States adopt regulatory measures to ensure business respect for human rights, including requirements of due diligence from companies that operate in the context of heightened human rights risks. State practices that integrate the corporate responsibility to respect in laws and policies can be constitutive of an international legal regime on business and human rights. Such regime would be integral to the emerging global system of business and human rights in which the three (law, civil, corporate) governance systems progress in a coordinated manner in the pursuit of reduced harm by business enterprises to human rights.[161]

Notes

1 John Ruggie, *Regulating Multinationals: The UN Guiding Principles, Civil Society, and International Legalization*, at 6 (Regulatory Policy Program, Working Paper RPP-2015–04, 2015).
2 J.A. Zerk, Multinationals and Corporate Social Responsibility: Limitations and Opportunities in International Law, at 70 (Cambridge University Press 2006).
3 Dinah Shelton, *Normative Hierarchy of International Law*, 100 The American Journal of International Law, at 319 (2006).
4 C.M. Chinkin, *The Challenge of Soft Law: Development and Change in International Law*, 38 International and Comparative Law Quarterly 850, at 851(1989).
5 Justin Nolan, *The Corporate Responsibility to Respect Human Rights: Soft Law or Not Law?*, *in* Human Rights Obligations of Business: Beyond the Corporate Responsibility to Respect? (Surya Deva & David Bilchitz eds. 2013).

6 The SRSG notes that 'soft law is "soft" in the sense that it does not by itself create legally binding obligations [but] derives its normative force through recognition of social expectations by States and other key actors'. Special Representative on the Issue of Human Rights and Transnational Corporations and Other Business Enterprises, *Business and Human Rights: Mapping International Standards of Responsibility and Accountability for Corporate Acts*, §45 A/HRC/4/35 (19 Feb. 2007) [hereinafter *Ruggie, 2007 Report*] (by John Ruggie). *See* further, Nolan, *id.* at 140.

7 According to the SRSG,

> The GPs are the first authoritative guidance that the Council and its predecessor body, the Commission on Human Rights, have issued for States and business enterprises on their respective obligations in relation to business and human rights; and it marked the first time that either body 'endorsed' a normative text on any subject that Governments did not negotiate themselves.
>
> *See* Ruggie, *supra* note 1

8 John Ruggie, *Business and Human Rights: Treaty Road Not Travelled*, Ethical Corporation (2008).

9 Ruggie, *supra* note 1, at 6.

10 Dinah Shelton, Commitment and Compliance: The Role of Non-Binding Norms in the International Legal System (Dinah Shelton ed. 2000).

11 Nolan, *supra* note 5, at 139.

12 Ruggie, *supra* note 1, at 42.

13 John Ruggie, Just Business Multinational Corporations and Human Rights, 57 (W.W. Norton & Company 2013).

14 Ruggie, *supra* note 1, at 10.

15 The SRSG referred to the Declaration on the Rights of Indigenous Peoples as an example, a soft law instrument which took 26 years to negotiate, and was adopted only in 2007. This was despite the relatively circumscribed nature of the subject. Ruggie, *supra* note 13, at 57. *See* further, John H. Knox, *The Ruggie Rules: Applying Human Rights Law to Corporations*, *in* The UN Guiding Principles on Business and Human Rights: Foundations and Implementation, at 64 (R. Mares ed. 2012).

16 This argument was elaborated upon by the SRSG in an issues-brief posted in January 2014 in contribution to discussions on the negotiation of a UN business and human rights treaty. Ecuador and South Africa supported an initiative to start a new process of formulating a treaty to clarify the human rights obligations of business enterprises and to establish an effective mechanism for remedies. This resulted in Human Rights Council Res 26/9, Elaboration of an international legally binding instrument on transnational corporations and other business enterprises with respect to human rights, 26th Sess., 10–27 June 2014, A/HRC/RES/26/9 (14 July 2014). J. Ruggie, A UN Business and Human Rights Treaty? An Issues Brief by John G. Ruggie (2014), www.hks.harvard.edu/m-rcbg/CSRI/UNBusinessandHumanRightsTreaty.pdf.

17 *Id.* at 3.

18 Ruggie, *supra* note 8, at 43.

19 John Ruggie, *Business and Human Rights: The Evolving International Agenda*, 23 (John F. Kennedy School of Government, Corporate Social Responsibility Initiative Working Paper No. 31, 2007).

20 Nicola Jägers, *Will Transnational Private Regulation Close the Governance Gap?*, *in* Human Rights Obligations of Business: Beyond the Corporate Responsibility to Respect?, 298 (Surya Deva & David Bilchitz eds. 2013).

21 Ruggie, *supra* note 1.

22 This was reflected in the terms of his mandate that called upon the SRSG to 'identify' and 'clarify' and to provide recommendations.

23 Ruggie, *supra* note 13, at 58.

24 The SRSG also discarded then the option of recommending a treaty of lesser complexity by stating that there was no foundation for *any* treaty negotiations at that time. Ruggie, *supra* note 13, at 56, 57.

25 The SRSG indicated that:

> [t]reaties form the bedrock of the international human rights system. Specific elements of the business and human rights agenda may become candidates for successful international legal instruments. But it is my carefully considered view that negotiations on an overarching treaty now would be unlikely to get off the ground and, even if they did, the outcome could well leave us worse off than we are today.
>
> John Ruggie, *Business and Human Rights: Treaty Road Not Travelled*, Ethical Corporation, at 48 (2008)

26 According to Knox, '[i]f Ruggie had introduced another draft of a legally binding agreement, or even a non-binding declaration, it seemed likely to meet the same fate [as the UN Norms]'. Knox, *supra* note 15, at 64.

27 Ruggie, *supra* note 13, at 58.

28 Dinah Shelton, *Introduction: Law, Non-Law and the Problem of 'Soft Law'*, *in* Commitment and Compliance: The Role of Non-binding Norms in the International Legal System, 13 (Dinah Shelton ed. 2003).

29 The SRSG indicated that:

> [a]ll Council members in 2011 were able to endorse the corporate responsibility to respect *all* human rights because, within the GPs' framework, that responsibility is based in a global social norm, not a legal obligation. In contrast, if the corporate responsibility to respect human rights were turned into an international treaty obligation, its applicability and the range of human rights to which it would apply would be determined by individual instances of state treaty ratification – not only involving the proposed new treaty, but also the variable human rights standards that individual states recognize as international legal obligations.
>
> Ruggie, *supra* note 1, at 9

30 Ruggie, *supra* note 13, at 59.

31 *Id.* at 63.

32 *Id.* at 62.

33 *Id.* at 43.

34 In the words of the SRSG:

> There are 77,000 transnational corporations, with about 800,000 subsidiaries and millions of suppliers – Walmart alone has 62,000. Then there are millions of other national companies. The existing treaty bodies have difficulty keeping up with 192 member States, and each deals with only a specific set of rights or affected group. How would one such committee handle millions of millions of companies, while addressing all rights of all persons?
>
> Ruggie, *supra* note 8

35 Shelton, *supra* note 28, at 12.

36 *Id.*

37 *Id.* at 13.

38 Nolan, *supra* note 5, at 142.

39 The SRSG notes that this multi-stakeholder approach endowed the UNGPs with

> what Joost Pauselyn, Ramses A Wessel, and Jan Wouters term 'thick stakeholder consensus' – which, they suggest, can be normatively superior in securing compliance to the 'thin state consent' validation requirement associated with traditional international law. Indeed, in this particular instance, thick stakeholder

consensus helped pave the way for unanimous Human Rights Council endorsement.

John Ruggie, *Global Governance and 'New Governance Theory': Lessons from Business and Human Rights*, 20 Global Governance 10 (2014)

40 '[T]he expertise of a large pool of regulators and other actors can lead to more dynamic regulation, sensitive to global and regional changes and evolution'. Joost Pauwelyn, et al., *When Structures Become Shackles: Stagnation and Dynamics in International Law Making*, 25 The European Journal of International Law (2014).

41 These arguments correspond with findings in the literature on the legal relevance of soft law, which point to soft law as a method to foster acceptance and compliance by States with international norms. As articulated by Shelton, the underlying assumption is that States adopt, accept and comply with international norms when it is in their interest to do so. The assumption is that soft law can accomplish compliance in a different way from hard law. More precisely, soft law can achieve compliance by way of managing incentives, rather than by coercion. Shelton notes that

soft law may be used precisely because compliance is expected to be difficult: it begins a dynamic process over time that may lead to hard law or the norm may remain soft at the international level but become hard law internally.

Shelton, *supra* note 10, at 17

42 *See* a similar argument by Backer in the context of the NCPs, noting that, precisely because the proceedings of NCPs are not binding, the flexibility of these NCPs allows the application of procedures that are detached from municipal law. Backer suggests that the OECD Guidelines on MNEs 'serve as something like an autonomous transnational system, subject principally to its own substantive rules that incidentally draw on an aggregated and generalized municipal and international law as a basis for the application of its norms'. Backer, *supra* note 79.

43 Nolan, *supra* note 5, at 144.

44 These factors are not entirely dissimilar from those explaining potential compliance by *States* with international norms, and relate to 'the form or process of adoption, the content of the instrument, the institutional setting, and the follow-up procedures envisaged'. Shelton, *supra* note 10, at 17.

45 Nolan, *supra* note 5, at 158.

46 Legitimacy is here understood in descriptive terms, that is, the belief of having the right to rule. Daniel Bodansky, *The Legitimacy and International Governance: A Coming Challenge for International Environmental Law?*, 93 The American Journal of International Law (1999). Allen Buchanan & Robert O. Keohane, *The Legitimacy of Global Governance Institutions*, 20 Ethics & International Affairs (2006).

47 Stéphanie Bijlmakers, *Business and Human Rights Governance and Democratic Legitimacy: The UN 'Protect, Respect and Remedy' Framework*, 26 Innovation: The European Journal of Social Sciences 288 (2013).

48 The SRSG has noted that States may turn to soft law for several reasons: (i) to chart possible future directions for, and fill gaps in, the international legal order when they are not yet able or willing to take firmer measures; where they (ii) conclude that legally binding mechanisms are not the best tool to address a particular issue; or (iii) in certain instances, to avoid having more binding measures gain political momentum.

49 Shelton notes how

soft law instruments often serve as an authoritative way to allow treaty parties to resolve ambiguities in a binding text or fill in gaps. This function is part of an increasingly complex international system with variations in forms of instruments, means, and standards of measurement that interact intensely and frequently, with the common purpose of regulating behavior within a rule of law framework.

Shelton, *supra* note 3, at 320

50 *Id.* at 320.
51 Nolan, *supra* note 5, at 159.
52 Special Representative on the Issue of Human Rights and Transnational Corporations and Other Business Enterprises, *Protect, Respect and Remedy: A Framework for Business and Human Rights*, ¶ 54, U.N. doc. A/HRC/8/5 (7 Apr. 2008) (by John Ruggie).
53 As a recent report notes, in relation to the UNGPs,

> national court systems might draw upon them to support their legal reasoning; parliaments might incorporate elements of them into regulations; they might become the basis for an international treaty; and they can be included as binding clauses in private party contracts.
>
> Foley Hoag LLP & UNEP FI, Banks and Human Rights: A Legal Analysis (Dec. 2015), www.unepfi.org/fileadmin/documents/BanksandHumanRights.pdf

54 *Id.*
55 Nolan, *supra* note 5, at 159.
56 *Id.*
57 For example, the business case is contested and the different commercial rationales that drive business responses may not apply at all times. The business case may not be sufficient, in and of itself, to ensure respect for human rights. IHBR, State of Play Human Rights in the Political Economy of States: Avenues for Application, 20–21 (2014).
58 *Report of the Working Group on the Issue of Human Rights and Transnational Corporations and Other Business Enterprises, Addendum: Uptake of the Guiding Principles on Business and Human Rights: Findings from a 2013 Questionnaire for Corporations*, 14, figure 7, Human Rights Council, U.N. doc. A/HRC/26/25/Add.1 [hereinafter *UN Working Group, Corporate Survey 2013*] (28 Apr. 2014).
59 IHBR, *supra* note 57, at 5.
60 *Id.* at. 5.
61 *UN Working Group, Corporate Survey 2013*, *supra* note 58, at 14.
62 Also *see* Shift & Mazars, The UN Guiding Principles Reporting Framework, 16 (2015).
63 *Id.* at 3–4, 5.
64 *Id.* at 3–4.
65 *Id.*
66 For instance, business enterprises have identified a lack of guidance on how to build leverage in operating contexts where human rights are not part of local law or applied in practice as a key obstacle in meeting their responsibility to respect human rights.
67 *Id.* at 20.
68 *Id.* at 20.
69 IHBR, *supra* note 57, at 20.
70 For instance, research points to a greater tendency among larger entities than among SMEs to focus on mapping high-risk operations as a priority. Also, smaller entities tend to focus more on improving complaints/grievance mechanisms as a priority than large entities. *UN Working Group, Corporate Survey 2013*, *supra* note 58, at 12.
71 European Commission, An Analysis of Policy References made by large EU Companies to Internationally Recognised CSR Guidelines and Principles, 9 (2013).
72 The corporate responsibility to respect human rights applies equally to SMEs. SMEs

facing severe risks that call for an elevated response and more dedicated resources may be constrained in their response by lack of resources. However, resource constraints need not be an issue, in and of themselves, because the human rights due diligence is a relative concept and responsive to, *inter alia*, the resource constraint of SMEs. 'Human rights due diligence is not an absolute, it is finite and limited by resources, time and context'. IHBR, *supra* note 57, at 22.

73 *Id.* at 14, § 42.

74 European Commission, An Analysis of Policy References made by large EU Companies to Internationally Recognised CSR Guidelines and Principles, 6, 10 (2013).

75 *UN Working Group, Corporate Survey 2013, supra* note 58, at 15.

76 *Id.* at 16, § 46–47.

77 A study suggests that disclosure on stakeholder engagement processes varied between companies active in different sectors. More precisely, according to the study, companies belonging to the extractive sector – 'where engagement centers on communities around their operations' – tend to show stronger disclosure on stakeholder engagement in their human rights impact assessments process. The study also suggests that companies in the apparel and the food, beverage, and agriculture sectors – 'where many companies have long-established audit programs that incorporate interviews with local stakeholders' – are more likely to disclose information on stakeholder engagement within their supply chains. Shift, Evidence of Corporate Disclosure relevant to the UN Guiding Principles on Business and Human Rights (2014), http://shiftproject.org/sites/default/files/Evidence%20of%20Corporate%20Disclosure%20Relevant%20 to%20the%20UN%20Guiding%20Principles%20on%20Business%20and%20Human%20Rights.pdf.

78 The SRSG notes, 'soft law is "soft" in the sense that it does not by itself create legally binding obligations [but] derives its normative force through recognition of social expectations by states and other key actors'. Ruggie, *2007 Report, supra* note 6, §6.

79 Backer makes this argument in relation to the OECD, noting that:

> Ultimately, under the guise of 'soft' law, the OECD may be able to construct a system of customary law and practice as binding as any hard-law system. What makes this soft law 'hard' *in effect* is precisely its naturalization of behavioural norms *within* entities that incorporate those practices in corporate culture, rather than its imposition from *outside* the community of actors by the formal fiat of positive legal command.
>
> Larry Catá Backer, *Rights and Accountability in Development ('Raid') v. DAS AIR and Global Witness v. Afrimex: Small Steps towards an Autonomous Transnational Legal System for the Regulation of Multinational Corporations*, 10 Melbourne Journal of International Law (2009)

Hill and Jones define culture as 'the specific collection of values and norms that are shared by people and ground in an organization and that control the way they interact with each other and with stakeholders outside the organisation'. Robert G. Eccles, et al., The Impact of a Corporate Culture of Sustainability on Corporate Behaviour and Performance, at 2 (Harvard Business School, Working Paper 12–035, 2011).

80 Melish & Meidinger, *Protect, Respect, Remedy and Participate: 'New Governance' Lessons for the Ruggie Framework, in* The UN Guiding Principles on Business and Human Rights: Foundations and Implementation (R. Mares ed. 2011).

81 *Id.*

82 Ruggie, *Life in the Global Public Domain: Response to Commentaries on the UN Guiding Principles and the Proposed Treaty on Business and Human Rights* (23 Jan. 2015), *available at* http://papers.ssrn.com/sol3/papers.cfm?abstract_id=2554726.

83 The Thun Group refers to the UNGPs as an example of 'hardening' soft law in the sense that they act as a catalyst to spark new policy requirements or binding regulation and are being multiplied by other international organizations and national legislators. UN Guiding Principles on Business and Human Rights: Discussion Paper for Banks on Implications of Principles 16–21, 4 (2013), http://business-humanrights.org/sites/default/files/media/documents/thun-group-discussion-paper-final-2-oct-2013.pdf.
84 *Ruggie, 2008 Report, supra* note 98, § 66. Casey & Scott define 'crystallization' as

> the process through which fluids are solidified, starting from a nucleus and then growing in a fashion which assumes a regular pattern in a very marked contrast to the boundaries from which it emerged. A process of crystallization thus gives shape to what was previously shapeless, defining and giving significance to elements of the structure. Drawing on this process, our particular understanding of the crystallization of norms suggests a process by which norms take on regulatory effect.
>
> Casey & Scott, cited in Eijsbouts, *supra* note 90, at 51, (2011)

85 The UN Guiding Principles indicate that the responsibility of business enterprises is 'distinct from issues of legal liability and enforcement, which remain defined largely by national law provisions in relevant jurisdictions'. Special Representative on the Issue of Human Rights and Transnational Corporations and Other Business Enterprises, *Guiding Principles on Business and Human Rights: Implementing the United Nations 'Protect, Respect and Remedy' Framework*. U.N.Doc. A/HRC/17/31, GP 12 (21 Mar. 2011) [hereinafter *UNGPs*] (by John Ruggie).
86 *Id.*, GP 23(c).
87 Special Representative on the Issue of Human Rights and Transnational Corporations and Other Business Enterprises, Business and human rights: further steps towards the operationalization of the 'protect, respect and remedy' framework, §66, A/HRC/14/27 (9 Apr. 2010) (by John Ruggie).
88 *Id.* § 66.
89 *Id.* § 66.
90 This corresponds with the view by Eijsbouts that a substantive social norm can find its way in various types of regulation: '(individual or collective) self-regulation, soft law, civil law, administrative law and, finally, criminal law'. Eijsbouts also notes that 'a substantive social norm can leave the territory of non-codified social norms and migrate back and forth among different forms of regulation and even return to the territory of non-codified social norms'. Jan Eijsbouts, Corporate responsibility, beyond voluntarism: Regulatory options to reinforce the licence to operate, at 32, (2011) (Inaugural Lecture, Maastricht University).
91 R. Mares, *Global Corporate Social Responsibility, Human Rights and Law: An Interactive Regulatory Perspective on the Voluntary-Mandatory Dichotomy*, 1 Transnational Legal Theory, at 256 (2010).
92 UNGPs, *supra* note 85, GP 3.
93 *Id.* GP 3.
94 *Id.* GP 3.
95 *Id.* General Principles.
96 *See*, for more detail, Chapter 5.
97 O. De Schutter, et al., Human Rights Due Diligence: The Role of States (2012).
98 The study indicated four ways in which States can use human rights due diligence in regulation: (1) as a means for companies to comply with laws and regulations (e.g. as a direct legal obligation or a as a defence against charges of criminal, civil or administrative violations); (2) as a means to provide incentives and benefits to companies for demonstrating human rights due diligence practice (e.g. through public procurement law or export credit policies); (3) through transparency and disclosure (disclosure requirements in securities laws, consumer protection laws and mandatory disclosure regulations); and (4) a combination of the above. *Id.*

99 Mark B. Taylor, *Human Rights Due Diligence: The Role of States, 2013 Progress Report* 4 (2013), *available at* http://icar.ngo/wp-content/uploads/2013/11/ICAR-Human-Rights-Due-Diligence-2013-Update-FINAL1.pdf.

100 Mark B. Taylor, *The Ruggie Framework: Polycentric Regulation and the Implications for Corporate Social Responsibility*, 5 Etikk i praksis – Nordic Journal of Applied Ethics 1, 27 (2011).

101 The concept of the corporate responsibility to respect already reflects certain well-established human rights principles in certain aspects. The concept reflects that all business enterprises can breach all human rights, which corresponds with the principle in international human rights law that all human rights are indivisible and interdependent. The requirement that it be implemented in a non-discriminatory manner corresponds with the human rights principle of non-discrimination (General Principles). The UNGPs recognize that business enterprises should involve meaningful consultation with relevant stakeholders at different stages of the human rights due diligence process. The concept reflects how human rights imposes certain process demands, in terms of meaningful stakeholder engagement and human rights expertise. UNGPs, *supra* note 85, GP 18(b), GP 20 (b).

102 A. Ramasastry, *Corporate Social Responsibility versus Business and Human Rights: Bridging the Gap between Responsibility and Accountability*, 238, 14 Journal of Human Rights (2015).

103 *UNGPs*, *supra* note 85, Commentary to GP 15.

104 Emphasis added. The UNGPs expressly note that the corporate responsibility to protect exists independent of the duty of States and 'over and above compliance with national laws and regulations protecting human rights', *id.* Commentary to GPs 11.

105 Report of the Special Representative of the Secretary-General on the issue of human rights and transnational corporations and other business enterprises, *Business and Human Rights: Towards Operationalizing the "Protect, Respect and Remedy" Framework*, § 47, U.N. doc. A/HRC/11/13 (22 Apr. 2009) (by John Ruggie).

106 *Id.* § 47.

107 Bonita Meyersfeld, *Business, Human Rights and Gender: A Legal Approach to External and Internal Considerations*, *in* Human Rights Obligations of Business: Beyond the Corporate Responsibility to Respect, at 207 (Cambridge ed. 2013).

108 *See*, for further detail, Chapter 5.

109 Backer, *supra* note 79, at 10.

110 Ruggie, *supra* note 13, at 91.

111 *Id.*

112 *Ruggie, 2007 Report*, supra note 6, at 17.

113 For instance, the UNGPs note that States could adopt laws setting out requirements for business enterprises to communicate on their respect for human rights and include provisions to 'give weight to such self-reporting in the event of a judicial or administrative proceeding'. *UNGPs*, *supra* note 85, Commentary to GP3.

114 Robert P. Barnidge, *The Due Diligence Principle under International Law*, International Community Law Review 81, 81–82 (2006).

115 States being best positioned to assess these facts and circumstances have a certain discretion to determine what due diligence measures are adequate to prevent and respond to human rights abuses by companies. Consequently, the due diligence standard allows States to rely on their circumstances as a defence precluding wrongfulness. *Id.* at 83.

116 Meyersfeld, *supra* note 107, at 207.

117 U.N. Comm. on the Rights of the Child, General Comment No. 16 on State obligations regarding the impact of business sector on children's rights, U.N. doc. CRC/C/GC/16, 62nd Sess. (14 Jan.–1 Feb. 2013).

118 U.N. Comm. on Economic, Social and Cultural Rights, *Statement on the Obligations of States Parties Regarding the Corporate Sector and Economic, Social and Cultural Rights*, U.N. doc. E/C.12/2011/1, 46th Sess. (12 July 2011).
119 *Id.* § 4.
120 *Id.* § 5.
121 *Id.* § 5.
122 *Id.* § 6.
123 U.N. Comm. on the Rights of the Child, General Comment No. 16 on State obligations regarding the impact of business sector on children's rights, U.N. doc. CRC/C/GC/16, 62nd Sess. (14 Jan.–1 Feb. 2013).
124 The Optional Protocol on the sale of children, child prostitution and child pornography and the Optional Protocol on the involvement of children in armed conflict.
125 U.N. Comm. on the Rights of the Child, General Comment No. 16 on State obligations regarding the impact of business sector on children's rights, U.N. doc. CRC/C/GC/16, 62nd Sess., § 4 (14 Jan.–1 Feb. 2013).
126 *Id.* § 5.
127 *Id.* § 7.
128 *Id.* § 8.
129 *Id.* § 26–27.
130 *Id.* § 28.
131 *Id.* § 28.
132 *Id.* § 50.
133 *Id.* § 51.
134 The General Comment indicates that 'a reasonable link exists when a business enterprise has its centre of activity, is registered or domiciled or has its main place of business or substantial business activities in the State concerned'. *Id.* § 43.
135 *Id.* § 41.
136 The CtR notes that this should be 'of major and equal concern to both host and home States of business enterprises' because the CRC has been 'nearly universally ratified'. *Id.* § 47.
137 *Id.* § 29.
138 *Id.* § 29.
139 *Id.* § 30.
140 Committee of Ministers, Council of Europe, *Recommendation CM/Rec (2016)3 of the Committee of Ministers to Member States on Business and Human Rights*, 1249th meeting, CM/Rec(2016)3 [hereinafter *Recommendation*] (2 Mar. 2016).
141 *Id.*
142 Steering Committee for Human Rights, *Explanatory Memorandum to Recommendation CM/Rec(2016)3 of the Committee of Ministers to Member States on Human Rights and Business*, 1249th meeting, CM(2016)18-addfinal [hereinafter *Explanatory Memorandum*] (2 Mar. 2016).
143 *Recommendation*, *supra* note 140.
144 *Id.*
145 The Recommendation also draws inspiration from Parliamentary Assembly Resolution 1757(2010) and Recommendation 1936(2010), which were both adopted on 6 October 2010. *Id.* § 9. For a discussion on the evolution of business and human rights and the reception of the UNGPs in the Council of Europe, *see* Augenstein et al., Business and Human Rights Law in the Council of Europe: Noblesse oblige (10 Feb. 2014), www.ejiltalk.org/business-and-human-rights-law-in-the-council-of-europe-noblesse-oblige/.
146 *Explanatory Memorandum*, *supra* note 142, § 12.
147 The Committee of Ministers by Art. 15b of the Statute of the Council of Europe can only provide recommendations to Member States, not to private entities. *Id.* § 10.

148 For the purpose of the Recommendation, domicile is defined within the meaning of the EU Brussels (No. 1215/2012) and Rome II (no. 864/2007) Regulations, *i.e.* 'as being the business's "statutory seat", "central administration" or "principle place of business"'. *Id.* § 8.
149 *Id.* § 28.
150 *Id.* § 14.
151 *Id.* § 29.
152 *Id.* § 36.
153 *Id.* § 36.
154 *Id.* § 36.
155 *Recommendation*, *supra* note 140, § 21.
156 *Explanatory Memorandum*, *supra* note 142, § 39.
157 *Recommendation*, *supra* note 140, § 21.
158 *Id.* § 22.
159 *Explanatory Memorandum*, *supra* note 142, § 40.
160 *Id.* § 36.
161 Taylor, *supra* note 100, at 27.

4 Human rights due diligence as a legal concept

Its characteristics and reformatory potential

Introduction

This chapter examines the corporate responsibility to respect human rights from a legal perspective. It focuses on the concept of human rights due diligence and its (legal) character as a standard of conduct and form of compliance. This involves an analysis of the interpretations of this concept and an evaluation of differences and similarities between this concept and other (legal) due diligence concepts used in various areas of law, including the duty of care concept under certain national (tort) laws of non-contractual obligations. The balancing act that the human rights due diligence concept entails will be explored further through a parallelism with the due diligence obligations that are applicable to States under international human rights law. The chapter will reflect on the functionality of the human rights due diligence concept in enabling and promoting future legal developments within legal systems. More specifically, it examines the potential of this concept to drive analytical improvements in and facilitate convergence across national laws affecting business behaviour. The human rights due diligence concept may be viewed as a reformatory concept, bound to fruitfully redefine the standards of due diligence that different areas of the legal order currently set out for business enterprises and thus also contribute to the reconceptualization of such laws.

The human rights due diligence concept

The human rights due diligence concept as defined in the UNGPs can be understood in relation to the traditional due diligence concept under corporate law, from which it originates.[1] Indeed, when framing the human rights due diligence concept, the SRSG drew on well-established due diligence and risk assessments practices in the areas of mergers and acquisitions and securities.[2] These practices respond, at least to some extent, to domestic laws that require companies to have information disclosure and control systems in place to assess and manage financial and related risks.[3] The American 'Securities Art of 1933' is an early example of such laws. Sections 11[4] and 12[5] of this Act created a standard of due diligence and care that could give rise to civil liability in case the information disclosed in relation to a security is inaccurate or misleading.

The construction of the human rights due diligence on the basis of the due diligence concept in corporate law aimed at establishing a relationship between corporate law and international human rights law, two areas of law that hitherto were often considered disconnected.[6] The establishment of a clear link between corporate law and international human rights law through the human rights due diligence concept brings business approaches to risk management to a closer relation with internationally recognized human rights standards and principles. It facilitates the acceptance of, and has the potential to incite, compliance by companies with their human rights responsibilities. Moreover, the concept of due diligence has the advantage of being readily understood by business enterprises: corporations could thus build on existing due diligence practices to integrate successfully human rights into their corporate practices. Doing so could also increase the capacity of business enterprises in risk management and incite compliance with the standards set by both systems. The nexus furthermore allowed for the integration of international human rights standards into risk management and related business practices, and for business enterprises to articulate their human rights concerns by reference to international human rights law. The human rights due diligence concept was a means to have companies accept a concept of corporate responsibility that is linked in substance to international human rights instruments.[7]

In short, the concept of due diligence was considered more resonant to business enterprises than compliance with international human rights norms, the applicability of which to business activities was, moreover, uncertain.[8]

Human rights due diligence: substantive measures required

This section will explain the human rights due diligence concept by comparison with existing approaches to due diligence in other areas of law. More precisely, the substantive and procedural aspects of human rights due diligence will be explained in relation to due diligence under corporate law and securities law. According to UNGP 17–24, an adequate human rights due diligence process requires the successful adoption of the following measures: (i) to investigate and take measures; (ii) to communicate that the measures have been adopted; (iii) to enable inclusive decision-making and participation; and (iv) to gather relevant human rights expertise.

The human rights due diligence concept can be understood as a forward-looking management process that is aimed at the prevention of adverse human rights impacts.[9] This concept as defined by the UNGPs in itself may not exist as a legal standard.[10] However, as will be set out in detail below, the diligence concept can be used and, as is argued below, should be used as a legal standard of conduct.[11]

To investigate and take measures (to know)

The requirement to investigate and take measures is threefold: (i) to carry out human rights impact assessments; (ii) to integrate the findings of these human rights assessments in the relevant process of the company; and (iii) to track responses.

Human rights impact assessments

One element of the human rights due diligence process is to undertake human rights risk assessments.[12] The main purpose of human rights impact assessments is to ascertain the nature of the impact of a company's activities on human rights. Unlike the traditional approaches to risk assessments in corporations, these assessments have an external, rather than an internal, focus.[13] They are not only (or, for that matter, mainly) aimed at identifying the material risks to and liabilities of the corporation from a financial viewpoint. The purpose is to identify the human rights risks of a company to right-holders, and from a right-holder perspective.

The UNGPs note that human rights impact assessment may be included within broader enterprise risk management systems; however, these assessments must extend beyond 'simply identifying and managing material risks to the company itself, to include risks to right-holders'.[14] The human rights assessments thus differ in purpose from traditional approaches to risk management in that they aim at analysing the risks that a company's operations pose to human rights, rather than the reverse.[15] These assessments must be undertaken in the interest of the right-holders whose risks might be adversely affected by the operations of the company, rather than in the interest of shareholders and investors. The aim of human rights impacts assessments is for companies and stakeholders to gain an understanding of the specific adverse human rights impacts on people, within the specific contexts of an operation. Special attention should be paid to 'particular human rights impacts on individuals from groups or populations that may be at heightened risk of vulnerability or marginalization, and bear in mind the risk that may be faced by women and men'.[16] In order to obtain an understanding of the human rights risk from a stakeholder perspective, the process should involve meaningful consultation with potentially affected groups and relevant stakeholders. This understanding serves to guide a company's decision-making on what due diligence steps are appropriate to manage these risks in the interest of right-holders.

The scope of the assessments mirrors that of the corporate responsibility to respect more generally. The assessments are aimed at identifying both actual and potential human rights impacts that the company's activities and business relationships may lead to. This process can be integrated into other risk assessments, provided that these assessments are undertaken by reference to international human rights. Human rights impact assessments must 'include all internationally recognized human rights as a reference point, since enterprises may potentially impact virtually any of these rights'.[17] For human rights impact assessments to conform to the human rights due diligence concept, such assessments should include references to international human rights. The UNGPs refer to the International Bill of Human Rights and the fundamental principles set out in the ILO Declaration on Fundamental Principles and Rights at Work as authoritative enumerations of human rights and a global minimum benchmark against which to assess performance.[18] These instruments provide a list of 'core internationally recognized human rights' standards.[19] While business enterprises must always consider the list of core rights,[20] they may also need to consider additional international human rights standards in certain specific scenarios.[21]

The human rights due diligence concept requires that business enterprises assess the actual and potential adverse human rights impacts under *all* internationally recognized human rights. The reason is that business enterprises can potentially impact virtually any of these rights.[22] Business enterprises should consequently opt for a comprehensive and non-selective approach to human rights and systematically identify relevant policies and practices accordingly. This challenges certain practices of business enterprises of identifying and addressing adverse human rights impacts in a targeted partial manner, focusing only on those human rights impacts that are of direct importance to the company from a financial perspective. By contrast, human rights due diligence requires companies to take into consideration all human rights, including those human rights they previously did not deal with, or even avoided: these are often human rights at greatest risk of being adversely affected. 'Cherry-picking' and selectively choosing at convenience a particular international framework and then focusing on the subset of human rights contained therein is, therefore, no longer acceptable.

Human rights impact assessment must be undertaken at 'regular intervals' in order to be responsive to the changes in human rights situations that are 'dynamic'. The UNGPs identify three intervals: (i) 'prior to a new activity or relationship; priori to major decisions or changes in the operation (e.g., market entry, product launch, policy change, or wider changes to the business)'; (ii) 'in response to or anticipation of changes in the operating environment (e.g., rising social tensions)'; and (iii) 'periodically throughout the life of an activity or relationship'.[23] This requirement that business enterprises consider human rights in a comprehensive manner is consistent with the requirement of 'objectivity and non-selectivity of the consideration of human rights issues' as recognized by the Vienna Plan of Action.[24] The Program of Action indicated that human rights globally must be treated 'in a fair and equal manner, on the same footing, and with the same emphasis'.[25] The Preamble to the Universal Declaration for Development also recognizes that the promotion of development requires equal attention and urgent consideration to all human rights and that, accordingly, 'the promotion of, respect for and enjoyment of certain human rights and fundamental freedoms cannot justify the denial of other human rights and fundamental freedoms'.[26]

Integrating the findings

The findings of the human rights impacts assessments must be horizontally integrated across relevant internal functions and processes of the company, and the company must take appropriate action.[27] The aim is for companies to ensure that the findings of the assessment 'are properly understood, given due weight, and acted upon' in order to prevent and mitigate potential human rights impacts.[28] Since human rights considerations are often isolated throughout the company, this element may constitute the biggest challenge for companies according to the SRSG.[29]

The UNGPs note the responsibility of companies to embed policy commitments into all relevant business functions.[30] This embedding is aimed at

> ensuring that all personnel are aware of the enterprise's human rights policy commitment, understand its implications for how they conduct their work, are trained, empowered and incentivized to act in ways that support the commitment, and regard it as intrinsic to the core values of the work place.[31]

This embedding is 'a macro process' that can enable the 'successful integration of findings and timely and sustainable responses'.[32] The 'integration' of findings entails a 'micro process of taking the findings about a potential impact, identifying who in the enterprise needs to be involved in addressing it and ensuring effective action'.[33] All those who are relevant for the identification and implementation of solutions should be identified and engaged. This includes those responsible for assessing adverse human rights impacts and those in control of decision-making and action to manage these impacts.[34] The responsibility for effectively addressing human rights impacts should be allocated to the appropriate level and function within the company.[35]

The UNGPs note that internal decision-making, budget allocations and oversight processes should be in place to enable effective responses.[36] Companies should adopt measures that are appropriate and proportionate to its capabilities. Large companies thus will likely be required to adopt a more systematized approach to ensure that findings are integrated effectively. A systemized approach may also be expected of smaller entities in the presence of potentially severe human rights impacts or a high probability of particular human rights impacts.[37]

In the case of a need to prioritize action, which might be due to resource constraints, the company should focus on preventing and mitigating those potential human rights impacts that are most severe[38] or likely to occur. Severity should be assessed in terms of the risks posed to human rights rather than to the company. The UNGPs make a distinction in this context to the way the company is involved in the adverse human rights impact (i.e. causation, contribution or direct linkage) and the extent of leverage by the company over the entity causing the harm. The conduct that is required from companies varies accordingly. In the case a company 'causes or may cause' an adverse human rights impact, a responsibility applies to the company to 'take the necessary steps to cease or prevent the impact'.[39]

In the alternative scenario where a company 'contributes or may contribute' to an adverse impact that is caused by another entity, the nature and extent of measures that a company should take to effectively integrate human rights can be determined less easily. A similar responsibility applies in that companies should adopt appropriate measures 'to cease or prevent its contribution'. Where the company does not control the other entity that causes the impact, the company should 'use its leverage to mitigate any remaining impact to the greatest extent possible'.[40] The UNGPs define leverage as 'the ability to effect change in the wrongful practices of an entity that causes a harm'.[41]

In the presence of potential adverse human rights impacts that are 'directly linked' to the operations, products or services of the company, and because the business relationship with another entity connects the company to the adverse human rights impact, a responsibility arises for the company to take appropriate action. In this scenario of 'direct linkage', appropriate action should be determined in relation to the following factors: 'the enterprise's leverage over the entity concerned, how crucial the relationship is to the enterprise, the severity of the abuse, and whether terminating the relationship with the entity itself would have adverse human rights impacts'.[42]

The nature and extent of conduct that is expected from companies to exercise leverage in situations where the company is involved in adverse human rights impacts through causation or direct linkage is not exactly defined. The UNGPs note that the company should exercise the leverage that it has to prevent or mitigate the adverse human rights impact. In the case the company lacks leverage, it should find ways to increase it (e.g. by 'offering capacity building or other incentives to the related entity, or collaborating with other actors').[43] The company should consider ending the relationship, where increasing the leverage is not possible. The potential human rights impacts of such withdrawal should be taken into account. Where the company decides to maintain the relationship and the abuse continues, the company 'should be able to demonstrate its own ongoing efforts to mitigate the impact and be prepared to accept any consequences – reputational, financial or legal – of the continuing connection'.[44]

Tracking responses

Another important element of the human rights due diligence process is the tracking of the effectiveness of businesses' responses. The purpose of tracking is aimed at verifying the effectiveness of companies' responses in addressing their human rights impacts. More specifically, the commentary to UNGP 20 notes that tracking 'is necessary to know if its human rights policies are being implemented optimally, whether it has responded effectively to the identified human rights impacts, and to drive continuous improvement'.[45]

The information that companies acquire through tracking can enable companies to improve the accountability of their human rights performance, both internally to management and communicating externally to shareholders and stakeholders.[46] Indicators can further assist companies in communicating more effectively.[47] Tracking can be of instrumental importance for companies to drive continued improvements in their human rights performance. The information that is acquired through tracking can be used 'to identify trends and patterns' and to highlight 'repeated problems that may require more systemic changes to policies and processes' and 'it brings out best practices that can be disseminated across the enterprise to further reduce risk and improve performance'.[48]

The UNGP notes that special efforts should go out to tracking the effectiveness of responses 'to impacts on individuals from groups or populations that may be at heightened risk of vulnerability and marginalization'.[49] Processes for tracking responses may be integrated within other tracking systems; however, these systems should allow for qualitative feedback, including from right-holders.[50] Such integration can contribute to 'normalizing' attention to human rights.[51] Companies are advised to undertake a root cause analysis, which can 'help pinpoint what actions by which parts of the enterprise, or by which other parties related to the enterprise, played a role in generating the impact, and how'.[52]

Business enterprises are required to rely on appropriate indicators in tracking the effectiveness of its responses.[53,54] Both quantitative and qualitative indictors should be used. Qualitative indicators can be important to verify that a company's own assessment about its human rights performance is accurate from the perspective of affected stakeholder groups. Companies may have arrived at this assessment on the basis of quantitative indicators.[55]

Businesses draw on relevant internal and external perspectives, in particular the perspectives of potentially affected stakeholders.[56] Such engagement is important to verify the accuracy of companies' responses to human rights. The process also creates opportunities for affected individuals to have a voice in the process and to contribute to the formation of an understanding based on the assessment of the performance of the company from a right-holder perspective.[57]

The UNGPs affirm that operational-level grievance mechanisms can be relevant for tracking business responses, for at least two reasons. First, they can support business enterprises in the identification of their adverse human rights impacts as part of their ongoing human rights due diligence, and in addressing systemic problems that trends and patterns in complaints may reveal. Second, they can enable the early and direct handling and remediation of adverse impacts, thereby 'preventing harms from compounding and grievances from escalating'.[58]

To communicate (to show)

One of the steps that business enterprises must undertake as part of the human rights due diligence process is communication. As stipulated by UNGP 17, business enterprises must 'account for' how the company goes about managing its human rights by 'communicating' this externally.[59] The purpose of such disclosure is for companies to 'show' their respect for human rights in practice. Companies should have reporting policies and processes in place by which they can provide transparency and accountability for their human rights due diligence. This responsibility to disclose is further elaborated in UNGP 21.

For companies to disclose in conformity to the UNGPs, certain modifications to current approaches to company disclosure should be undertaken. These changes relate to the type of information that should be disclosed, the nature and form of disclosure, and the audience companies should address their disclosure to and who is entitled to the information. Communications should meet a minimum standard in all instances. This minimum standard relates to both the content and process of disclosure. As previously indicated, unlike traditional disclosure under corporate law, the focus should be on both external and internal disclosure.[60,61] The purpose of disclosure is to improve business respect for human rights. The focus of disclosure should therefore not only 'be the corporation's risk and liability, but the risks towards third parties'.[62]

The responsibility to disclose is based on human rights risks. The scope for disclosure mirrors the scope of the corporate responsibility to respect more generally. Business enterprises must disclose on their potential and actual adverse human rights impacts. The disclosure should reflect the human rights risks that a company causes by its own activities, contributes to or is directly linked to through the business relationships it enters into. The occurrence of adverse human rights impacts that a company is involved in gives rise to the responsibility to communicate. When stakeholders bring human rights issues to the attention of business enterprises, the need to communicate becomes apparent.

Disclosure must include anything relevant for human rights. Since human rights impacts involve right-holders and affected stakeholders, disclosure must provide an adequate depiction of these impacts and a company's response thereto, and one focusing on the perspective of the right-holder. Unlike in traditional disclosure, this information is not primarily owed to shareholders[63] or investors[64] but to all affected stakeholders, and most importantly, to individuals and groups whose human rights may be adversely impacted by the activities of the company. Since disclosure is owed to affected stakeholders, and, in particular, to right-holders, the responsibility to communicate requires that business enterprises disclose the type of information that is useful for these right-holders. Consequently, companies must be transparent and account for their human rights due diligence in a manner that is meaningful to these stakeholders.

The purpose of disclosure is not only to inform the company's own conduct, but also to inform the conduct of these stakeholders (and, in particular, right-holders), in relation to business conduct.[65] This requires that disclosure must be of a type and form that allows right-holders to obtain an accurate depiction of a company's human rights due diligence. Partly also for this reason, business enterprises must be responsive to the concerns raised by or on behalf of these stakeholders. Disclosure must be timely in order to be responsive to changes in human rights situations, which are often dynamic and evolving. For right-holders to fully understand the impact and responses of a company, the latter may need to establish a dialogue with the former.[66,67] It has been argued that communication must be useful for right-holders in order to meaningfully participate and respond in consultations and to serve as a basis for an exchange of information between stakeholders.

The UNGP 21 further elaborates on the implications of the responsibility to communicate information from a right-holder perspective for business enterprises, noting that communications should:

a Be of a *form* and *frequency* that reflect an enterprise's human rights impacts and that are accessible to its intended audiences;
b Provide information that is *sufficient* to evaluate the adequacy of an enterprise's response to the particular human rights impact involved.

This principle indicates that disclosure must be of a form that is accessible to its intended audiences. Since the responsibility to disclose is also owed to right-holders, companies must ensure that right-holders can access the information on their human rights risks and responses. Doing so would give effect to the right to information, which is itself, of course, a human right.[68]

As is the case for the human rights due diligence process more generally, the responsibility is pragmatic in that discretion is left to companies to communicate through means that are appropriate to the circumstances of the company. These means can take on various forms, including '"in-person" meetings, online dialogues, consultation with affected stakeholders, and formal public reports'.[69] The responsibility to disclose shifts from pragmatic means of disclosure to more technical means when the adverse human rights impacts reach a certain threshold of severity. Severe human rights impacts prompt a responsibility to report formally on how companies address these adverse human rights impacts.[70] Such formal reporting can range from 'traditional annual reports and corporate responsibility/sustainability reports, to include on-line updates and integrated financial and non-financial reports'.[71]

The responsibility to disclose under the UNGPs is often more demanding than the transparency that is commonly expected under a corporate law/financial regulation regime.[72] The UNGPs suggest that companies should disclose information on human rights risks and responses, even when such disclosure goes beyond what is perceived as materially relevant for the company from a financial viewpoint. A restriction is built into the responsibility to disclose in the sense that disclosure should not pose 'risks to affected stakeholders, personnel or to legitimate requirements of commercial confidentiality'.[73] Thus the responsibility to disclose entails in practice a balancing exercise, between disclosing information in a manner that provides the most optimal representation of a businesses' respect for human rights while minimizing the potential adverse impacts that such disclosure may have on the human rights of individuals.

In short, the communications of business enterprises must be frequent,[74] accessible,[75] sufficient,[76] balanced and informed in order to provide an adequate measure of transparency and accountability for respect for human rights.[77]

To enable inclusive decision-making and participation

Human rights due diligence requires that business enterprises involve in meaningful consultations with relevant stakeholders, at different stages of the due diligence process. The decision of business enterprises should be made in an inclusive and participatory manner that allows for the evaluation of potential risks to human rights.

The reason is that human rights due diligence does not relate only to the risks to a company's economic interests,[78] but to the interests of stakeholders more generally, and right-holders in particular. In this regard, the human rights due diligence challenges the presumption under corporate law that business enterprises should manage only those risks that are material to the company. Human rights due diligence entails that companies should manage the risks that their activities and relationships may pose to the rights of affected individuals and communities.[79] Understanding these risks and the appropriate care that a company should take from a right-holder perspective requires engagement with these right-holders or those who may legitimately represent them.

The meaningful consultation with potentially affected groups and other relevant stakeholders is expected at various stages of the human rights due diligence process. A company should 'involve in meaningful consultation' when undertaking a human rights impact assessment in order to identify and assess the nature of human rights impacts. The assessment is aimed at obtaining an accurate account of the 'specific impacts on specific people, given a specific context of operations'.[80] This entails that companies should consult affected stakeholders directly for the purpose of understanding their concerns.[81] Special attention must be paid to the human rights impacts on individuals from groups or populations at heightened risk of vulnerability and marginalization, and gender-sensitive human risks.

Companies should furthermore draw on feedback from affected stakeholders when tracking the effectiveness of their responses to verify whether their adverse human rights impacts are addressed.[82] The purpose is for business enterprises to develop an understanding of the nature of the human rights impacts to inform their human rights due diligence processes and policies and to consider the stakeholder experiences.

Whether stakeholders can meaningfully participate in consultations with business enterprises and respond to the assessments of risks and care by a company will depend on the information that is available to them. The UNGPs have been criticized in relation thereto. More specifically, it has been rightly argued that the UNGPs recognize as the main function of corporate disclosure providing information that demonstrates human rights due diligence and that limits liability for the company. The disclosure of information that is useful for right-holders in order to meaningfully participate and respond in consultations and can serve as a basis for an exchange of information between stakeholders appears to be of less importance to the UNGP. The UNGPs do not expressly note that business enterprises should have such an information exchange with stakeholders. Only in relation to 'severe' risks do the UNGPs recognize a responsibility for business enterprises to report formally. In the absence of mandatory disclosure obligations, there is no guarantee that companies will provide the necessary degree of transparency, and in a timely manner for right-holders to be able to meaningfully participate in consultations.[83]

The introduction of meaningful stakeholder consultation as an integral part of the human rights due diligence process aligns due diligence by companies with the considerations that underlie the human rights principles of participation and democracy. The enjoyment of human rights is tied to the requirement that individuals can participate in decision-making that affects their lives. The right to participate is in itself a human right, and stakeholder consultations are an important means to realize this right. Participation is also an important foundational element of democracy, and a means to achieve it.[84] Promoting participation in decision-making through consultations can potentially empower individuals, which is particularly relevant for persons from groups or populations at heightened risk of vulnerability or marginalization, or facing gender-specific risks.[85]

Business enterprises are invited to exercise discretion to right-holders when interpreting their human rights due diligence.[86] Since business enterprises must consult with relevant stakeholders, there is less room for companies to avoid critical views. Stakeholder consultations can enhance the credibility of interpretations of due diligence. Such consultations constitute a method to clear up ambiguities, identify and address potentially conflicting understandings of how business enterprises ought to satisfy their human rights due diligence requirements and to arrive at a common understanding. Dialogue can facilitate relationships of trust that are essential for the effectiveness of the measures. Consultations thus provide incentives for companies to comply. Business performance will be subject to review, hence companies will seek to avoid being identified by stakeholders as non-compliant. Involvement of stakeholders in the tracking and measurement of compliance makes non-compliance more difficult to conceal. In this regard, stakeholder consultations can serve to distinguish genuine implementation of human rights responsibility from public relations exercises.

To consult human rights expertise

Business enterprises should be adequately informed by relevant human rights expertise. They are expected to draw from internal and/or external expertise in formulating their human rights policy.[87] As a company's operations become more complex, the reliance on such expertise becomes more important to an assessment of how to best respond.[88] When operating in intricate countries or local contexts that complicate efforts to respect for human rights, business enterprises should also rely on expertise to determine how best to meet their responsibility. Business enterprises should draw on human rights expertise as part of their human rights impact assessment process.[89] Sources of expertise may be written or non-written, internal or external to the company. When facing complex operating environments, companies are advised to consult not only expertise internal to the enterprise, but also 'to consult externally with credible, independent experts, including from governments, civil society, national human rights institutions (NHRIs) and relevant multi-stakeholder initiatives'.[90]

The decision of business enterprises should be made in a manner that is objective and credible and that allows for optimal responses to the corporate responsibility to respect.[91] The concept challenges the practices of business enterprises of practically self-redefining existing standards by applying an interpretation of human rights of their own, one that is most convenient for corporate interests. Business enterprises have sometimes referenced international human rights instruments, extracted certain provisions, and then interpreted the standards codified therein in a manner that altered their meaning and protection as intended by the respective instrument.[92] Reliance on relevant expertise can result in a more objective assessment of appropriate business responses in complex environments. It can promote greater consistency and coherence in interpretations of human rights standards across business enterprises.[93]

Human rights due diligence as a standard of conduct: a balancing exercise

In this section, human rights due diligence will be explained as a standard of conduct which entails a judgement about whether a company exercises or has exercised reasonable care and a balancing exercise. The nature of this balancing exercise is similar and can be understood in reference to the duty of care concept which currently exists under certain national (tort) laws of non-contractual obligations. This legal duty of care concept requires companies to exercise reasonable care, the legal definition of which is determined by reference to legal and non-legal standards. The human rights due diligence can inform the *indicia* that factor into a determination of whether a company has struck the right balance between risk and care in meeting its legal obligations under these laws.[94]

The human rights due diligence concept entails a judgement as to whether the policies and processes that business enterprises must have in place to meet their responsibility to respect are sufficient and appropriate, having regard to the circumstances of the company.[95] This entails a balancing act in practice.

The balancing exercise that is integral to human rights due diligence differs from the one that is characteristic to the due diligence concept under corporate law. The concept as it has been applied to define the scope of directors' duties of care in corporate law is traditionally oriented towards finding a balance between the company's economic risks and opportunities.[96] In many jurisdictions, corporate law adopts a 'shareholder approach', in the case of which the balancing act centres around the impact of decision-making on the best interest of the company, which is equivalent to the maximization of shareholders' value as owners. The factors that are determinate for striking this balance are often private interests that are of concern to the corporation only.

Corporate law may opt for the 'enlightened shareholder value approach'. This approach permits or, in limited cases, requires directors to have regard to a wider range of stakeholder interests. Then human rights may be among the non-shareholder interests that inform the balancing act, provided doing so keeps within the director's duty to act in the company's best interest.[97] Depending on the jurisdiction, the company's best interest may be understood in a broader sense as encapsulating the combined interests of society at large. This seems to be a recent trend, however, and in the most common scenario the directors may have regard for these broader interests, but ultimately owe their duty of care to the company's shareholders.[98]

The balancing exercise that is at the core of the human rights due diligence concept more closely resembles the balancing act that courts undertake under civil tort law, more specifically in their normative judgement as to whether a company has committed a tort of negligence by having failed to meet a legal duty of care under national tort law. Before arriving at a verdict as to whether a company is liable for having acted negligently, the court undertakes a balancing act in order to determine whether the company has taken the measures that it was reasonably expected to take in order to prevent foreseeable harm to legal interest from materializing. More exactly, the court's balancing act

> boils down to an assessment of whether the parent company has exercised due care towards the foreseeable and legally protected interests of the host country plaintiffs, in light of the potential risks inherent in the multinational corporation's host country activities.[99]

This balancing act centres around the impact of corporate decision-making on human rights, rather than the company.

It is similar to the balancing act related to the human rights due diligence concept in that it seeks to find a balance between care of the company and risks to human rights. The human rights due diligence concept as set out in the UNGPs reflects that a balance should be struck between taking sufficient due diligence measures and managing the actual and potential human rights impacts that a company is involved in through its own activities and business relationships. The nature of this balancing exercise is pragmatic in that it revolves around the aim of avoiding and mitigating the adverse human rights impacts and the means by which this is achieved. These means must commensurate to the capabilities of the company in terms of their scale and complexity.[100]

The following factors are determinants for striking the right balance: the severity of the adverse human rights impacts, the likelihood of adverse human rights impacts occurring (operating context and sector) and the ability of the company (size, ownership and structure).[101] These resemble the four factors that are balanced by a court in a tort liability case under civil tort law, namely: 'the probability that the risk will materialize; the seriousness of the expected damage;

the character and benefit of the activities in question; and the burden of taking precautionary measures'.[102]

The UNGPs suggest that a proportionality test applies, in that the company acts in accordance with its due diligence responsibility if it adopts measures that are sufficient to manage human rights risks that it is involved in. These measures should be suitable to their objective and, provided they are indeed sufficient, should commensurate to the capabilities of the company. As small and medium-size enterprises have lesser capacity and more informal processes and management structures, their responsibility might be limited to measures of lesser complexity and scale.[103] The means by which a company can discharge its responsibility can also vary according to whether a company conducts its business through a corporate group or individually.[104] In case of the presence of a more significant probability of adverse human rights occurring, which may be explained in relation to the particular industry or operational contexts of the company, business enterprises may need to take measures of greater scale and complexity.[105]

The responsibility of companies requires more from companies if the operations of a company or the operating context give rise to human rights risks of a more serious nature. If human rights risks reach a threshold of severity, which is judged in relation to 'scale, scope and irremediable character of the impact', the responsibility to respect requires corresponding measures.[106] The responsibility will be less contingent on practical considerations of what means suit the economic interests of the company and more on technical considerations of what measures are needed to effectively mitigate or avoid the adverse human rights impacts.[107] The due diligence concept would require companies to adopt technical measures, thereby removing the scope of discretion of companies by imposing a requirement on companies to act in a certain manner. Since certain measures would be required regardless of economic considerations, the responsibility to respect would be more oriented towards achieving the desired result of effectively avoiding or prioritizing adverse human rights impact.[108]

Upon identification of human rights situations and risks, a company must begin to take action to address those human rights impacts that are 'most severe' or 'where delayed response would make them irremediable'. It is further stipulated that '[s]everity is not an absolute concept in this context, but is relative to the other human rights impacts the business enterprise has identified'.[109] A company must also prioritize those areas where the risks of adverse human rights impacts occurring are greatest.[110]

The human rights due diligence concept from an international human rights perspective

This section will explain the human rights due diligence concept from the perspective of international human rights law. The human rights concept will be compared to the due diligence concept to which international human rights law has resorted in order to define the requirement that States ensure an adequate protection of human rights.[111,112] The UNGPs' premise on the understanding that the duties and responsibilities of States and business enterprises are differentiated and mutually reinforcing. The section will compare the balancing exercise that underpins the human rights due diligence concept to the one that courts apply in their assessment of qualified human rights under international human rights law.

International human rights law prescribes certain limitations to the exercise of human rights, which are premised on the understanding that the realization of human rights is not only an individual's rights, but also a community interest and commitment. Courts have commonly applied the method of a balancing exercise in their interpretation of 'qualified' human rights.[113] States are required to strike a balance between securing the rights and freedoms of individuals and the interests of a community, e.g. national security, public safety or public order.[114] In their evaluation of this balancing act, courts often apply the principle of proportionality, meaning that 'the objective of the communal aim or interest has to be sufficiently important to limit the right; the measure of the limitation has to be suitable and no more than necessary to defend the communal interest in question'.[115]

Overall, these provisions of international human rights treaties or international instruments that contain such 'qualified' human rights have to be interpreted strictly.[116,117] For instance, the International Covenant on Civil and Political Rights (the ICCPR) under Art. 18 (3) stipulates that the freedom to manifest one's religion or beliefs 'may be subject only to such limitations as are prescribed by law and are necessary to protect public safety, order, health, or morals or the fundamental rights and freedoms of others'.[118] The UN Human Rights Committee in its General Comment 22 states that this provision must be interpreted strictly, meaning that restrictions are not allowed on grounds not specified in the provision, may only be applied for the purpose prescribed, must be 'directly related and proportionate to the specific need on which they are predicated', must not be 'imposed for discriminatory purposes or applied in a discriminatory manner' and if applied for the purpose of protecting morals, the restriction 'must be based on principles not deriving exclusively from a single tradition'.[119,120] This means that 'the objective of the communal aim or interest has to be sufficiently important to limit the right; the measure of the limitation has to be suitable and no more than necessary to defend the communal interest in question'.[121]

The balancing exercise that is integral to international human rights law differs in several aspects from the one that underpins the human rights due diligence concept under the UNGPs. The due diligence concept in international human rights law attempts to strike a balance between the communal interest and the human right of the individual. The balancing exercise that relates to the human rights due diligence concept is aimed at finding a balance between the private interests of the company and individual and/or community interests. The factors that are a determinant for finding this balance are private interest factors related to risk to human rights and care by the company.

The balancing of economic interests against individual/communal interests may not be controversial from a human rights perspective. One could argue that the realization of human rights is not only the prerogative of the human rights of individuals, but also that of the community in promoting economic development. The relation between international peace and security, the creation of conditions of economic and social progress and development, and the promotion and protection of human rights is recognized in Art. 55 of the UN Charter. The positive impacts that business enterprises and markets can have on the realization of human rights are well known. These can entail achieving concrete outcomes for the realization of human rights, for instance by providing access to credit, education, food and water through private service delivery. Business enterprises can also contribute to improvement of social conditions or economic development.

The significance of the positive contribution of business enterprises to human rights was acknowledged in HRC Resolution 17/4. The Resolution signalled next to the importance of effectively mitigating the negative, also the significance of fully realizing the positive impacts of globalization and of deriving maximally the benefits of the activities of business enterprises.[122] The HRC also recognized that proper regulation, including through national legislation, of business enterprises can assist in channelling the benefits of business towards contributing to the enjoyment of human rights and fundamental freedoms.[123,124]

The balancing exercise that underpins the human rights due diligence concept as set out in the UNGPs thus could be justified from a human rights perspective. The due diligence concept seems to require companies to adopt measures that are sufficient to prevent and mitigate their potential and actual adverse human rights impacts without interrupting companies in their pursuit of economic objectives more than necessary, with the aim of achieving the most optimal outcome for human rights. This seems to align with the objective of the UNGPs, which is 'enhancing standards and practices with regard to business and human rights so as to achieve tangible results for affected individuals and communities, and thereby also contributing to a socially sustainable globalization'.

When comparing the human rights due diligence concept as defined by the UNGPs with the due diligence concept as it exists in international human rights law, however, several concerns arise. These concerns can be explained in relation to the fact that the human rights due diligence concept builds on the language of corporate law and is not human rights-based.

The balancing exercise is oriented towards the business enterprise and whether it acted to the best of its abilities, in view of its capabilities and circumstances. The interests of individuals are balanced against the economic/business interests of a company to take action that is sufficient and commensurate to the capabilities of the company. Depending on one's viewpoint, the corporate responsibility to respect human rights may encourage a 'good enough' due diligence[125] or does not allow companies to get away lightly. The former viewpoint suggests that the focus is not on achieving the maximum level of outcome in its objective of managing the adverse human rights risk, but on achieving the minimal constraints possible on business enterprises while managing adverse human rights impacts. The human rights due diligence that is sufficient and the least burdensome on the company ought to be chosen. The corporate responsibility to respect human rights may also be understood as an assessment of whether all measures that are within the companies' capabilities have been taken to manage risk to human rights. The human rights due diligence concept appears to supply arguments that point in the direction of business enterprises and their interests. Both interpretations reflect that the due diligence concept originates from corporate law and the human rights due diligence concept is business-oriented.

Consequently, business interests in managing adverse human rights impacts seem to be at the centre of the balance act. If human rights risks had been at the centre, the balancing exercise would have been oriented towards strengthening and reinforcing the processes and policies of companies to achieve full respect for human rights, rather than finding the most practical and economically efficient solution for business enterprises.[126] Only when the risk of adverse human rights impacts meets a threshold of severity, the focus of responsibility shifts towards the technical measures that are necessary to achieve the objective of effectively avoiding and mitigating adverse human rights impacts, and the practical economic/business interests of the company become of lesser importance.

The balancing exercise is also corporate-centric in that the company is the broker, and will ultimately be responsible for finding the appropriate balance.[127] This is in part because the balancing exercise evolves around what constitutes 'appropriate' policies and processes. To the extent that what constitutes as 'appropriate' depends on the circumstances of the company, which the company is in the best position to assess, the company seems best positioned to determine which policies and policies are 'appropriate' to discharge its responsibility. This is more so because the balancing exercise is determined by factors that are not only related to human rights but also to economic/business interests (e.g. size and structure of the company). The requirement for meaningful engagement and consultation of expertise in order to obtain a proper understanding of the adverse human rights risks from a right-holder perspective may expose the decision-making of the company to external scrutiny and influence, the ultimate decision falls to the company.

Business enterprises thus seem to be in the driver seat. Insofar that human rights due diligence allows for discretion to companies to determine by what policies and practices to manage adverse human rights risks, companies may want to influence the balancing act to their advantage, as a function of the company's pursuit of economic objectives. Business enterprises may exercise influence over this balancing act not only to safeguard their own commercial interests within particular situations, but also to ensure that interpretations of human rights due diligence keep within their convenience. This is in part because the activities of business enterprises are conditioned by their legal and incentive structures that are coupled to economic normative frameworks. While the human rights due diligence concept is intended to revolutionize existing approaches to due diligence in the interest of human rights, the question arises whether this can be achieved in practice. Can these economic legal and incentive structures be reconciled with the human rights due diligence concept?

One may also consider the complexities involved in the balancing exercise where human rights interests are concerned.[128] The balancing exercise is complicated by the different and possibly conflicting interests that decision-making by the company can give rise to and the possible conflicting priorities that call for choices and trade-offs between human rights interests. The prerogative to conduct a balancing exercise between human rights interests commonly falls to the State and within the public national and international state/law system. The human rights due diligence concept entails that business enterprises may also need to consider and make difficult trade-offs in relation to conflicting human rights interests, which is something that business enterprises are commonly not familiar with. This raises the question whether undemocratic private corporations should exercise the ample discretion that comes with such policy decisions and balancing acts.[129]

Depending on the situation, resolving conflicting interests can involve complexity in terms of the diversity and range of interest that need to be considered, and competing priorities and trade-offs. Conflicting interests may arise over competing human rights risks or issues, competing human rights claims of different social groups or communities, long-term v. short-term interests in considering human rights impacts, human rights that are enjoyed in the community (e.g. freedom of association, rights of members of minorities, the freedom to manifest one's religion or belief) and those enjoyed by individuals, the human rights interests of a more disadvantaged group and a more advantaged group, and the community interests of long-term economic success of business enterprises and short-term human rights interests.

Human rights due diligence as an open-ended and adaptable concept

The section will reflect on the open-ended character of the human rights due diligence concept. The concept is clearly defined in that it provides for concrete parameters as to how business enterprises should respect human rights, but it is also articulated at a certain level of abstraction. This open nature of the concept should not necessarily be problematic. In fact, such open-ended character may be intentional since it allows the details as to what human rights due diligence requires or entails within a particular contexts or issue area to be further tailored to that specific scenario. As the SRSG appears to agree, States should provide further details and clarity through guidance on how business enterprises should respect human rights.[130]

The human right due diligence concept as formulated in the UNGPs is undefined to a certain degree. The fact that it is articulated at a level of abstraction can be explained by its nature as a principle. The concept is a baseline normative standard that reflects an interpretation of existing international social expectations. The SRSG derived this concept by a process of interpretation of existing standards and practices, which involved fact-based research projects and extensive consultations. The corporate responsibility to respect and the human rights due diligence concept enjoy acceptance by business enterprises. As a result of the anonymous consensus reached on the UNGPs within the HRC, the concept also enjoys certain recognition among States. The corporate responsibility to respect reflects a core concept, the elements and parameters of which, as outlined above, are not supposed to be challenged.[131]

Beyond this core, however, there is discretion to business enterprises and other actors to translate the human rights due diligence concept to practice. There is discretion for companies to decide the type and scope of the measures business enterprises seek to meet their responsibility. Its effective implementation may require means of different scale and complexity depending on the circumstances of the company, in terms of the size of a company, its nature and operational context, and the severity of its adverse human rights impacts.[132] The human rights due diligence concept supplies arguments that point to the direction of striking an appropriate balance between risks and care, without prescribing a particular outcome.

The ambiguity and openness of the human rights due diligence concept may not be desirable to the extent that it reduces the clarity that the UNGPs in themselves were set out to provide. It can lead to uncertainty about what conduct is required from companies for the effective implementation of their responsibilities. Uncertainty can incite non-compliance or diverging compliance between companies. It can also complicate efforts to monitor compliance and to hold business enterprises to account. The vague language of the UNGPs was a major point of critique by civil society organizations.[133]

Where the State duty to protect is concerned, the lack of specificity seems less of an issue. The State duty to protect reflects the existing legal standards established in international human rights law. If the State duty to protect had been specified in greater detail, this may have introduced a standard that would go beyond the existing standard. The normative contribution of the UNGPs was not to create any new legal obligations or to affect the human rights obligations of States as existed. 'Nothing in these Guiding Principles should be read as creating new international law obligations, or as limiting or undermining any legal obligations a State may have undertaken or be subject to under international law with regard to human rights.'[134]

While raising legal standards for States is desirable and morally justifiable from a human rights viewpoint, doing so would have undermined the SRSG's claim that the UNGPs did not create new legal obligations. To the extent that the UNGPs were intended to reflect international human rights law as it exists, rather than as it should be, openness in language can be considered on point.

International human rights law does not prescribe how States should legislate in order to prevent and remedy human rights abuses within their jurisdictions. The SRSG acknowledged that '[w]ithin these parameters, States have discretion as to how to fulfil their duty', while noting that '[t]he human rights treaties generally contemplate legislative, administrative and judicial measures'.[135] The discretion left to States is intended and justified by various considerations.

First, if international human rights were to prescribe State action, this may result in States being obligated to adopt measures that are inappropriate to conditions and situations in a respective State. Discretion is left to the State to identify and design the measures that best correspond to the conditions and factors in domestic jurisdictions, in order to deliver the most optimal results in protecting human rights in practice. It is not uncommon, as Kinley and Chambers have pointed out, that international human rights instruments are formulated in open-ended language and accommodate for flexibility in their interpretation.[136,137] While more detailed language can reduce ambiguity, some level of abstraction seems necessary to facilitate interpretations of substantive treaty provisions that are in conformity with the object and purpose of international human rights law and evolving circumstances. International human rights treaties are 'living instruments' that must be interpreted in light of present-day conditions.[138] Since the object and purpose of international human rights law is to protect individual human beings, its provisions must 'be interpreted and applied so as to make its safeguards practical and effective'.[139]

Second, discretion also gives States a degree of flexibility to adopt measures in proportion to their capacities. The ICESCR appreciates this when considering that States enjoy certain discretion when adopting measures to discharge their international legal duties under the ICESCR. The economic, social and cultural rights in this convention are to be achieved progressively. It follows that States have an obligation to take appropriate measures towards the full realization of these human rights, to the maximum of their available resources.[140] That what constitute 'appropriate' measures is relative to the resources that a State has at its disposal. States are free to decide what means are most appropriate in light of circumstances with respect to each right.[141] Means can include, but are not limited to administrative, financial, educational and social measures.[142] The CtESCR has held that legal measures may be indispensable in certain purposes.[143] The discretion of States to choose 'appropriate' measures allows States to adopt legislation, or other measures, that are right for achieving the most optimal protection of human rights under prevailing circumstances.

The jurisprudence of the ECHR shows that courts generally exercise restraint in reviewing State's practices in implementing their international human rights obligations under domestic legislation.[144] In cases where the ECHR was asked to review the necessity of restrictive measures a State adopted in protection of the public interest, the court upheld the doctrine of the 'margin of appreciation'. The ECHR has left a margin to the State and its legislative and judicial bodies charged with interpreting and applying the laws.[145] The difficulty of discerning the existence of uniform human rights standards in the case of disparities among legal situations in Member States due to the rapid evolution of opinions on a subject has served as a justification for upholding this doctrine. States are better positioned than judges to assess the national circumstances in this context, because they are in more direct and continuous contact with the vital forces in their country, the argument holds.[146] The Court also has pointed to its subsidiary role in safeguarding human rights, hence showing deference to States whose authority derives from its democratic mandate and who is first in line to secure the protection of rights of the ECHR.[147]

What could explain the openness in the language of the UNGPs in relation to the corporate responsibility to respect? The openness seems to provide companies with a measure of discretion to design their human rights policy and human rights due diligence process in a manner that is mindful of the contextual factors external and internal to the business, while keeping within the parameters set by the UNGPs. The UNGPs thus do not prescribe means that would be inappropriate or ineffective in factual situations.[148] Rather than assuming that certain means are appropriate a priori, the suitability of measures is to be determined on a case-by-case basis. The UNGPs suggest that business responses are to be determined inductively and in consultation with stakeholders and expertise.

The lack of specificity allows for responsiveness to contextual changes and for business enterprises to adjust their means over time. This is important, for instance, where evolving operations and operating contexts of a company create changes in human rights risks and call for different responses.[149] The UNGPs' emphasis that human rights due diligence should be 'ongoing' testifies to the importance of being responsive to changing business challenges.[150] Arguably, if human rights due diligence would have been formulated in more strict terms, this may have impeded companies from responding most optimally to such changing challenges posed by changing contexts. If more specific language had inhibited an optimal response, this may have incentivized non-compliance by companies.

To the extent that it cannot be determined a priori what measures will be most appropriate in light of diverging contexts, distinct challenges, evolving social expectations and conditions,[151] openness in language seems suited. Openness serves the function of achieving the objective of the UNGPs in a most optimal manner, which may require different conduct and combinations of measures by States and companies.[152] The introduction to the UNGPs stipulates:

> While the Principles themselves are universally applicable, the means by which they are realized will reflect the fact that we live in a world of 192 United Nations Member States, 80,000 transnational enterprises, 10 times as many subsidiaries and countless millions of national firms, most of which are small- and medium-sized enterprises. When it comes to means for implementation, therefore, one size does not fit all.[153]

Greater specificity in the UNGPs could have undermined the global and universal applicability of the corporate responsibility to respect human rights. The SRSG noted, 'situational variations will always exist, but they cannot and should not become the basis for general and universally applicable principles'.[154] The corporate responsibility to respect human rights was intended to reflect a globally applicable social norm. Specifying this norm in further detail may have been premature, in part because of the complexity involved.[155]

The vague wording of the corporate responsibility to respect human rights can be said to reflect the indeterminate nature of international social expectations, and the extent to which a more detailed norm may not grasp acceptance of these social expectations globally. This does not negate the in-principle universal nature of a more detailed social norm, or the justification of such a norm from a moral viewpoint.[156] The social expectations of business enterprises may be difficult to discern where they are unwritten, and in the process of formation.

If the UNGPs had been drafted in greater detail, global support and acceptance for the UNGPs furthermore may not have been forthcoming. Founding the corporate responsibility to respect on social expectations rather than legal obligations lifted certain legal and political constraints from the development of norms. The political and legal constraints that applied to the mandate were hardly conducive to opting for a progressive interpretation on the corporate responsibility to respect human rights. Knox notes that the SRSG felt the need to underspecify some aspects of the corporate responsibility to protect to avert criticism and build political support for his project.[157]

According to some who adopt a more critical stance, stakeholders were prepared to support the UNGPs because they lacked detail. This was despite the different agendas of these stakeholders. Openness in the language of the UNGPs thus seemed to have facilitated consensus building. Kinley and Chambers make a similar observation in relation to the vague wording of the UN Norms: 'the fact that they are open-ended is not only unexceptional, it is also necessary to achieve international consensus on the subject and to enable all parties to relate to the initiative'.[158] Mares goes further by pointing to human rights due diligence as an instrumental concept that, because of its match to business operations, was uniquely able to facilitate this process of securing convergence between stakeholders and to set in motion a governance regime evolution.[159]

The openness of the due diligence concept thus allows for flexibility in the application of the due diligence concept, and can therefore maximize the transformational potential of the human rights due diligence concept. The importance of the reformatory potential of the human rights due diligence concept can be explained in relation to legal norm-creation at the national and international level. The human rights due diligence concept lends itself to implementation in different areas of law, which facilitates its further crystallization into legal obligations at the national (or even supranational, i.e. EU) level. The further 'hardening' of the human rights due diligence concept into a legal obligation under different national laws is not only desirable to foster corporate cultures respectful of human rights. States have a legal obligation to consider adopting such regulatory measures in order to ensure that business enterprises meet their responsibility to respect human rights in practice.[160]

Conclusion

This chapter argues that the human rights due diligence concept should be assessed in its ability to drive conceptual improvements in, and facilitate convergence across, national laws that affect business behaviour. It is a reformatory concept that is bound to redefine fruitfully the standards of due diligence that different areas of the legal order currently set out for business enterprises. The purpose is to construe an institutional framework that supports business respect for human rights.

This chapter focused on human rights due diligence as a standard of performance. The UNGPs define the corporate responsibility as a negative obligation that business enterprises 'should avoid infringing on the human rights of others and should address adverse human rights impacts with which they are involved'.[161,162] This responsibility imposes on companies a requirement to be proactive in order to avoid and address human rights impacts. Companies are responsible for undertaking a human rights due diligence process to 'identify, prevent, mitigate and account for how they address their impacts on human rights'. This process should, at a minimum, encompass the following elements: 'assessing actual and potential human rights impacts, integrating and acting upon the findings, tracking responses, and communicating how impacts are addressed'.[163] This chapter reflected on the implications of the effective operationalization of this human rights due diligence requirement by comparison with existing approaches to due diligence in corporate law.

The SRSG articulates the human rights due diligence concept in open-ended language, hence the exact conduct that is expected from business enterprises is not exactly clear. This quality allows for flexibility of facts and circumstances in the application of the human rights due diligence concept to companies. The due diligence standard entails a judgement of whether the policies and processes that a company has in place are sufficient and appropriate to avoid and address adverse human rights impacts. This test and corresponding balancing exercise resembles the duty of care standard that exists under national (tort) law of non-contractual obligations.

This flexibility furthermore makes the human rights due diligence concept adaptable, capable of transcending different areas of law and lends the concept for effective implementation and enforcement in different areas of national law. This openness allows for further clarification, which should be provided by States through the integration of the human rights due diligence concept into law. The legitimacy and authority that derives from their democratic mandate entails that the clarifications by States carry authoritative weight, and more weight than those provided by private voluntary initiatives, for instance. While the UNGPs view a role for private/hybrid voluntary initiatives in the further crystallization of the human rights due diligence concept, their interpretations cannot be treated as equivalent or be given the same recognition as the definition of public institutions, mainly for this reason. The human rights due diligence concept would furthermore need to be defined in line with constitutional and human rights provisions that bind the State under national and international law. States may contribute to the clarification of the due diligence concept through the implementation of the concept in domestic legislation and regulation, or as a result of domestic adjudication.[164]

National authorities can refer to the human rights due diligence concept to address gaps in human rights protection. This concept can give direction to national authorities when revisiting rules and regulations for the purpose of realigning them with the expectation that business enterprises respect human rights by reference to universally recognized human rights standards and principles. It provides minimum substantive content and parameters around which conflicting concepts in these laws can be resolved and convergence created. At the same time, the exact definition and implications of the concept may be further defined by reference to the respective objectives of these laws and regulations. The exact definition of human rights due diligence would thus be the result of the interaction between the international human rights law that provides the benchmark that business conduct should be assessed against, the national laws and regulations that give rise to the human rights due diligence obligation and their object and purpose, and the conditions identified in the UNGPs and their strategic objective.

Notes

1 Tineke Lambooij, Corporate Social Responsibility: Legal and Semi-Legal Frameworks Supporting CSR, 278 (2010) (Ph.D. dissertation, University of Leiden).

2 John Gerard Ruggie, Just Business Multinational Corporations and Human Rights, 100–101 (W.W. Norton & Company 2013).

3 Special Representative on the Issue of Human Rights and Transnational Corporations and Other Business Enterprises, *Protect, Respect and Remedy: A Framework for Business and Human Rights*, U.N. doc. A/HRC/8/5, ¶ 57 (7 Apr. 2008) (by John Ruggie).

4 Section 11 provided that any person who had acquired a security could sue the defendant specified if the respective security 'contained an untrue statement of a material fact or omitted to state a material fact required to be stated therein or necessary to make the statements therein not misleading'. There would, however, be no liability if the defendant had met a standard of care. As stipulated in section 11 (b) (3), this standard of care required that the defendant had undertaken 'reasonable investigation' that provided 'reasonable ground to believe and did believe' that the registration statements 'were true and that there was no omission'. Sect. 11.(a) of the Securities Act of 1933.

5 Section 12 provided that a person could sue the defendant who sold or offered a security by means of a prospectus or oral communication that contained 'an untrue statement of a material fact or omits to state a material fact necessary in order to make the statements [...] not misleading'. The section created a standard of reasonable care, stipulating that the defendant should not be held liable if 'he did not know, and in the exercise of reasonable care could not have known, of such untruth or omission'. Sect. 12.(a)(2)(a) of the Securities Act of 1933.

6 It has been highlighted, in this regard, that 'traditional American corporate law speaks the language of economics and perhaps politics. It generally does not speak the language of human rights'. Lucien J. Dhooge, *Due Diligence as a Defense to*

Corporate Liability Pursuant to the Alien Tort Statute, 22 Emory International Law Review 455, 437 (2009).
7 Ruggie, *supra* note 2, at 101.
8 Dhooge, *supra* note 6, at 473.
9 Sabine Michalowski, *Due Diligence and Complicity: A Relationship in Need of Clarification*, *in* Human Rights Obligations of Business: Beyond the Corporate Responsibility to Respect?, 218–242, 231 (Cambridge University Press ed. 2013).
10 Mark B. Taylor, *The Ruggie Framework: Polycentric Regulation and the Implications For Corporate Social Responsibility*, 5 Etikk i praksis – Nordic Journal of Applied Ethics 1, 25 (2011).
11 Jonathan Bonnitcha & Robert McCorquodale, *Is the Concept of 'Due Diligence' in the Guiding Principles Coherent?* (2013), *available at* http://papers.ssrn.com/sol3/papers.cfm?abstract_id=2208588.
12 Special Representative on the Issue of Human Rights and Transnational Corporations and Other Business Enterprises, *Guiding Principles on Business and Human Rights: Implementing the United Nations 'Protect, Respect and Remedy' Framework*, U.N. Doc. A/HRC/17/31, GP 8 (21 Mar. 2011) [hereinafter *UNGPs*] (by John Ruggie).
13 Tara van Ho, *'Due Diligence' in 'Transitional Justice States': An Obligation for Greater Transparency?*, in Human Rights and Business: Direct Corporate Accountability for Human Rights, 243 (Jernej Letnar Černič & Tara Van Ho eds. 2015).
14 UNGPs, *supra* note 12, Commentary to GP 17.
15 Van Ho, *supra* note 13, at 246.
16 UNGPs, *supra* note 12, Commentary to GP 18.
17 *Id.* Commentary to GP 8.
18 *Id.* GP 12.
19 *Id.* Commentary to GP 12.
20 *Id.*
21 *Id.* Commentary to GP 12 reflects this:

> Depending on circumstances, business enterprises may need to consider additional standards. For instance, enterprises should respect the human rights of individuals belonging to specific groups or populations that require particular attention, where they may have adverse human rights impacts on them. In this connection, United Nations instruments have elaborated further on the rights of indigenous peoples; women; national or ethnic, religious and linguistic minorities; children; persons with disabilities; and migrant workers and their families. Moreover, in situations of armed conflict enterprises should respect the standards of international humanitarian law.

22 *Id.* Commentary to GP 18.
23 *Id.*
24 Vienna Declaration and Programme of Action, Adopted by the World Conference on Human Rights in Vienna, 25 June 1993, ¶ 32.
25 *Id.* ¶ 5.
26 The Declaration on the Right to Development, Annex to U.N. G.A. Res 41/128, 97th Sess. Preambule (4 Dec. 1986).
27 UNGPs, *supra* note 12, GP 19.
28 *Id.* Commentary to GP 19.
29 *Id.* ¶ 62.
30 *Id.* Commentary to GP 19.
31 OHCHR, The Corporate Responsibility to Respect Human Rights: An Interpretive Guide (2012).
32 *Id.* at 46–47.
33 *Id.* at 46–47 (emphasis added).

34 *Id.* at 19.
35 UNGPs, *supra* note 12, GP 19(a)(i).
36 *Id.* GP 19(a)(ii).
37 Appropriate action might require that large companies create cross-functional decision-making groups that engage experts and staff from relevant functions or departments. Companies may combine these with internal reporting requirements. Senior management may need to be involved in decision-making and oversight in the presence of high-risk context or severe impacts. European Commission, Employment & Recruitment Agencies Sector Guide on Implementing the UN Guiding Principles on Business and Human Rights, 45 (2013), www.ihrb.org/pdf/eu-sector-guidance/EC-Guides/E&RA/EC-Guide_E&RA.pdf.
38 UNGPs, *supra* note 12, GP 24.
39 *Id.* Commentary to GP 19.
40 *Id.*
41 *Id.*
42 *Id.*
43 *Id.*
44 *Id.*
45 *Id.* Commentary to GP 20.
46 OHCHR, *supra* note 31, at 52.
47 UNGPs, *supra* note 12, GP 20.
48 OHCHR, *supra* note 31, at 53.
49 UNGPs, *supra* note 12, GP 20.
50 OHCHR, *supra* note 31, at 53.
51 *Id.* at 53.
52 *Id.* at 54.
53 UNGPs, *supra* note 12, GP 20(a).
54 Indicators have the potential to serve as measurement tools. For a detailed assessment of existing human rights indicator systems, *see* K. Starl, et al., Human Rights Indicators in the Context of the European Union, FRAME Deliverable 13.1 (24 Dec. 2014), *available at* www.fp7-frame.eu/wp-content/materiale/reports/12-Deliverable-13.1.pdf.
55 OHCHR, *supra* note 31, at 55.
56 UNGPs, *supra* note 12, Commentary to GP 20.
57 OHCHR, *supra* note 31, at 55.
58 UNGPs, *supra* note 12, GP 29. *See* Bijlmakers, et al., Report on Tracking CSR Responses FRAME Deliverable 7.4 (Nov. 2015, 2014), *available at* www.fp7-frame.eu/wp-content/uploads/2016/09/Deliverable-7.4.pdf.
59 *Id.* GP 17.
60 Van Ho, *supra* note 13, at 246.
61 It is true that companies already disclose externally under securities legislation; however, this disclosure is of a somewhat different character and serves a different function. The purpose of mandatory disclosure at a stage of the public offering of shares is to address the information asymmetry between inside and outside investors and to ensure that investors are protected when purchasing securities from an issuer. The purpose of mandatory disclosure on the secondary market is to maximize the information efficiency of the market. Louise Gullifer & Jennifer Payne, Corporate Finance Law: Principles and Policy, 524 (2nd ed., Hart Publishing 2015).
62 Van Ho, *supra* note 13, at 246.
63 For instance, the requirements as to annual reports and accounts set out in the UK 2006 Company Act are primarily oriented towards the disclosure of information to shareholders. Gullifer & Payne, *supra* note 61, 547–548.
64 For instance, Art. 5 of Directive 2004/109/EC (Transparency Directive) notes that issuers of shares or debt securities shall make public a half yearly financial report

that covers a condensed set of financial statements and an interim report. This disclosure requirement has been implemented by EU Member States through securities legislation and aims primarily at the disclosure of information to the market. Directive 2004/109/EC, of the European Parliament and the Council of 15 December 2004 on the harmonization of transparency requirements in relation to information about issuers whose securities are admitted to trading on a regulated market and amending Directive 2001/34/EC, art. 5(1) 2004 O.J. (L 390) 38, Art. 5(1). Directive 2013/50/EU, of the European Parliament and of the Council of 22 October 2013 amending Directive 2004/109/EC of the European Parliament and of the Council on the harmonization of transparency requirements in relation to information about issuers whose securities are admitted to trading on a regulated market. Directive 2003/71/EC, of the European Parliament and of the Council on the prospectus to be published when securities are offered to the public or admitted to trading and Commission Directive 2007/14/EC laying down detailed rules for the implementation of certain provisions of Directive 2004/109/EC, art. 1(4) amending art. 5(1), 2013 O.J. (L 294) 13. Gullifer & Payne, *supra* note 61, at 547–548.

65 Van Ho, *supra* note 13, at 246.

66 *Id.*

67 For instance, Van Ho notes that, in transitional justice States that face a higher likelihood of recidivism to conflict, there is a need for a heightened level of transparency in order 'to assess unusual impacts on the economic, political and social inequalities between identified ethnic and social groups'. *Id.* at 248.

68 See, *e.g.* Article 19(2) International Covenant on Civil and Political Rights, Adopted and opened for signature, ratification and accession by General Assembly resolution 2200A (XXI) of 16 December 1966, entry into force 23 March 1976.

69 UNGPs, *supra* note 12, GP 21 (21 Mar. 2011).

70 Absent an element of severity, the form of disclosure is discretionary and business enterprises may communicate through alternative, informal forms of communications. Examples of informal forms of disclosure are 'in-person meetings, online dialogues, consultation with affected stakeholders'. *Id.* Commentary to GP 21.

71 *Id.* GP 21.

72 Van Ho, *supra* note 13, at 247.

73 UNGPs, *supra* note 12, GP 21.

74 *Id.* GP 21 (a).

75 *Id.* GP 21 (a).

76 *Id.* GP 21 (b).

77 *Id.* Commentary to GP 21.

78 It should be noted, however, that the failure to identify and manage human rights risks can result in significant financial costs, including 'opportunity costs, financial costs, legal costs and reputational costs'. [Interview with Ruggie.] Also *see* a study by Davis and Franks re: the potential costs that arise for extractive companies due to company-community conflicts. Rachel Davis & Daniel M. Franks, *The Costs of Conflict with Local Communities in the Extractive Industry*, SRMining2011 (21 Oct. 2011), *available at* http://shiftproject.org/sites/default/files/Davis%20&%20Franks_Costs%20of%20Conflict_SRM.pdf.

79 Commentary to GP 17. Ruggie, *supra* note 2, at 99. Muchlinski, *Implementing the New UN Corporate Human Rights Framework: Implications for Corporate Law, Governance, and Regulation*, 22 Business Ethics Quarterly 145, 145–177, 149 (2012).

80 UNGPs, *supra* note 12, Commentary to GP 18.

81 *Id.* GP 18 and Commentary.

82 *Id.* GP 20.

83 Van Ho, *supra* note 13.

84 Democracy is widely considered as one of the general principles of human rights governance that sustains its legitimacy, *see* J.O. McGinnis & I. Somin, *Democracy*

and International Human Rights Law, 84 Notre Dame Law Review (2009). It is founded on 'the freely expressed will of people to determine their own political, economic, social and cultural systems and their full participation in all aspects of their lives'. Human Rights Council Res. 19/36, Human rights, democracy and the rule of law, 19th Sess., 19 Apr. 2012, U.N. A/HRC/RES/19/36 (19 Apr. 2012). The consent of the people is recognized as a writ for the legitimate right to govern. Article 23(1) of the UDHR states,

> [T]he will of the people shall be the basis of authority of government; this shall be expressed in periodic and genuine elections which shall be by universal and equal suffrage and shall be held by secret voting or by equivalent free voting procedures.

Article 25 of the ICCPR furthermore enunciates the democratic values of political equality and control as anchors of democratic governance, outlining equal rights, opportunities for citizens to participate in public affairs 'directly or through freely chosen representatives', to vote and to be elected and to have access to public service without discrimination. Scholarship has advanced the view that democracy is not only a prerequisite for legitimate governance, but it may in fact be a legal entitlement. T.M. Frank, The Emerging Right to Democratic Governance, 86 The American Journal of International Law 46–91 (1992).

85 The UNDRIP recognizes that indigenous people have the right to participate in decision-making in matters that would affect their human rights. This entails that States must consult with indigenous peoples in order to obtain their free and informed consent prior to the adoption and implementation of legislative and administrative measures that may affect them, or the approval of any project affecting their lands, territories or other resources. Free, prior and informed consent is an expression of indigenous peoples right to self-determination, by virtue of which they 'freely determine their political status and freely pursue their economic, social and cultural development'. United Nations Declaration on the Rights of Indigenous Peoples, G.A. Res. 61/295, U.N. Doc. 61/295, Art.3, 18, 19, 32.2. (13 Sept. 2007). *UN WG, 2013 Report, supra* note 114, ¶ 10 (6 Aug. 2013). International Covenant on Civil and Political Rights, Art. 4.1, 16 Dec. 1966, G.A. Res. 2200A (XXI). The Declaration on the Right to Development, Annex to U.N. G.A. Res 41/128, 97th Sess. (4 Dec. 1986), Preambule.

86 Ruggie, *supra* note 2, at 99.

87 UNGPs, *supra* note 12, GP 16.

88 *Id.* Commentary to GP 16.

89 *Id.* GP 18 (a).

90 *Id.* Commentary to GP 23.

91 *Id.* GP 16.

92 Bob Hepple, A *Race to the Top? International Investment Guidelines and Corporate Codes of Conduct*, 20 Comparative Labor Law & Policy Journal 358 (1999).

93 The importance of consistency was signalled by the 1993 Vienna Declaration and Program of Action that recognized 'the need to maintain consistency with the high quality of existing international standards'. Vienna Declaration and Programme of Action, Adopted by the World Conference on Human Rights in Vienna, 25 June 1993, ¶ 6.

94 *See* Cees van Dam, *Tort Law and Human Rights: Brothers in Arms on the Role of Tort Law in the Area of Business and Human Rights*, 2 Journal of European Tort Law 3, 221, 244 (2011).

95 UNGPs, *supra* note 12, GP 15.

96 Tara Van Ho, *Operationalizing Human Rights in the Business Context*, University of Essex (31 Mar. 2015), http://blogs.essex.ac.uk/hrc/2015/03/31/operationalizing-human-rights-in-the-business-context/.

97 According to Mushlinski, the acting to promote the success of the company entails in practice to strike a balance between 'the needs of the company and its members to be protected from incompetent management and the need to give directors flexibility and freedom to engage in entrepreneurial activity'. Muchlinski, *supra* note 79, at 161.

98 Report of the Special Representative of the Secretary-General on the issue of human rights and transnational corporations and other business enterprises, Addendum: Human Rights and Corporate Law: Trends and Observations from a Cross-National Study Conducted by the Special Representative, at 15–18, A/HRC/17/31/Add.2. (23 May 2011) (by John Ruggie). Tara Van Ho, *supra* note 96.

99 Liesbeth F.H. Enneking, *Foreign Direct Liability and Beyond: Exploring the Role of Tort Law, in* Promoting International Corporate Social Responsibility and Accountability, 232–233 (Eleven International Publishing 2012).

100 *Id.* at 232–233.

101 *Id.* at 232–233.

102 *Id.* at 233.

103 UNGPs, *supra* note 12, GP 14.

104 *Id.* GP 14.

105 *Id.* GP 12.

106 *Id.* Commentary to GP 14.

107 Note the resemblance with: Enneking, *supra* note 99, at 232–233.

108 For similar argument, *see, id.* at 233–234.

109 UNGPs, *supra* note 12, Commentary to GP 24.

110 This is for instance the case where the value chains of a business enterprise comprises of such a large number of entities that the conduct of human rights due diligence across all entities in the chain is unreasonably difficult. In such cases, 'business enterprises should identify general areas where the risk of adverse human rights impacts is most significant, whether due to certain suppliers' or clients' operating context, the particular operations, products or services involved, or other relevant considerations, and prioritize these for human rights due diligence'. *Id.* Commentary to GP 17.

111 For an analysis of due diligence in human rights law, *see* Tineke Lambooij, *supra* note 1, at 293–309.

112 The concept of due diligence was not entirely new to the discourse of business and human rights. For instance, the UN Norms recognized a due diligence responsibility for corporations 'in ensuring that their activities do not contribute directly or indirectly to human rights abuses, and that they do not directly or indirectly benefit from abuses of which they were aware or ought to have been aware'. *Commentary on the Norms on the Responsibilities of Transnational Corporations and Other Business Enterprises with Regard to Human Rights*, U.N. Doc. E/CN.4/Sub.2/2003/38/Rev.2 (2003), at Commentary A. (b).

113 The act of balancing is a method that has been employed by the ECtHR, the CJEU and many national Constitutional Courts for the interpretation and implementation of qualified human rights. This balancing exercise entails the identifying, qualifying and weighing of the interests of the individual and the community/public interest, to ultimately decide on the most optimal outcome. Başak Çali, *Balancing Human Rights? Methodological Problems with Weights, Scales and Proportions*, 259 Human Rights Quarterly 251, 253 (2007).

114 Working Group on the issue of human rights and transnational corporations and other business enterprises, *Report of the Working Group on the Issue of Human Rights and Transnational Corporations and Other Business Enterprises in Accordance with Human Rights Council Resolution 17/4, Transmitted by Note of the Secretary-General*, U.N. doc. A/68/279, ¶ 7, ftn 18 [hereinafter *UN WG, 2013 Report*] (6 Aug. 2013).

115 Çali, *supra* note 113, at 253.

116 *UN WG, 2013 Report, supra* note 114, ¶ 7, ftn 18.

117 For instance, limitations on human rights must be avoided, community interests cannot justify the wholesale violation of human rights, and must be in conformity with the objective of the respective human rights instrument. Bertrand G. Ramcharan, The Fundamentals of International Human Rights Treaty Law, 15 (Martinus Nijhoff Publishers 2011). Ramcharan refers to Article 9(2) of the African Charter on Human and People's Rights that stipulates: 'Every individual shall have the right to express and disseminate his opinions within the law.' The Commission held that national law could not offset the right to express and disseminate one's opinions:

> To allow national law to have precedence over the international law of the Charter would defeat the purpose of the rights and freedoms enshrined in the Charter. International human rights standards must always prevail over contradictory national law. Any limitation on the rights of the Charter must be in conformity with the provisions of the Charter.

118 International Covenant on Civil and Political Rights, Art 18.3, 16 Dec. 1966, G.A. Res. 2200A (XXI).

119 U.N. Human Rights Committee, General Comment No. 22: Article 18 (Freedom of Thought, Conscience or Religion), CCPR/C/21/Rev.1/Add. 4, 48th Sess. (30 July 1993).

120 Another example can be found in the context of indigenous people's rights. The Declaration on the Rights of Indigenous People (UNDRIP) stipulates in Art. 46 that the exercise of the human rights set forth in the Declaration:

> Shall be subject only to such limitations as are determined by law and in accordance with international human rights obligations. Any such limitations shall be non-discriminatory and strictly necessary solely for the purpose of securing due recognition and respect for the rights and freedoms of others and for meeting the just and most compelling requirements of a democratic society.
>
> United Nations Declaration on the Rights of Indigenous Peoples, Art. 46, G.A. Res. 61/295, U.N. Doc.61/295, Annex (13 Sept. 2007) (UN General Assembly 2007)

121 Çali, *supra* note 113.

122 Human Rights Council Res. 17/4, Human rights and transnational corporations and other business enterprises, 17th Sess., 30 May–17 June 2011, U.N. Doc A/HRC/RES/17/4 (17 July 2007).

123 *Id.*

124 In a draft of the UNGP, the SRSG noted the following:

> Business is the major source of investment and job creation, and markets can be highly efficient means for allocating scarce resources, capable of generating economic growth, reducing poverty, and increasing demand for the rule of law, thereby contributing to the realization of a broad spectrum of human rights.
>
> Special Representative on the Issue of Human Rights and Transnational Corporations and Other Business Enterprises, *Draft: Guiding Principles For The Implementation Of The United Nations 'Protect, Respect and Remedy' Framework*, ¶ 1 (2010)

125 Van Ho, *supra* note 13, at 245.

126 *See e.g.* the following provisions contain language that endorses a human rights approach: Human Rights Council Res. 11/3, Trafficking in persons, especially women and children, 27th Sess., 17 June 2009, A/HRC/RES/11/3, ¶ 1 (17 June 2009) and 3(f), Trafficking in women and girls, Resolution adopted by the General Assembly on 18 December 2008, G.A. Res. 63/156, A/RES/63/156, ¶ 18. (2–18 June 2009).

127 Van Ho, *supra* note 13, at 246.
128 *Id*. at 240.
129 Larissa van den Herik & Jernej Letnar Černič, *Regulating Corporations under International Law: From Human Rights to International Criminal Law and Back Again*, Journal of International Criminal Justice 742 (2010).
130 Van Ho, *supra* note 13, at 242. UNGPs, *supra* note 12, GP 3(c), GP 7 (21 Mar. 2011).
131 The same applies for the interpretation of the State duty to protect, which has not been without criticism. The UNGPs have been criticized for 'locking-in' an interpretation of international human rights law where this core cannot be challenged. This may impede the development of alternative regulatory approaches to business and human rights, and thus, restrict innovation, Lopéz argues. '[T]he supposed comprehensiveness and authority of [the Guiding Principles] leaves nearly no room for improvement or further development of additional standards and norms.' This position is 'contrary to the evolving nature of international law standards'. *See* Carlos Lopéz, *The 'Ruggie Process': From Legal Obligations to Corporate Social Responsibility?*, *in* Human Rights Obligations of Business: Beyond the Corporate Responsibility to Respect?, 60 (Surya Deva & David Bilchitz eds. 2013).
132 UNGPs, *supra* note 12, GP 14, 17(b).
133 In a joint statement, civil society notes:

> In Principles 1, 5, 6, 8, 10, 13, 14, 17, 23, 24, and 25, the draft refers to 'appropriate steps', 'appropriate actions', and steps that should be taken 'where appropriate' when referring to State regulation of business activity. However, the draft UNGPs provide little guidance as to what is or is not appropriate and, in so doing, fail to provide concrete recommendations for enhanced protection of human rights against abuse involving business.
>
> Joint Civil Society Statement on the draft Guiding Principles on Business and Human Rights (Jan. 2011), www.fidh.org/IMG/pdf/Joint_CSO_Statement_on_GPs.pdf

134 UNGPs, *supra* note 12, General Principles.
135 J. Ruggie, *Building on a 'Landmark Year' and Thinking Ahead*, institute for Human Rights and Business, para. 14 (12 Jan. 2012). www.ihrb.org/commentary/board/building_on_landmark_year_and_ thinking_ahead.html.
136 David Kinley & Rachel Chambers, *The UN Human Rights Norms for Corporations: The Private Implications of Public International Law*, 20 Human Rights Law Review (2006).
137 The 'margin of appreciation' granted to States in the fulfilment of their obligations under the European Convention of Human Rights, is one example. The doctrine has been applied by the Court in cases were differences and disparities among legal situations of Member States make it difficult to identify a uniform human rights standard. It rests on the understanding that in certain contexts, States are considered to be in a better position than judges to assess their national circumstances. Social conditions and developments must be taken into account in function of the special object and purpose of human rights treaties, which call for an objective and dynamic reading. Clare Ovey & Robin C.A. White, Jacobs and White: European Convention on Human Rights, 52–55 (2006).
138 *Tyrer v. the United Kingdom*, App. No. 5856/72, 2 Eur. H.R. Rep. 1, 15–16 (1978). *Lozidou v. Turkey*, App. No. 15318/89, 20 Eur. H.R. Rep. 99, ¶ 71, (1995).
139 *Lozidou v. Turkey*, *id.* ¶ 72. *Soering v. The United Kingdom*, App. No. 14038/88, 11 Eur. H.R. Rep. 439, at 34 (1989). *Artico v. Italy*, App. 6694/74, Eur. H.R. Rep. 4, at 16 (1980).

140 The ICESCR states in Art. 2:

> Each State Party to the present Covenant undertakes to take steps, individually and through international assistance and co-operation, especially economic and technical, to the maximum of its available resources, with a view to achieving progressively the full realization of the rights recognized in the present Covenant by all appropriate means, including particularly the adoption of legislative measures.
>
> International Covenant on Economic, Social and Cultural Rights, art. 2, 16 Dec. 1966, General Assembly resolution 2200A (XXI)

141 U.N. Committee on Economic, Social and Cultural Rights General Comment No. 3: The Nature of States Parties' Obligations (Art. 2, Para. 1, of the Covenant), E/1991/23, 5th Sess. (14 Dec. 1990).

142 *Id.* ¶ 7.

143 *Id.* ¶ 3.

144 Christian Tomuschat, *Democracy and the Rule of Law*, *in* Oxford Handbooks of International Human Rights Law, 14 (Dinah Shelton ed. 2013).

145 *Handyside v. The United Kingdom*, App. No. 5493/72, 1 Eur. H.R. Rep. 737, ¶ 48 (1976).

146 *Id.* ¶ 48.

147 *Id.* ¶ 48.

148 Hence, the UNGPs refer to 'one size does not fit all'. *See* UNGPs, introduction, para. 15. The leeway left by the UNGPs can be seen as a deliberate step by the SRSG to respond to critique of the business community about a 'one-size-fits-all approach' not being able to accommodate for the diversity in factors that affect the capacity of a company to impact on human rights. David Weissbrodt & Muria Kruger, *Norms on the Responsibilities of Transnational Corporations and Other Business Enterprises with Regard to Human Rights*, 97 The American Journal of International Law 901, 911 (2003).

149 UNGPs, *supra* note 12, GP 17(c).

150 *Id.* GP 17(c).

151 The SRSG seems to deliberately frame this responsibility in vague wording to accommodate business concerns about a 'one-size-fits-all' approach that would not provide companies with the flexibility they deemed necessary to address unique human rights challenges faced in their operations and operating contexts.

152 UNGPs, *supra* note 12, at 1.

153 *Id.* Introduction, ¶ 15.

154 J. Ruggie, Note on ISO 26000 Guidance Draft Document, 3 (Nov. 2009), www.business-humanrights.org/media/bhr/files/Ruggie-note-re-ISO-26000-Nov-2009.PDF.

155 A company survey by the German Global Compact Network and ecosense on the usage of tools to implement the UNGPs found that a high degree of abstraction of the UNGPs was illustrative of the complexity of the topic of business and human rights.

156 From a moral viewpoint, there is widespread support for the argument that the need to protect human dignity demands that both states and non-state actors observe fundamental rights. Business enterprises are no exception. Peter Muchlinski, *Corporate Social Responsibility*, *in* The Oxford Handbook of International Investment Law, 655 (Peter Muchlinski, et al. eds. 2008). *See* Philip Alston, Non-State Actors and Human Rights (Oxford University Press 2005) and A. Clapham, Human Rights Obligations of Non-State Actors (Oxford University Press 2006).

157 John H. Knox, *The Ruggie Rules: Applying Human Rights Law to Corporations*, *in* The UN Guiding Principles on Business and Human Rights: Foundations and Implementation, 66 (R. Mares ed. 2012).

158 Kinley & Chambers, *supra* note 296, *at* 20.

159 R. Mares, 'Respect' Human Rights: Concept and Convergence, 53–54 (forthcoming in Law, Business and Human Rights: Bridging the Gap (Robert C. Bird, Daniel R. Cahoy, & Jamie Darin Prenkert, eds., Elgar Publishing Ltd. forthcoming 2014).

160 Olivier de Schutter makes this argument:

> Potentially most important of all, however, is the fact that the 'business case' for CSR produces, at the rhetorical level, a powerful consequence: it serves to create the impression that the development of CSR will make natural progress, in a sort of evolutionary growth driven by market mechanisms, without such progress having to be encouraged or artificially produced by an intervention of public authorities. There is a very thin line between the idea that 'CSR is profitable for business' and the idea that 'CSR may take care of itself'. This consequence should be avoided at all costs. There is a need, clearly identifiable, for a regulatory framework to be established, if CSR is to work. This is not in contradiction with the voluntary character of CSR. On the contrary, it attaches its meaning to voluntary commitments.
>
> Olivier de Schutter, *Corporate Social Responsibility: European Style*, 14 European Law Journal 219 (2008)

161 UNGPs, *supra* note 12, at 11.

162 The linkage of the responsibility to respect human rights to the human rights due diligence concept is a departure from the 'sphere of influence' concept that had been adhered to until then to apply human rights responsibilities to business enterprises. The scope of this obligation is delineated on the basis of the potential and actual impacts that a company's operations or business relationships have on internationally recognized human rights and that the company is involved in by way of causation, contribution or direct linkage.

163 UNGPs, *supra* note 12, GP 17.

164 Humberto Fernando Cantú Rivera, *Business & Human Rights: From a 'Responsibility to Respect' to Legal Obligations and Enforcement*, in Human Rights and Business: Direct Corporate Accountability for Human Rights, 320 (Jernej Letnar Černič & Tara Van Ho eds. 2015).

5 The EU's contribution to the implementation of CSR and the corporate responsibility to respect human rights

Critical reflections on the European Commission's strategy on CSR[1]

Introduction

This chapter takes measure of the EU's commitment and concrete efforts to promote responses to the UNGPs. It focuses on how and to what extent the UNGPs have been codified in EU law and policy and to what extent this codification is effectively implementing CSR, and business responsibilities for human rights, at EU and national level. This chapter will focus on the EU CSR Strategy through which the EU coordinates its business and human rights-related activities. The European Commission (the Commission) presented this strategy in a Communication entitled 'A renewed EU Strategy 2011–14 for Corporate Social Responsibility' (the EU CSR Strategy[2]) on 25 October 2011. This communication provides the European Commission's internal policy framework for the promotion of CSR, and business respect for human rights, and sets out a renewed European Strategy for CSR.[3] This chapter assesses the EU's approach and concrete efforts to foster compliance and changes in business behaviour in relation to human rights. It argues that there is scope for the EU to increase its level of engagement with the UNGPs. The Charter of Fundamental Rights of the European Union (CFREU) and the objective that the EU has set itself 'to make the fundamental rights provided for in the Charter as effective as possible',[4] may entail an obligation for the EU to seriously consider taking all actions that are within its competences to do so. The chapter also notes that the substance of the efforts of the EU and the regulatory responses by the EU, States, business enterprises and other actors to the UNGPs provide indication of evolving CSR standards and practices.

The origins of EU CSR policy

CSR made its debut in the EU political sphere in 1993, when the then-President of the Commission, Mr Jacques Delors, called on European business enterprises to mobilize and join the fight against social exclusion.[5,6] It was only in 2001, however, that CSR formally became an item on the EU political agenda. At a special meeting organized in Lisbon, 23–24 March 2000, the European Council made an appeal to the sense of social responsibility of corporations with regards to 'best practices on lifelong learning, work organisation, equal opportunities, social inclusion and sustainable development'.[7] The concept can be understood in relation to the strategic Lisbon goals set out for 2010. At a meeting in Gothenburg later that year, the European Council noted that the EU Sustainability Agenda 'completes' the political commitments set out in the 2000 Lisbon Strategy by adding a third environmental dimension to this Strategy.[8] The European Council thereby recognized that 'in the long term, economic growth, social cohesion and environmental protection must go hand in hand'.[9] It appears that the idea behind the CSR concept was for business enterprises to engage in learning practices and the sharing of experiences on the implementation of the shared objectives, from which best practices may be discerned.[10]

In July 2001, the Commission issued its Green Paper, 'Promoting a European Framework for corporate social responsibility' (the Green Paper). This document officially launched the EU CSR Policy.[11] In the Green Paper the Commission defined CSR as 'a concept whereby companies integrate social and environmental concerns in their business operations and in their interaction with their stakeholders on a voluntary basis'.[12] CSR was conceived as business driven and process oriented, in that business enterprises through CSR could manage stakeholder relations and increase their 'license to operate'.[13] Stressing the business case for CSR, the communication noted that such an inclusive approach could result in 'long term strategy minimising risks linked to uncertainty'.[14] CSR was not seen as a substitute for the development of relevant regulation or legislation. The communication noted that

> in countries where such regulations do not exist, efforts should focus on putting the proper regulatory or legislative framework in place in order to define a level playing field on the basis of which socially responsible practices can be developed.[15]

The main aim of the Green Paper was to ignite innovative practices, greater transparency, new partnerships and business initiatives on CSR. CSR was presented as an instrumental value in the advancement of the strategic goal decided in Lisbon for the Union: 'to become the most competitive and dynamic knowledge-based economy in the world, capable of sustainable economic growth with more and better jobs and greater social cohesion'.[16] The Green Paper also intended to stimulate innovative thinking about the manner in which the EU could assume a meaningful role of promoting CSR, at the European and international level. The European approach was to mirror and correspond with international initiatives, *inter alia*, the OECD Guidelines for Multinational Enterprises, the active promotion to which the Commission was committed. The EU approach was aimed to 'complement and add value to existing activities' by:

- providing an overall European framework, aiming at promoting quality and coherence of CSR practices, through developing broad principles, approaches and tools, and promoting best practice and innovative ideas,
- supporting best practice approaches to cost-effective evaluation and independent verification of CSR practices, ensuring thereby their effectiveness and credibility.[17]

The Communication 'Corporate Social Responsibility: A business contribution to Sustainable Development', issued by the Commission in 2002, presented an EU Strategy for CSR.[18] Despite calls by trade unions and civil society for a regulatory framework to set 'minimum standards' and ensure 'a level playing field', the renewed Strategy aligned with the business case for CSR. Business enterprises had largely discarded a regulatory approach as an inapt 'one-size-fits all solution' that would 'stifle creativity and innovation' and could 'lead to conflicting priorities for enterprises in different geographical areas'.[19] In the face of an increasingly polarized debate, the EU opted for the strictly voluntary approach favoured by the business community. The tools that the EU thus introduced to put its CSR policy to practice included only non-mandatory 'soft' tools, e.g. the increase of knowledge about the positive impact of CSR, the exchange of experiences and good practices, the facilitation of convergence and transparency and the promotion of CSR management skills.

The Communication set the stage for the creation of an EU Multi-Stakeholder Forum (the MSF) on CSR. The MSF was intended to serve as a forum for dialogue that, through the exchange of good practices and experiences, the development of a common EU approach and guiding principles, and the identification of areas for action, could contribute to transparency and convergence of CSR practices and instruments. Greater transparency and convergence was desirable especially in the areas of codes of conduct, management standards, accounting, auditing and reporting, labels, and socially responsible investment.[20,21] Convened in 2002, the MSF brought together representatives of business networks, trade unions, employer organizations and civil society to fulfil a mandate that was more restricted than the 2002 Communication initially had advocated. The objective of 'identifying and exploring areas where additional action is needed at the European level' had been omitted, hence the exclusion of the possibility to table proposals for a regulatory framework.[22] The MSF's Final Report, presented at its final High-Level Meeting in June 2004, did not push for greater commitments in the form of legal engagement.[23] The outcome left many disappointed, especially NGOs that expressed that the EU should assume 'the lead role in the development of an effective EU framework for CSR',[24] a view the European Parliament shared. As certain NGOs did not endorse the findings in the report, no consensus was reached in the end.[25]

The Commission's 2006 communication 'Implementing the Partnership for Growth and Jobs: Making Europe a Pole of Excellence on Corporate Social Responsibility' redirected EU CSR policy towards the objectives of the relaunched Lisbon Partnership, i.e. growth and jobs. The Lisbon 2005 Strategy marked the marginalization of the EU's social dimension: as social policy was relegated to the benefit of economic growth,[26] so was EU CSR policy. The Commission's acknowledgement that 'enterprises are the primary actors in CSR' and that the Commission 'can best achieve its objectives by working more closely with European enterprises' constitute examples of this trend.[27] The 2006 communication introduced the creation of the European Alliance for CSR, a business-led initiative that sought to create a wider partnership between enterprises, States and relevant stakeholders. The creation of the Alliance prompted civil society organizations to abandon the MSF in 2006, and to boycott a later attempt by the EU to reconvene the forum in 2009.[28] The Alliance further narrowed interests and participants to a powerful coalition of like-minded anti-regulation actors.[29]

The EU CSR Policy since 2001 has been correctly depicted as a 'business-driven, voluntary and process-oriented' approach.[30] This approach triumphed under the 2006 communication, which set out the ambition of the Commission to further through its EU CSR Policy the priorities set by the Lisbon Strategy and at making the EU 'a Pole of Excellence on CSR in support of a competitive and sustainable enterprise and market economy'.[31] The Commission's 2006 communication also indicated that the Commission would follow the work of the SRSG.[32] When the MSF was reconvened in November 2010, and business enterprises and NGO representatives reunited to discuss CSR developments and ways forward towards the creation of a new communication,[33] a special session was devoted to the integration of the PRR Framework.[34]

The renewed EU CSR Strategy 2011–2014

The Commission issued the EU CSR Strategy on 25 October 2011.[35] This Strategy was launched against the backdrop of the financial and economic crisis, which had negative effects on the general level of trust in corporations. The crisis encouraged EU Member States to call on business enterprises to address these negative effects, including by taking responsibility for the adverse impacts of their operations on human rights, in conformity with international standards. The magnitude of these impacts had become increasingly visible through a number of high-profile cases of human rights violations committed by business enterprises.[36]

The EU renewed its CSR policy with the aim 'to create conditions favourable to sustainable growth, responsible business behaviour and durable employment generation in the medium and long term'.[37] The Commission

> introduces new elements which can help further extend the impact of the policy [...] and seeks to reaffirm the EU's global influence in this field, enabling the EU to better promote its interests and values in relations with other regions and countries [...] to guide and coordinate EU Member State policies and so reduce the risks of divergent approaches that would create additional costs for enterprises operating in more than one Member State.[38]

The EU coordinates its approach to CSR and business responsibilities related to human rights through the EU CSR Strategy.[39] There are various elements to the Strategy that are of particular relevance to human rights.

First, the EU CSR Strategy clarifies that the EU commitments and policies on business and human rights are framed as part of this broader EU CSR Strategy and agenda for action. The first two instalments of the EU's CSR Strategy, as above mentioned, dated respectively 2002 and 2006, hardly referred to human rights. These instruments conceived of CSR as a voluntary initiative by business enterprises to 'integrate social and environmental concerns in their business operations and in their interaction with their stakeholders'.[40] The EU CSR Strategy identifies '[t]he need to give greater attention to human rights, which have become a significantly more prominent aspect of CSR'.[41] Human rights are thus viewed as part of a comprehensive CSR concept. This also suggests that human rights should be read in light of the aforementioned purpose of CSR, which is to promote sustainable growth, responsible business conduct, and durable employment generation.

The Commission seeks alignment with global approaches in its efforts to promote CSR, including its human rights aspect. The Commission lists five 'internationally recognised principles and guidelines' in this context. These instruments are the OECD Guidelines for MNEs, the UNGC, the ISO 26000, the ILO Tripartite Declaration, and the UNGPs. According to the Commission, these instruments in combination represent 'an evolving and recently strengthened global framework for CSR'.[42] Where the promotion of the human rights aspect of CSR is concerned, the EU notes that it 'fully endorses' the UNGPs and points to the other instruments aforementioned as 'support for businesses in addressing the UNGPs'.[43]

Second, the EU redefined its understanding of CSR as 'the responsibility of enterprises for their impacts on society'. This definition corresponds to the expectations set out under the UNGPs that business enterprises have a responsibility to respect human rights.[44] The absence of an express reference to CSR as *voluntary* marked a significant departure from the EU's previous definition of CSR.[45] In particular, the fact that the EU definition no longer expressly refers to CSR as voluntary, suggests that the EU no longer rejects, a priori, regulatory measures as a means to promote CSR. Indeed, the EU CSR Strategy now expressly recognizes '[t]he need to acknowledge the role that complementary regulation plays in creating an environment more conducive to enterprises voluntarily meeting their social responsibility'.[46]

Third, the Commission presents a new agenda for action. This agenda reflects a greater focus on human rights, as 'a significantly more prominent aspect of CSR', and a 'smart mix' approach to promoting CSR and business respect for human rights. This 'smart mix' approach, next to voluntary measures, views a role for State regulation in promoting corporate responsibility and for human rights. This approach somewhat differs from the (also referred to as 'smart mix') approach that the UNGPs advance, in that, under the EU approach, business enterprises are expected to take the lead in the development of CSR, while

States have only a complementary role.[47,48] The Strategy notes 'the need to acknowledge the role that complementary regulation plays in creating an environment more conducive to enterprises voluntarily meeting their social responsibility'.[49]

The following sections undertake a more detailed examination of the new EU CSR definition and Plan for Action. The aim is to determine how well the EU's approach corresponds with the concepts and intent of the UNGPs.[50] The focus is on aspects that bring the EU's CSR Policy into greater alignment with the UNGPs. The analysis focuses on actions that have been identified in the EU Plan of Action 2010–2014, and that are especially relevant for fostering business respect for human rights. The analysis draws from the EU 'Staff Working Document' that the EU published in 2015, which surveys the measures the EU has taken in order to implement the UNGPs.[51] The EU CSR Strategy expired in December 2014, and for the moment, no new strategy is forthcoming.

EU competences in the area of business and human rights

A question that arises when examining the contribution of the EU to the promotion and implementation of the UNGPs is the competences the EU has to act in the area of business and human rights. The defining characteristics of EU law in this domain are the principles of conferral and subsidiarity. According to Article 5(1) of the Treaty on European Union (TEU): '[t]he limits of Union competences are governed by the principle of conferral. The use of Union competences is governed by the principles of subsidiarity and proportionality'. Pursuant to the principle of conferral, enshrined in Article 5(2) of the TEU, 'the EU shall only act within the confines of the competences conferred upon it by the Member States in pursuance of the objectives set out in the Treaties'. Pursuant to the principle of subsidiarity, as provided for in Article 5(3) TEU,

> [...] in areas which do not fall within its exclusive competence, the Union shall act only if and in so far as the objectives of the proposed action cannot be sufficiently achieved by the Member States, either at central level or at regional and local level, but can rather, by reason of the scale or effects of the proposed action, be better achieved at Union level.[52]

These principles are relevant for understanding how the role of the EU in advancing business and human rights objectives relates to the role of EU Member States, which have their own sphere of competence. As the Commission Staff Document notes, the EU may only exercise those regulatory competences that are conferred upon it by the EU Treaties,[53] the scope and content of which furthermore varies according to different legal and political fields. The Commission recognizes that business and human rights is cross-cutting and touches upon a wide range of such areas, *inter alia*, 'human rights law, investment and trade law, consumer protection law, civil law, and commercial law, corporate or penal law'.[54]

The Commission Staff Document recalls the status of EU fundamental rights under EU law. It refers to Article 2 of the Treaty that recognizes the pre-imminence of respect for human rights as one of the values upon which the EU has been founded. According to Article 2 TEU: '[t]he Union is founded on the values of respect for human dignity, freedom, democracy, equality, the rule of law and respect for human rights'. The document also refers to the EU Charter of Fundamental Rights, which was 'solemnly proclaimed' on 7 December 2000, and acquired the same legal value as Treaties when the Treaty of Lisbon entered into force. According to Article 6(1) TEU:

> The Union recognises the rights, freedoms and principles set out in the Charter of Fundamental Rights of the European Union of 7 December 2000, as adapted at Strasbourg, on 12 December 2007, which shall have the same legal value as the Treaties.

Also relevant, but not expressly referred to in the EU Staff document, is Art. 6(3) TEU that codifies the case law of the European courts according to which EU fundamental rights are general principles of EU law:[55]

> Fundamental rights, as guaranteed by the European Convention for the Protection of Human Rights and Fundamental Freedoms and as they result from the constitutional traditions common to the Member States, shall constitute general principles of the Union's law.

All EU actions, including legislative proposals,[56] must thus be defined and implemented in a manner compatible with the CFREU as a legally binding instrument and general principles of EU law (and in particular EU protected human rights). This also entails that EU Member States, when implementing EU rules or acting within the scope of EU law, are bound by EU protected human rights.[57]

The Commission Staff Document furthermore specifies that the Charter 'does not extend the EU competencies' and applies only to EU member States when implementing Union law. The EU thereby places emphasis on due regard for Art. 51(2) of the Charter, which could be argued to apply the principle of subsidiarity to this field, meaning that the promotion of the application of the EU Charter by EU institutions and bodies should occur within the bounds of their respective powers. Art. 51(2) of the CFREU specifies that '[t]his Charter does not establish any new power or task for the Community or the Union, or modify powers and tasks defined by the Treaties'.

The Commission Staff Document identified a number of fields where the EU has competences to take action to promote the implementation of the UNGPs, in the areas of external action (Art. 21 TEU), the right to equality and non-discrimination (Art. 10 TEU), trade relations and agreements (Art. 207(1) Treaty on the Functioning of the European Union (TFEU)), development cooperation (Art. 208(1) TFEU), economic, financial and technical cooperation

(Art. 212 TFEU), humanitarian aid (Art. 214 TFEU) and migrant workers' rights. This list of fields is not exhaustive and the EU has competences in other areas that might be relevant for business and human rights not referred to in the document, such as, e.g. the EU internal market.

A new definition and approach to CSR

The renewed EU CSR Strategy presents a new definition of CSR as 'the responsibility of enterprises for their impacts on society'.[58] There are certain aspects of the EU definition of CSR that bring closer alignment between the EU approach and the expectations set out in the UNGPs.

A prominent example is that the definition does not include an express reference to its voluntary nature. This is, in and of itself, striking, in that it constitutes a clear departure from the previous EU definition of CSR, which referred to the *voluntary* integration of social and environmental concerns into business operations.[59] The new definition thus accommodates for the recognition set out in the UNGPs that CSR is not a strictly voluntary exercise by nature. Indeed, the EU CSR strategy notes that '[r]espect for applicable legislation, and for collective agreements between social partners, is a prerequisite for meeting that responsibility'.[60]

The core concepts that constitute the foundation of the EU's new definition of CSR, i.e. 'responsibility' and 'impact', also bring the EU definition closer to the conceptual framework of the UNGPs. The UNGPs recognize that business enterprises have a 'responsibility' to respect human rights by managing their actual or potential adverse 'impacts' on human rights. Also the two elements that the EU views as integral to CSR bring its new definition into greater alignment with the UNGPs. Apart from respect for applicable law, business enterprises should have in place a process to integrate, *inter alia*, human rights 'into their business operations and core strategy in close collaboration with their stakeholders'.[61]

The EU CSR Strategy notes that the aim of this responsibility is two-fold: (1) 'maximising the creation of shared value for their owners/shareholders and for their other stakeholders and society at large'; and (2) 'identifying, preventing and mitigating their possible adverse impacts'.[62] By referring to maximizing the 'creation of shared value', the EU CSR Strategy suggests an approach that views the simultaneous creation of economic and social value as key to the long-term success of business and, ultimately, beneficial to society at large.[63] This approach supports the understanding that human rights and economic objectives are compatible and can be pursued simultaneously. The EU strategy encourages business enterprises 'to adopt a long-term strategic approach to CSR, and to explore opportunities for developing innovative products, services and business models that contribute to societal wellbeing and lead to higher quality and more productive jobs'.[64]

Next to the positive, the communication also points to the negative as integral to CSR: business enterprises are expected to conduct CSR for the purpose of addressing their possible adverse impacts on society. This corresponds with the notion also set out in the UNGPs that business enterprises have a responsibility for their adverse human rights impacts, and that promoting positive impacts on human rights is desirable but in itself not sufficient for business enterprises to meet this responsibility. The EU language of 'identifying, preventing and mitigating' is clearly inspired by and aligns with the human rights due diligence responsibility set out under UNGP 15(b). Business enterprises are encouraged 'to carry out risk-based due diligence, including through their supply chain' in order to discharge their responsibility.

The EU CSR Policy recognizes that CSR is a flexible concept that leaves discretion to companies to meet their responsibility in a manner appropriate to their circumstances.[65] While this responsibility is applicable to all business enterprises, the text notes that the complexity of the CSR process that enterprises should have in place to integrate human rights into their operations and core strategy 'will depend on factors such as the size of the enterprise and the nature of its operations'.[66] With regards to SMEs, this process 'is likely to remain informal and intuitive'.[67] To be noted is that the EU definition of CSR is primarily oriented towards the responsibility of business enterprises for the prevention of potential adverse human rights impacts. There is no mention of corporate responsibility for the remediation of actual human rights impacts.[68]

The conceptual alignment between the corporate responsibility to respect human rights as defined by the UNGPs and the new EU CSR definition can thus be clearly discerned. The EU's renewed definition of CSR is thus broadly aligned with the UNGPs. The EU furthermore gives recognition to the concept of the corporate responsibility to respect human rights in its EU agenda for action. The EU Agenda for Action 2011–14 recognizes that business enterprises have a responsibility to respect human rights, and notes that this concept conforms to international principles, *inter alia*, the UNGPs. The EU thus sets out a clear expectation that business enterprises should respect human rights. The EU's action plan notes that it '[e]xpects all European enterprises to meet the corporate responsibility to respect human rights, *as defined in the GPs*'.[69] The EU Agenda for Action 2011–14 is examined next.

An agenda for action 2011–2014

On 25 October 2011, the Commission presented a new agenda for action for the period 2011–2014. This agenda contains EU actions aimed at promoting CSR, as well as business respect for human rights more specifically. The agenda indicates that the EU seeks greater alignment between the European and global approaches to CSR. The Commission notes that it will 'promote European interests in international CSR policy developments, while at the same time ensuring the integration of internationally recognised principles and guidelines into its own CSR policies'.[70] Moreover, the new agenda advances a 'smart mix approach' that comprises, next to voluntary measures, regulatory action.

The section first identifies aspects of this agenda that bring the EU's approach closer to that of the UNGPs. This will be followed by an examination of concrete EU actions that are especially relevant in terms of fostering compliance and promote changes in business conduct related to human rights, in and outside the EU. The sections are organized in relation to the addressees of EU action: the EU itself, EU Member States, business enterprises and NGOs and other relevant stakeholders. The following section focuses on the EU regulatory measures.

The impact of EU action on fostering business responses to the UNGPs

EU action to promote the Union's response to the UNGPs

The EU CSR Policy articulates actions that are aimed at strengthening the Union's own responses to the UNGPs. As mentioned above, the Commission seeks a better alignment between European and global approaches to CSR. It is in this context that the plan of action notes that the Commission aims 'to advance a more level global playing field' and that it 'will step up its cooperation with Member States, partner countries and relevant international fora to promote respect for internationally recognised principles and guidelines, and to foster consistency between them'.[71]

A section of the renewed EU CSR policy agenda is thus devoted to the implementation of the UNGPs. The Commission in this section identifies 'coherence of EU policies relevant to business and human rights as a critical challenge'.[72] The Commission has pointed to the need for coherence at different levels ('within different EU institutions; between those institutions; and between the EU and its Member States'). The EU promotes policy coherence through the EU CSR Strategy and the coordination of the implementation of different aspects of this strategy through various processes and procedures. The Staff document also points to the legally binding force of the CFREU, which applies to all the actions that the institutions and bodies of the Union undertake within their respective mandates.[73] The Commission also views the implementation of the UNGPs as instrumental in furthering the human rights objectives of EU policy (e.g. 'child labour, forced prison labour, human trafficking, gender equality, non-discrimination, freedom of association and the right to collective bargaining').[74]

The EU also seeks to promote CSR through its external policies. The EU promotes coherence between internal and external EU policies, and policy consistency with human rights and fundamental freedoms, through the Action Plans on Human Rights and Democracy, which are further strengthened by the cooperative efforts of the European Council's Working Group on Human Rights aimed at mainstreaming human rights in all aspects of EU external relations.[75] The Commission indicated that it would 'make relevant proposals in the field of trade-and-development'.[76] A study has shown that none of the trade agreements that are in force in the EU today contain within their human rights clauses an express reference to the UNGPs (or, for that matter, any other CSR instruments). Also, no such reference to the UNGPs can be found in the sustainable development chapters of the so-called 'new generation agreements', including that which has been concluded with Canada most recently.[77]

With regards to development policy, the EU has a legal commitment to promote coherence based on Art. 208(1) of the TFEU,[78] which entails 'avoiding that other policies undermine the primacy development objective of poverty eradication, and creating synergies between other policies and the objectives of development policy'.[79] The EU agenda signals the EU's support for private sector development in EU development cooperation, indicating that 'by promoting respect for social and environmental standards, EU enterprises can foster better governance and inclusive growth in developing countries'. The Commission indicated that, where appropriate, it would 'propose to address CSR in established dialogues with partner countries and regions'.[80] An example of concrete action related to development policy is the Commission's intention to 'identify ways to promote responsible business conduct in its future policy initiatives towards more inclusive and sustainable recovery and growth in third countries'.[81]

The Staff EU Document points to various partnerships that the EU has engaged in to support responsible business practices among European companies in developing countries and responsible supply chain management. A prominent example is the 'Sustainability Compact for Continuous Improvement in Labour Rights and Factory Safety in Ready-Made Garment and Knitwear Industry in Bangladesh' (the Sustainability Compact). The Sustainability Compact is a partnership between the EU, the ILO, Bangladesh and the US initiated in response to the Rana Plaza factory fire, that has as its objective 'to improve labour, health and safety conditions for workers as well as to encourage responsible businesses in the ready-made garment industry in Bangladesh'.[82] Also mentioned in the Staff EU Document is an initiative by the EU, the Government of Myanmar/Burma, the US, Japan, Denmark and the ILO to 'Promote Fundamental Labour Rights and Practices in Myanmar/Burma'.[83]

For 2013, the Commission committed to issue a report stipulating the EU priorities in the implementation of the UNGPs. This report has not been delivered. Instead, the Commission issued the aforementioned Staff document that surveys the measures that the EU has taken, in order to implement the UNGPs.

EU action to promote state responses to the UNGPs

The EU furthermore seeks to foster State responses to the UNGPs. The EU sees itself as having an enabling and coordinating role for what concerns fostering State responses to the UNGPs. Important in this regard is the invitation by the Commission to EU Member States to develop national plans for CSR.[84][85] More specifically, the EU has invited:[86]

> Member States to develop or update by 2012 their own plans or national lists of priority actions to promote CSR in support of the Europe 2020 strategy, with reference to internationally recognised CSR principles and guidelines and in cooperation with enterprises and other stakeholders, taking account of the issues raised in this communication.

The EU has also asked EU Member States to develop 'national plans for the implementation of the UN Guiding Principles'.[87] The Commission's Action plan furthermore noted the EU's intention to 'create with Member States in 2012 a peer review mechanism for national CSR policies'.[88] The EU organized this peer review process in 2013–2014, and also issued a new Compendium on CSR National Public Policies in the EU.[89,90]

The National Action Plans (NAPs) on business and human rights, or NAPs, are useful as a tool for implementing the UNGPs.[91] This is partly because the policy actions that EU Member States outline in these NAPs provide an indication of the approaches, priorities and measures that EU Member States select and how and to what extent these respond to the country-specific factors and regulatory environments that shape business responses to the UNGPs.[92]

The UK was the first to publish a NAP on business and human rights in September 2013. Several other EU Member States have followed suit, though far passed the deadline that had been set; there is no comprehensive EU-wide coverage in this regard. According to the Commission Staff Working Document:

> Several governments have adopted CSR statements or policies that mention human rights. To date, six Member States (United Kingdom, Netherlands, Italy, Denmark, Finland and Lithuania) have published their plans and at least seven more EU Member States are currently preparing national action plans on business and human rights. Likewise, more than half of the EU Member States [...] have adopted National Action Plans on CSR, which incorporate human rights issues. Several other Member States are also preparing national action plans on CSR, with final versions expected to be released in 2015 and 2016.[93]

Sweden published its NAP on business and human rights in August 2015.[94] The NAPs – either CSR or specifically on the UNGPs – are thus in different stages of development. Some are still at the stage of intentions, others are in an early drafting phase, while others would be close to finalized.[95] Some CSR NAPs have however been in existence for a while and have already undergone review and been updated.[96] Some NAPs on the UNGPs are also currently undergoing review, or are scheduled for review in the near future. To sum up, all EU Member States except for one have developed, formally committed to, or started to develop a NAP on CSR,[97] but timings and practices greatly diverge as to this.

The EU issued a new Compendium on CSR National Public Policies in the EU with the objective to provide clarity on the state of play in the development of proposed EU Member State policy actions on CSR, including in relation to business and human rights.[98] The Compendium takes the EU understanding of CSR as outlined in the EU CSR strategy as its starting point: 'the responsibility of enterprises for their impacts on society'. It provides transparent information on actions taken and progress achieved by the European Commission towards the implementation of its EU CSR Strategy, the policy approaches of EU Member States on CSR, including the state of play of their NAPs, and the rationales for the priorities set by NAPs. It is based on the findings of the abovementioned CSR peer reviews, a questionnaire,[99] and the existing NAPs on CSR and the UNGPs.

The Compendium points to various country-specific factors – cultural, economic, institutional and political – that EU Member States consider in their national priority setting. Some are especially relevant for shaping policies and priorities on business and human rights.[100] The Compendium indicates that legislative approaches are more common in countries that place greater emphasis on the *responsibility* of business enterprises. This suggests that a national definition of CSR that expressly refers to the *responsibility* of companies, rather than merely to CSR as a voluntary activity, may lend itself more easily to the development of a regulatory approach.[101]

The Compendium also reflects on thematic priorities related to business and human rights that emerge across many EU Member States and elaborates on initiatives by EU Member States in these thematic areas. One finding is that EU Member States have a tendency to 'integrat[e], disseminat[e] and shap[e]' their UNGP actions within their broader CSR policy,[102] thereby mirroring the EU approach. A strong thematic area is the support to SMEs in the development of CSR approaches. EU Member States also tend to focus on company reporting and disclosure requirements.[103] This may be partly explained in relation to the new EU Directive on Non-Financial Disclosure[104] which entered into force on 6 December 2014.

The Compendium practices evidence that many EU Member States have integrated the full range of the UNGPs into their national policy frameworks and commonly address the key thematic issues of supply chain management, support for SMEs, reporting and public procurement. Moreover, it would seem that EU Member States are putting the smart mix approach into practice, which the UNGPs recommend and the Commission supports and encourages. This is illustrated by the mix of different types of instruments that EU Member States employ, ranging from legal instruments to partnering instruments to promote business respect for human rights.[105]

EU action to promote business responses to the UNGPs

The EU seeks to foster compliance by business enterprises by promoting the recognition by business enterprises of their corporate responsibility to respect human rights. The Commission invites companies to renew their efforts which respect to these internationally recognized principles and guidelines. The EU invites certain companies to commit to these initiatives and to monitor the commitments made. More specifically, the Commission asks all European-based multinational companies to make a commitment by 2014 to respect the ILO Tripartite Declaration.[106] All large European enterprises furthermore are invited to commit to take account of at least one of the following instruments: the UNGC, the OECD Guidelines for MNEs, or ISO 26000.[107] The Commission further expresses its intention to 'monitor the commitments made by European enterprises with more than 10.000 employees to take account of internationally recognised CSR principles and guidelines'.[108]

In March 2013, the Commission issued a study of policy references made by 200 randomly selected large EU companies to internationally recognized CSR Guidelines and Principles.[109,110] The EU agenda includes action aimed at fostering business compliance by promoting self- and co-regulatory processes. The Commission committed to improve the effectiveness of such processes by developing a code of good practice for self- and co-regulation exercises in cooperation with enterprises and other stakeholders. In addition, the Commission seeks to provide clarity about the implications of this responsibility for companies, which can vary according to their circumstances.

The Commission has thus developed human rights guidance for three business sectors: (i) 'employment and recruitment agencies'; (ii) 'information and communication technology'; and (iii) 'oil and gas'.[111] These instruments embody an effort by the Commission to add precision to the concept and elaborate on the implications that the definition may have for business enterprises operating in the respective sectors. The guides provide practical steps for translating the UNGPs into business, without imposing a 'one-size-fits-all' approach.[112] The Commission has furthermore issued guidance for small and medium-sized enterprises,[113] and five case studies, which reflects a similar effort to leverage through the impact that this definition may have on this size-related type of enterprise.

The Commission also sets out actions aimed at promoting awareness about business respect for human rights and the capacities that may need to be developed for business enterprises to be able to abide by this norm in practice. Relevant action in this regard is the Commission's commitment to raise awareness about business respect for human rights in areas where the State fails to meet its duty to protect. This involves a process with the relevant stakeholders ('enterprises, EU Delegations in partnering countries, and local civil society actors, in particular human rights organisations and defenders').[114] Other relevant actions focus on promoting business responses to CSR more generally through capacity-building activities. Relevant actions are, *inter alia*, the creation of a multi-stakeholder platform in relevant industrial sectors and the launch of a European award scheme for CSR partnerships.[115] The Commission also takes action for the purpose of a better integration of CSR into education, training and research.

EU action to promote responses to the UNGPs through markets and social pressure

The EU policy agenda furthermore includes actions that promote compliance through market and social compliance mechanisms. The plan of action notes that the EU seeks to leverage policies in the area of 'consumption, public procurement and investment to strengthen market incentives for CSR'. A prominent example that may affect business conduct in relation to human rights is the aforementioned commitment of the Commission to facilitate a better integration of social and environmental considerations into EU Public Procurement Directives.[116] Another example is the EU's invitation to European asset managers and asset owners, especially pension funds, to sign up to the UN Principles for Responsible Investment.[117] The Commission furthermore promotes various initiatives to enhance supply chain transparency. In 2017, an EU regulation was adopted introducing mandatory due diligence requirements in the minerals sector.[118]

EU regulatory and 'smart mix' measures

The EU policy agenda furthermore includes regulatory measures that the EU committed to adopt, as part of its smart mix of measures. The legislative proposal for the (in the meantime adopted) Directive on non-financial disclosure is expressly referred to as an example of such regulatory action.[119] This Directive further harmonized at Union level the disclosure requirements for certain companies related to, *inter alia*, human rights. Also expressly mentioned in the EU agenda is the 2011 review of the Public Procurement Directives and the commitment of the Commission to facilitate the better integration of social and environmental considerations into these Directives.[120] This review resulted in the adoption on 11 February 2014 of a new set of public procurement Directives.[121] These regulatory measures, by harmonizing national legislations, can contribute to greater coherence and convergence in State regulation of business conduct across the EU. Such regulation can foster EU Member State responses to the UNGPs,[122] as well as improve the functioning of the internal market.

Analysis

The Commission indicates in the EU CSR Strategy that the 'European policy to promote CSR should be made fully consistent with this framework'. The Commission refers to the global framework for CSR that comprises of a core set of internationally recognized principles and guidelines, including the UNGPs. This commitment by the Commission to consistency with, *inter alia*, the UNGPs may not be binding, however it is not without potential legal effects.[123] The analysis indicates that there is scope for the EU to increase its level of engagement with the UNGPs in order to actively implement this commitment.

This chapter considered the extent to which the EU approach to fostering the human rights aspect of CSR aligns with the UNGPs. The adoption by the EU of the 'smart mix' approach to promoting business respect for human rights constitutes a positive development in this regard. The EU presents a combination of legally binding and voluntary measures that aim at strengthening and coordinating EU Member State responses to the EU, which are combined with voluntary measures that promote soft law initiatives and self-regulatory measures.

A commitment to full consistency with the UNGPs needs to be taken into consideration to the extent to which these EU measures promote responses that conform with the UNGPs. Full consistency can only be realized if the UNGPs and their core concepts are effectively integrated within such measures. The extent to which the EU relies on regulatory measures to promote business respect for human rights and the extent to which corporate respect for human rights has been integrated into such EU regulatory measures varies considerably across different areas.

The renewed and consolidated EU Public Procurement Directive extend the leeway for States to use public procurement in support of advancing social policies. While these Directives allow authorities to take social concerns into account in the procurement process, there is no express reference to corporate respect for human rights, or the UNGPs for that matter, in these Directives, which is a significant gap. While awareness of any violation of an international law provision may be sufficient for a bidder to be excluded, the international human rights standards mentioned are (unduly narrowly) focused on international labour standards.[124]

The EU Directive on non-financial disclosure sets out requirements for certain companies to make disclosure on, *inter alia*, human rights, which align with the concepts of the UNGPs. The Directive expressly refers to the UNGPs as an instrument that business enterprises can use in their reporting. However, and as set out in the next chapter, the Directive is deficient in certain important aspects. As a consequence, there may be disparities among national implementation measures, which may reduce the effectiveness of the Directive in ensuring a minimum level of disclosure that is necessary for the protection of human rights. While it is therefore particularly important that the EU proactively monitors the national implementation of the Directive, the Directive makes no provision for such a process.[125]

The EU has adopted disclosure requirements for EU companies that are active in the extractive industry or the logging of primary forests, which are furthermore combined with due diligence requirements.[126] These disclosure requirements have not been extended to other sectors.[127] An EU regulation was adopted in 2017 introducing mandatory due diligence requirements in the minerals sector.[128] The EU has not considered adopting mandatory disclosure in other sectors, or regulatory measures that enable stakeholders to obtain the information they need to hold business enterprises to account.[129] There seems to be a clear gap in engagement with human rights in these law-making processes.

This lack of engagement with human rights does not sit easily with the objective that the EU has set 'to make the fundamental rights provided for in the Charter as effective as possible'.[130] The Commission has issued a communication in which it sets out a strategy for the effective implementation of the CFREU. The Communication notes that the CFREU should serve as a 'compass for the Union's policies and their implementation by the Member States'.[131]

This entails that the EU promotes a 'fundamental rights culture' at all stages of the procedure, from the initial drafting of a proposal within the Commission to the impact analysis, and right up to the checks on the legality of the final text.[132]

The Communication notes that the Commission 'routinely checks its legislative proposals and the acts it adopts to ensure that they are compatible with the Charter'.[133] As highlighted by Monti and Chalmers,

> there is a thin line between verifying that EU law-making does not violate fundamental rights and moving to a human rights policy in which EU institutions see EU goals as increasingly about realisation of the rights and principles in the [Charter] rather than other more discrete tasks.[134]

Whilst a case can be made for the former, it sets a more ambitious agenda for the Union with a wider remit. As Monti and Chalmers also note:

> Beyond this debate, few would oppose the idea that legislative proposals be verified for their impact on fundamental rights. However, there remains the question of the rigour of this process. If it is simply box-ticking, fundamental rights become a rhetorical instrument to justify EU law making. In that regard, it is a pity that the Court of Justice has not yet had the opportunity to rule on whether a procedural failure to engage sufficiently with fundamental rights in the legislative process is, by itself, a violation of fundamental rights insofar as it shows inadequate care for these.[135]

As was noted previously, all EU actions, including legislative proposals,[136] must be defined and implemented in a manner that is compatible with the CFREU and general principles of EU law (and in particular EU protected human rights). The EU also may need to give greater attention to the UNGPs in this regard. The CJEU held in *Kadi*:

> In addition, according to settled case-law, fundamental rights form an integral part of the general principles of law whose observance the Court ensures. For that purpose, the Court draws inspiration from the constitutional traditions common to the Member States and from the guidelines supplied by international instruments for the protection of human rights on which the Member States have collaborated or to which they are signatories.[137]

The UNGPs as an international instrument could thus serve as a source of inspiration for the EU courts in their interpretation of the scope of general principles of EU law, especially when considering that the EU and its Member States have actively engaged in the process of their development.[138]

The focus in the EU engagement with the UNGPs has been primarily on EU external policy. This is reflected in the EU Staff Document. The imbalance between internal and external competencies is likely to stem from the incongruence between the internal and external dimension of EU policy, as reflected in TEU Art. 3(3) and 3(5).[139]According to De Burca:

> Thus the strategy has been to identify the fields of EU internal policy in which human rights concerns are considered relevant by reference to the precise scope of the EU's powers in fields such as social inclusion or anti-discrimination. This strategy is not however used in the external domain, in which human rights protection is treated as a cross-cutting goal relevant to all domains of EU external action. It is certainly not the case that the EU's remit or powers are more extensive in the international domain than internally, indeed the opposite is arguably true. However, the EU and more specifically the Member States have been unwilling to treat respect for human rights as a cross-cutting concern of internal EU policies, whereas they have asserted it to be such a concern in all areas of external policy.[140]

The EU internal and external policy dimensions cannot be kept separate in a satisfactory manner however, because, according to Alston and Weiler, '[t]hey are, in fact, two sides of the same coin'. There are four reasons for this, Alston and Weiler note:

> In the case of the Union, there are several additional reasons why a concern with external policy also necessitates a careful consideration of the internal policy dimensions. Firstly, the development and implementation of an effective external human rights policy can only be undertaken in the context of appropriate internal institutional arrangements. Secondly, in an era when universality and indivisibility are the touchstones of human rights, an external policy which is not underpinned by a comparably comprehensive and authentic internal policy can have no hope of being taken seriously. Thirdly, [...], a credible, human rights policy must assiduously avoid unilateralism and double standards and that can only be done by ensuring reciprocity and consistency. Finally, the reality is that a Union which is not prepared to embrace a strong human rights policy for itself is highly unlikely to develop a fully-fledged external policy and apply it with energy or consistency. As long as human rights remain a suspect preoccupation within, their status without will remain tenuous.[141]

TEU Art. 17(1) read in combination the Articles 2 and 3 of the TEU impose an obligation on the Commission to ensure secondary legislation and national implementing measures are in compliance with the CFREU, *ad intra* and *ad extra*. Arguably, these articles should be interpreted more broadly as encompassing within their applicable scope all areas of EU internal policy in which the EU has competencies, including areas that are not expressly recognized under Article 3(3) as promoting human rights powers directly but that can affect the enjoyment of the rights and fundamental freedoms set out in the Charter. There is nothing in the case law that expressly rejects the notion that the EU should treat human rights as a cross-cutting issue that is relevant for all areas of internal and external policy.

It follows that the Commission should review all EU internal policies and laws in which the EU has competencies, in order to ensure their alignment with EU fundamental human rights. It should also pay due regard to the development and implementation of these measures, and whether this is undertaken in a manner that is not merely compliant with the Charter, but also gives full effect to the rights and principles within the Charter. Amongst the areas of EU internal policies in which the EU has competencies and that are not covered but can, and arguably should, be used to foster demand for business respect for human rights is corporate and securities law. Research has shown that there is a nexus between securities and company law and human rights, and that the existence or absence of these laws in national jurisdictions can encourage or impede companies' respect for human rights.[142] The link between the EU regimes in the area of financial regulation and respect for human rights remains to a great extent unexplored, *inter alia*, securities (prospective and trading on the security market), market safeguards and EU mergers.

It is reasonable to expect that EU Member States when acting within their sphere of influence will take legislative measures to require human rights due diligence from companies. International human rights law imposes a positive obligation on States to adopt such legislative measures as necessary in particular circumstances. EU Member States that have adopted NAPs have indicated regulatory measures as part of a smart mix. An example of an initiative to introduce a legally binding duty of human rights due diligence is France's *Proposition de loi relative au devoir de vigilance des sociétés mères et des entreprises donneuses d'ordre* ('law about the duty of due diligence of parent companies and main contractors'), which came into force 28 March 2017.[143,144] A proliferation of such legislation in the future may lead to the EU to take regulatory measures in order to avoid it creating distortions in the internal market.

Conclusion

This chapter examined how and to what extent the UNGPs have been codified in EU law and policy and to what extent this codification is effectively implementing CSR, and businesses' responsibilities for human rights, at EU and national level. It examined the EU CSR Strategy, which introduced an EU policy framework for the promotion of CSR. It was found that the EU views human rights as an integral and prominent aspect of CSR, and seeks policy consistency with internationally recognized principles and guidelines, including the UNGPs. The EU CSR Strategy features various new elements that bring the EU CSR Policy into greater alignment with the approach advanced by the UNGPs. A prominent example is the updated definition of CSR, 'the responsibility of enterprises for their impact on society'. The EU CSR Strategy also presents a plan of action that advances a 'smart mix' approach that, next to voluntary measures, views a role for complementary regulation.

The efforts by the EU, States, business enterprises and other actors to advance in the implementation of the UNGPs provide indication of evolving practices in relation to corporate responsibility and accountability for human rights in the EU context. There is an emerging understanding in the EU of the need for business enterprises to respect human rights. The negative effects of the financial and economic crisis and the high-profile cases of human rights violations had made this need apparent. There is also an emerging understanding in the EU of international human rights being directly applicable to business enterprises. Illustrative is the alignment of EU policy with global approaches in its efforts to promote CSR and its 'full endorsement' of the UNGPs. There is also increased recognition of a shared understanding of the substantive requirements of the responsibility of business enterprises in relation to human rights, which, as the analysis of the EU definition and the Plan of Action suggest, corresponds with the expectations set out in the UNGPs.

The EU, EU Member States, business enterprises and other non-state actors have adopted a range of voluntary and mandatory measures in their efforts to actively promote the implementation of the UNGPs. The EU Directives in the area of non-financial disclosure and public procurement have been adapted. These instruments are supplemented by, *inter alia*, NAPs on CSR and the implementation of the UNGPs that EU Members have published at national level, EU guidance material for business enterprises operating in the key business sectors (employment and recruitment agencies, ICT companies, oil and gas companies), and EU policy documents and reports.

These initiatives take on added significance when considered in combination, indicating that the corporate responsibility to respect human rights is crystallizing into a more binding norm in soft and hard-law sources.[145] These measures, to the extent that these embed the UNGPs, potentially affect compliance and foster positive changes in the behaviour of companies. As a consequence of the regulatory dynamics that arise out of the combined effects of this 'smart mix' of measures, business enterprises are, and should be, increasingly bound to implementing this corporate responsibility to respect human rights. Business enterprises face a binding responsibility to respect human rights under various sources of law, ranging from transnational laws at national and EU level to soft law mechanisms by State and non-state actors at all levels.

This chapter argued that there is scope for the EU to scale up its level of engagement with the UNGPs, however, in order to actively implement its commitment to make the EU policy to promote CSR fully consistent with the global framework for CSR, which comprises of a core set of international recognized principles and guidelines, including the UNGPs. The Charter of Fundamental Rights and the objective that the EU has set itself 'to make the fundamental rights provided for in the Charter as effective as possible',[146] may entail an obligation for the EU to seriously consider taking all actions that are within its competences to do so.

Notes

1 This chapter is based on a report written for the FRAME Project, *see* Bijlmakers, et al., Report on Tracking CSR Responses FRAME Deliverable 7.4 (Nov. 2015, 2014), www.fp7-frame.eu/wp-content/uploads/2016/09/Deliverable-7.4.pdf.
2 Commission Staff Working Document on Implementing the UN Guiding Principles on Business and Human Rights – State of Play, 6, SWD (2015) 144 final (14 July 2015) [hereinafter *Commission Staff Working Document*].
3 *Id.*
4 *Communication from the Commission Strategy for the Effective Implementation of the Charter of Fundamental Rights by the European Union*, 3, COM (2010) 573 final (19 Oct. 2010) [hereinafter *Commission Communication CFREU*].
5 *Commission Green Paper on Promoting a European Framework for Corporate Social Responsibility*, COM (2001) 366 final, at 3 (18 July 2001) [hereinafter *Commission, Green Paper*].
6 Business networks were created in response to this call, including CSR Europe. CSR Europe, CSR Europe: A key partner for EU engagement on CSR, www.csreurope.org/sites/default/files/CSR%20Europe%20-%20A%20Key%20Partner%20for%20EU%20engagement%202014.pdf.
7 Presidency Conclusions, Lisbon European Council (23–24 Mar. 2000).
8 In Lisbon, the European Council set the strategic goals 'to become the most competitive and dynamic knowledge-based economy in the world capable of sustainable economic growth with more and better jobs and greater social cohesion'. Presidency Conclusions, Lisbon European Council (23–24 Mar. 2000), ¶ 5.
9 *Communication from the Commission. A Sustainable Europe for a Better World: A European Union Strategy for Sustainable Development*, COM (2001) 264 final (15 May 2001).
10 Olivier De Schutter, *Corporate Social Responsibility: European Style*, 14 European Law Journal 203, 206 (2008).
11 *Commission, Green Paper*, *supra* note 5.
12 *Id.* at 6.
13 *Id.* at 12.
14 *Id.* at 6.
15 *Id.* at 22. De Schutter, *supra* note 10, at 207.
16 *Commission, Green Paper*, *supra* note 5, at 6.
17 *Id.* at 18.
18 *Communication from the Commission Concerning Corporate Social Responsibility: A Business Contribution to Sustainable Development*, COM (2002) 347 final (2 July 2002).
19 *Id.* at 4.
20 *Id.* at 17.
21 De Schutter notes that the Commission diverged from prevailing business views to CSR by recognizing a role for the EU to facilitate convergence in a proliferating body of CSR instruments in order to (i) avoid confusion and market distortions and (ii) to ensure a proper functioning of the EU internal market and a level playing field. De Schutter, *supra* note 10, 203, 208.
22 *Id.* at 213. Jan Wouters & Leen Chanet, *Corporate Human Rights Responsibility: A European Perspective*, 6 Northwestern Journal of International Human Rights, 277 (2008).
23 The report pointed to the soft-tools of awareness raising and knowledge improvement, developing capacities and competences to mainstream CSR, and ensuring an enabling environment for CSR. The report did recommend that public authorities ensure that there is both a legal framework and the right economic and social conditions in place to allow corporations that wish to go further through CSR to benefit from this in the market place, both in the EU and globally. However, as no concrete

proposals were tabled as to what such a framework could entail, the legal ramifications of EU CSR policy remained ambiguous. *European Multistakeholder Forum on CSR: Final Results & Recommendations*, 12, 15 (29 June 2004), *available at* www.indianet.nl/EU-MSF_CSR.pdf. *See* Jan Wouters & Nicolas Hachez, *The EU Corporate Social Responsibility Strategy: A Business-Driven, Voluntary and Process-Oriented Policy*, 1 Journal of European Social Policy, 19 (2009).

24 Loew Thomas, The Results of the European Multi-stakeholder Forum on CSR in the View of Business, NGO and Science. Discussion Paper (2005), *available at* www.4sustainability.de/fileadmin/redakteur/bilder/Publikationen/2005-Results-of-the-EMS-Forum-in-the-View-of-Business-N..pdf. Social Platform, et al., NGOs Call on Commission and Council to Shift Gears after Multi-Stakeholder Forum: European CSR Process Must Move from Dialogue to Action (2004), *available at* www.corporatejustice.org/IMG/pdf/NGOCSRopenletterFINAL290604.pdf.

25 De Schutter, *supra* note 10, 214.

26 Ipek Eren Vural, Converging Europe Transformation of Social Policy in the Enlarged European Union and in Turkey, 10 (Routledge 2011).

27 *Communication from the Commission to the European Parliament, the Council and the European Economic and Social Committee, Implementing the Partnership for Growth and Jobs: Making Europe a Pole of Excellence on Corporate Social Responsibility*, COM (2006) 136 final, 2 (22 Mar. 2006).

28 NGOs succinctly reorganized themselves in the Corporate Coalition for Corporate Justice. W. Benedek, et al., *supra* note 127, at 16–17.

29 J Fairbrass, *Exploring Corporate Social Responsibility Policy in the European Union: A Discursive Institutional Analysis*, 49 Journal of Common Market Studies, 962 (2011).

30 *European Multistakeholder Forum on CSR: Final Results & Recommendations*, *at* 12, 111, *supra* note 23.

31 *Commission*, *Partnership for Growth*, *supra* note 27, at 11.

32 *Id.* at 8.

33 For further information on the EU Multi-stakeholder forum, *see*, www.csr-in-commerce.eu/news.php/en/26/forum-discusses-future-eu-csr-policy.

34 *Executive Summary: EU Multi Stakeholder Forum on Corporate Social Responsibility* (3–4 Feb. 2015), *available at* http://ec.europa.eu/DocsRoom/documents/8774/attachments/1/translations/en/renditions/native.

35 *Communication from the Commission to the European Parliament, the Council, the European Economic and Social Committee and the Committee of the Regions: A Renewed EU Strategy 2011–14 for Corporate Social Responsibility*, COM (2011) 681 final [hereinafter *Commission, A Renewed EU CSR Strategy*] (25 Oct. 2011).

36 European Commission, Corporate Social Responsibility: National Public Policies in the European Union: Compendium 2014, at 7 (31 Oct. 2014)

37 *Commission*, *A Renewed EU CSR Strategy*, *supra* note 35, ¶ 1.3.

38 European Commission, *supra* note 36, at 6.

39 Commission Staff Working Document, *supra* note 2, at 2.

40 *Commission*, *Green Paper*, *supra* note 5, ¶ 61, at 20.

41 *Commission*, *A Renewed EU CSR Strategy*, *supra* note 35, at 5. *Commission*, *Partnership for Growth*, *supra* note 26, at 4.

42 *Commission*, *A Renewed EU CSR Strategy*, *id.* at 5. *Commission*, *Partnership for Growth*, *id.*, at 7.

43 Commission Staff Working Document, *supra* note 2, at 22.

44 *Commission*, *A Renewed EU CSR Strategy*, *supra* note 35, at 6.

45 Previously CSR was explained as the voluntary integration of social and environmental concerns into business operations. *Commission*, *Green Paper*, *supra* note 5, §20.

46 *Commission*, *A Renewed EU CSR Strategy*, *supra* note 35, at 5.

47 The EU CSR Strategy points to a shift in the attitude of the Commission towards accepting a supporting role for public authorities to ensuring CSR through 'a smart

mix of voluntary policy measures and, where necessary, complementary regulation, for example to promote transparency, create market incentives for responsible business conduct, and ensure corporate accountability'. *Id.* at 7.

48 This is the reverse of the approach promoted by the UNGPs, which is premised on the understanding that States are primarily responsible for ensuring business respect for human rights, though the UNGPs have been interpreted differently in relation to this point. Footer notes that UNGP 18 'underscores the fact that a company or business enterprise bears primary responsibility to ensure that its activities do not cause or contribute to adverse human rights impacts'. *See* Mary E. Footer, *Human Rights Due Diligence and the Responsible Supply of Minerals from Conflict-affected Areas: Towards a Normative Framework?*, *in* Human Rights and Business: Direct Corporate Accountability for Human Rights, 186 (Wolf Legal Publishers ed. 2015).

49 *Commission*, *A Renewed EU CSR Strategy*, *supra* note 35, at 5.

50 Special Representative on the Issue of Human Rights and Transnational Corporations and Other Business Enterprises, *Guiding Principles on Business and Human Rights: Implementing the United Nations 'Protect, Respect and Remedy' Framework.* U.N.Doc. A/HRC/17/31 (21 Mar. 2011) [hereinafter *UNGPs*] (by John Ruggie).

51 *Id.*

52 *Commission Staff Working Document*, *supra* note 2, at 4.

53 *Id.* at 4.

54 *Id.* at 4.

55 Case 11/70, *Internationale Handelsgesellschaft mbH v. Einfuhr- und Vorratsstelle für Getreide und Futtermittel 1970*, E.C.R. 1125.

56 *Commission Staff Working Document*, *supra* note 2, at 17.

57 C-617/10, Akerberg Fransson, E.C.R. (2013).

58 *Commission*, *A Renewed EU CSR Strategy*, *supra* note 35, at 6.

59 *Commission*, *Green Paper*, *supra* note 5.

60 *Commission*, *A Renewed EU CSR Strategy*, *supra* note 35, at 6.

61 *Id.* at 6.

62 *Id.* at 5, 6.

63 Me Porter & Mr Kramer, *Creating Shared Value* 89 Harvard Business Review, 62–77 (2011). Eijsbouts & Kemp, *Over maatschappelijk verantwoord ondernemen*, *waardecreatie*, *ondernemingsrecht en vennootschapsbelang*, *tijdschrift voor vennootschapsrechtspersonenrecht* 5 Tijdschrift voor vennootschapsrecht, rechtspersonenrecht en ondernemingsbestuur, 120–132 (2012).

64 *Commission*, *A Renewed EU CSR Strategy*, *supra* note 35, at 6.

65 *Id.* at 7.

66 *Id.* at 6.

67 *Id.* at 6.

68 To be noted is GP 22 stipulating that business enterprises have a responsibility to provide for or cooperate in the remediation of adverse human rights impacts that they have caused or contributed to. UNGPs, *supra* note 50, GP 22.

69 *Commission*, *A Renewed EU CSR Strategy*, *supra* note 35, at 14 (emphasis added).

70 *Id.*

71 *Id.* at 13.

72 *Id.* at 14.

73 *Commission Staff Working Document*, *supra* note 2, at 17.

74 *Commission*, *A Renewed EU CSR Strategy*, *supra* note 35, at 14.

75 *Commission Staff Working Document*, *supra* note 2, at 17.

76 *Id.* at 14.

77 The Commission published a Joint Communication with the European External Action Service on the Action Plan on Human Rights and Democracy (2015–2019) titled 'Keeping human rights at the heart of the EU agenda'. The Communication proposes to 'aim at the systematic inclusion in trade and investment agreements of

references to internationally recognised principles and guidelines on [CSR]'. *Commission Staff Working Document*, *supra* note 2 at 8.

78 Article 208(1) TEU states that '[t]he Union shall take account of the objectives of development cooperation in the policies that it implements which are likely to affect developing countries'.

79 *Commission Staff Working Document*, *supra* note 2, at 18.

80 *Commission*, *A Renewed EU CSR Strategy*, *supra* note 35, at 13.

81 *Id.* at 14.

82 *Commission Staff Working Document*, *supra* note 2, at 4.

83 This initiative focuses on labour law reforms, institutional capacity building as well as the full involvement of stakeholders, including business, employers' and workers' organisations'. *Commission Staff Working Document*, *supra* note 2, at 13.

84 *Commission*, *A Renewed EU CSR Strategy*, *supra* note 35, at 13.

85 *Id.* at 13.

86 *Id.* at 13.

87 *Id.* at 14.

88 *Id.* at 13.

89 European Commission, *supra* note 36, at 7.

90 This publication follows previous editions of the EU Compendium on CSR policies, issued in 2006, 2007 and 2011, respectively. European Commission, *id.*

91 European Commission, Notes: Corporate Social Responsibility European Annual Review Meeting: EU Member States High-Level Group on CSR, EU CSR Multi-Stakeholder Forum Committee International Organisations, 6 (20 Dec. 2013), www.asktheeu.org/en/request/1168/response/4544/attach/11/FINAL%20Notes%20CSR%20HLG%20meeting%2020%20December%202013.pdf.

92 NAPs also have limitations as they are not a measure of State's actual compliance to the UNGPs. A NAP does not necessarily provide a complete picture of all activities that a State plans or undertakes, or an accurate depiction of the State's implementation measures instituted. Also NAPs may not provide an adequate depiction of the effectiveness of such measures, and the extent to which these measures foster business compliance. The fact that most NAPs have not been subject to monitoring or revision is relevant in this regard.

93 *Commission Staff Working Document*, *supra* note 2 at 7.

94 The Swedish NAP for business and human rights is *available at* www.government.se/contentassets/822dc47952124734b60daf1865e39343/action-plan-for-business-and-human-rights.pdf.

95 The Belgian NAP for business and human rights is *available at* www.sdgs.be/sites/default/files/publication/attachments/nationaal_actieplan_ondernemingen_en_mensenrechten_2017.compressed.pdf.

96 The UK released an updated NAP on business and human rights on 12 May 2016. The updated NAP is *available at* www.gov.uk/government/uploads/system/uploads/attachment_data/file/522805/_Business_Implementing_the_UN_Guiding_Principles_on_Business_and_Human_Rights_updated_May_2016.pdf. The original UK Plan of Action entitled '*Good Business: Implementing the UNGPs on Business and Human Rights*' is *available at* www.gov.uk/government/uploads/system/uploads/attachment_data/file//BHR_Action_Plan_-_final_online_version_1_.pdf.

97 Luxemburg has no formal plans to develop a formal NAP. European Commission, *supra* note 36, at 14.

98 *Id.* at 7.

99 *Id.* at 12.

100 One of these factors mentioned is the structure of the economy, in terms of the number and share of multinational companies, SMEs and micro-economies. States that are the seat of many multinational enterprises may focus on different problems and measures than countries that have a relatively higher number of SMEs. States

that are home to business enterprises that experience higher vulnerability to brand risks due to exposure to foreign trade or because they have complex supply chains with participating units in less economically developed countries tend to have more advanced policies. European Commission, *supra* note 36, at 13.

101 *Id.* at 14.

102 *Id.* at 20–22.

103 *Id.* at 8.

104 Directive 2014/95/EU of the European Parliament and of the Council of 22 October 2014 amending Directive 2013/34/EU as regards disclosure of non-financial and diversity information by certain large undertakings and groups, 2014 O.J. (L 330) 1.

105 The Commission distinguishes between the following types of instruments: legal instruments that require CSR practices through the application of legislative, executive and judicial power, economic and financial instruments that drive CSR practices by using financial incentives and market forces, informational instruments that disseminate knowledge on CSR, partnering instruments that aim at voluntary cooperation between stakeholders, and hybrid instruments that combine two or more of these instruments. European Commission, *supra* note 36 at 10.

106 *Commission, a Renewed EU CSR Strategy*, *supra* note 35, at 13.

107 *Id.*

108 *Id.*

109 European Commission, *An Analysis of Policy References Made by large EU Companies to Internationally Recognised CSR Guidelines and Principles* (2013).

110 For an analysis, see Bijlmakers, et al., Report on Tracking CSR Responses FRAME Deliverable 7.4, at 48 (Nov. 2015, 2014), www.fp7-frame.eu/wp-content/uploads/2016/09/Deliverable-7.4.pdf.

111 *See*, http://ec.europa.eu/enterprise/newsroom/cf/itemdetail.cfm?item_id=5752&lang=en.

112 *Commission Staff Working Document*, *supra* note 2, at 2.

113 European Commission, My business and human rights: A guide to human rights for small and medium-sized enterprises (2012), http://ec.europa.eu/enterprise/policies/sustainable-business/files/csr-sme/human-rights-sme-guide-final_en.pdf.

114 *Commission, a Renewed EU CSR Strategy*, *supra* note 35, at 14.

115 *See* www.csreurope.org/pages/en/european_csr_award_scheme.html.

116 *Commission, a Renewed EU CSR Strategy*, *supra* note 35, at 20.

117 The Commission indicated it would 'consider a requirement on all investment funds and financial institutions to inform all their clients [...] about any ethical or responsible investment criteria they apply or any standards and codes to which they adhere'. *Id.* at 11.

118 Regulation (EU) 2017/821 of the European Parliament and of the Council of 17 May 2017 laying down supply chain due diligence obligations for Union importers of tin, tantalum and tungsten, their ores, and gold originating from conflict-affected and high-risk areas, O.J. (L130) 1.

119 The Commission draws attention to the international reporting frameworks, including the GRI and indicates its interest to advance towards the approach of integrated financial and non-financial reporting and the work of the International Integrated Reporting Committee in relation thereto. The Commission not only encourages business enterprises, but all organizations to improve their disclosure, including civil society organizations and public authorities. *Commission, a Renewed EU CSR Strategy*, *supra* note 35, at 11–12.

120 *Id.* at 20.

121 For an analysis of the revised EU Public Procurement Directives, see Bijlmakers, et al., Report on Tracking CSR Responses FRAME Deliverable 7.4, at 151–154 (Nov. 2015, 2014), www.fp7-frame.eu/wp-content/uploads/2016/09/Deliverable-7.4.pdf.

122 More specifically, these regulatory measures may foster State responses to GP 3 that requires States to '[e]ncourage, and where appropriate require, business enterprises to communicate how they address their human rights impacts', and to UNGPs 5 and 6 that require States to promote corporate respect for human rights in their commercial transactions with business enterprises, including by exercising adequate oversight when they 'contract with, or legislate for, business enterprises to provide services'. UNGPs, *supra* note 50, GPs 3, 4, 6.

123 The Commission can only depart from its own statements of policy in a reasoned and motivated manner – and in compliance with the general principles of EU law, including equal treatment and legitimate expectations (Joined cases C-189/02 P, C-202/02 P, C-205/02 P to C-208/02 P and C-213/02 P *Dansk Rørindustri A/S* et al. *v. Commission* [2005] I-5425, ¶ 211).

124 *Commission, a Renewed EU CSR Strategy*, *supra* note 35, at 20.

125 The Commission has a duty pursuant to Art. 17.1 TEU to ensure 'the application of the Treaties and of measures adopted by the institutions pursuant to them'. To be noted also is that EU protected fundamental rights are applicable to EU Member States not only when implementing acts of the EU, but also to all situations falling within the scope of EU law. *See*, C-617/10, *Akerberg Fransson*, E.C.R. (2013).

126 The EU Accountancy Directive notes the following:

> In order to provide for enhanced transparency of payments made to governments, large undertakings and public interest entities which are active in the extractive industry or logging of primary forests (2) should disclose material payments made to governments in the countries in which they operate in a separate report, on an annual basis. Such undertakings are active in countries rich in natural resources, in particular minerals, oil, natural gas and primary forests. The report should include types of payments comparable to those disclosed by an undertaking participating in the Extractive Industries Transparency Initiative (EITI). The initiative is also complementary to the Forest Law Enforcement, Governance and Trade Action Plan of the European Union (EU FLEGT) and the provisions of Regulation (EU) No 995/2010 of the European Parliament and of the Council of 20 October 2010 laying down the obligations of operators who place timber and timber products on the market (3), which require traders of timber products to exercise due diligence in order to prevent illegal wood from entering the Union market.

Directive 2013/34/EU, of the European Parliament and of the Council of 26 June 2013 on the annual financial statements, consolidated financial statements and related reports of certain types of undertakings, amending Directive 2006/43/EC of the European Parliament and of the Council and repealing Council Directives 78/660/EEC and 83/349/EEC, Recital 44, 2013 O.J. (L 182) 19. Also *see* Directive 2013/50/EU, of the European Parliament and of the Council of 22 October 2013 amending Directive 2004/109/EC of the European Parliament and of the Council on the harmonization of transparency requirements in relation to information about issuers whose securities are admitted to trading on a regulated market, Directive 2003/71/EC of the European Parliament and of the Council on the prospectus to be published when securities are offered to the public or admitted to trading and Commission Directive 2007/14/EC laying down detailed rules for the implementation of certain provisions of Directive 2004/109/EC, Recital 7, 2013 O.J. (L 294) 13. Regulation (EU) No 995/2010 of the European Parliament and of the Council of 20 October 2010 laying down the obligations of operators who place timber and timber products on the market, Recital 15–17, 2010 O.J. (L 295) 23. The due diligence requirements introduced by the EU Timber Regulation do not cohere with the UNGPs 'as regards the substance or normative sources for the exercise of due diligence'. K. Buhmann, *Defying Territorial Limitations: Regulating Business Conduct Extraterritorially Through Establishing Obligations, in EU Law and National Law, in* Human Rights and Business: Direct Corporate Accountability for Human Rights, 296 (Jernej Letnar Černič & Tara Van Ho eds. 2015).

127 W. Benedek, et al., Improving EU Engagement with Non-State Actors, FRAME Deliverable 7.2, at 71.

128 Regulation (EU) 2017/821 of the European Parliament and of the Council of 17 May 2017 laying down supply chain due diligence obligations for Union importers of tin, tantalum and tungsten, their ores, and gold originating from conflict-affected and high-risk areas, O.J. (L130) 1.

129 *See* Steering Committee for Human Rights, Explanatory memorandum to Recommendation CM/Rec(2016)3 of the Committee of Ministers to Member States on human rights and business, § 36, 1249th meeting, COM (2016) 18-addfinal (2 Mar. 2016).

130 *Commission Communication CFREU*, *supra* note 4, at 3.

131 *Id.* at 4.

132 *Id.* at 4.

133 *Id.* at 4.

134 D. Chalmers, G. Davies, and G. Monti, European Union Law: Cases and Materials, (Cambridge University Press 2014). According to these authors, particularly noteworthy examples of judicial feebleness are Case C-540/03 *Parliament v. Council* [2006] ECR 1–5769; Case C-303/05 *Advocaten voor de Wereld* [2007] ECR 1–3633; Case C-396/ 11 *Radu*, Judgment of 29 Jan. 2013.

135 Chalmers, et al., *id.*

136 *Commission Communication CFREU*, *supra* note 4, at 17.

137 Joined Cases C-402/05 and C-415/05, *Yassin Abdullah Kadi and Al Barakaat International Foundation v. Council and Commission*, 2008 E.C.R. I-461, ¶ 283.

138 Also noted, Art. 3(5) TEU according to which the Union shall contribute to, among other goals, 'the strict observance and the development of international law, including respect for the principles of the United Nations Charter'.

139 De Búrca explains this discrepancy as follows. Art. 2 TEU recognizes respect for human dignity and human rights as foundational principles of the Union;

> The Union is founded on the values of respect for human dignity, freedom, democracy, equality, the rule of law and respect for human rights, including the rights of persons belonging to minorities'. Whilst Art. 3(5) TEU involving human rights in external relations is formulated broadly, asserting that the protection of human rights is an overarching objective in all EU external relations, Art. 3(3) TEU dealing with human rights within internal EU policies, on the other hand, specifically names the internal EU policy fields that implicate human rights-related objectives; 'It shall combat social exclusion and discrimination, and shall promote social justice and protection, equality between women and men, solidarity between generations and protection of the rights of the child'. Its scope is hence delimited to 'those areas of EU power or competence which directly promote human rights – i.e., mainly anti-discrimination and social inclusion policy'. The enactment of the Charter of Fundamental Rights has changed little in this respect. The restrictive clauses of Art. 51(2), 51 and 6 TEU inhibit the Charter from modifying the powers and tasks in the Treaty in any way.
>
> *See* Gráinne de Búrca, *The Road Not Taken: The EU as a Global Human Rights Actor*, 105 American Journal of International Law, 38 (2011)

140 *Id.* 38.

141 Philip Alston & J.H.H. Weiler, *An 'Ever Closer Union in Need of a Human Rights Policy'*, 9 European Journal of European Law, 664 (1998).

142 Mandate of the Special Representative of the Secretary-General (SRSG) on the Issue of Human Rights and Transnational Corporations and other Business Enterprises, Corporate Law Project: Overarching Trends and Observations, 1 (2010).
143 *See*, www.senat.fr/dossier-legislatif/ppl14–376.html.
144 *See*, Bjorn Fasterling, Vigilence or Compliance? On the New French 'Vigilence' Law (19 June 2017), https://bhr.stern.nyu.edu/blogs/french-vigiliance-law.
145 For a similar argument, *see* Wood, *Reinforcing Participatory Governance Through International Human Rights Obligations of Political Parties*, 28 Harvard Human Rights Journal, 147 (2015).
146 *Commission Communication* CFREU, *supra* note 4, at 3.

6 The role of mandatory disclosure in operationalizing human rights due diligence

The case of the EU Directive on non-financial disclosure and board diversity

Introduction

This chapter examines the legal implications of giving effect to the corporate responsibility to respect human rights as defined in the UNGPs, through EU and national mandatory disclosure legislation. The focus of this chapter is on Directive 2014/95/EU, of 22 October 2014, *as regards disclosure of non-financial and diversity information by certain large undertakings and groups* (hereinafter the 'Non-Financial Reporting Directive' or the 'Directive').[1] This Directive amended Directive 2013/34/EU, of 26 June 2013, *on the annual financial statements, consolidated financial statements and related reports of certain types of undertakings*.[2] These EU Directives provide a minimum harmonization of the EU regime for non-financial disclosure by requiring EU Member States to enforce on certain business entities ('undertakings' in the Directive's jargon) and groups minimum disclosure requirements on certain non-financial matters including, *inter alia*, human rights.

The chapter analyses the so-called 'indirect' and 'direct' effect of the Directive. It concludes that by enacting the Directive, the EU opted for a *type of legal instrument* that has potentially sweeping implications for the rights of stakeholders when it comes to the disclosure obligations of corporations. However, as will be explained, in particular, in relation to the 'comply or explain' framework, it is uncertain whether the *content* of the Directive will contribute to further the rights of stakeholders. This chapter also argues that the Directive, in the light of its objectives and pursuant to well-established case law supporting a purposive interpretation of secondary EU legislation should have certain extraterritorial effects.

Preliminary considerations

Recent years have seen the adoption and revision of mandatory disclosure rules in the EU and beyond. These rules set out requirements for companies to disclose externally information that is necessary not only to obtain an understanding of the economic performance of companies, but also the impact of business enterprises on non-financial issues that are of public interest, including human rights. There is an increasing number of mandatory disclosure rules that require companies to disclose on human rights risks, policies and due diligence. The impetus for the adoption (or revision) of such instruments comes from regulators and increasing stakeholder expectations that business enterprises release such information. In order to enhance regulatory coherence and legal certainty, the more recent instruments adopted in this domain also include among their objectives to foster greater convergence between the existing disclosure requirements.

The chapter departs from conventional wisdom, according to which the national and EU mandatory disclosure legislation are a method for indirectly regulating business respect for human rights. As will be gathered from the following pages, the reporting on human rights issues by corporations has the potential to result in improved human rights performance.[3] Mandatory reporting requirements, alongside other multi-stakeholder and self-regulatory reporting initiatives, contribute to the regulatory dynamics affecting business conduct, which the UNGPs set out to promote. This chapter will examine the legal implications of ensuring the effective operationalizing of the responsibility to communicate in particular (as an integral part of human rights due diligence, in conformity with the expectations set out in the UNGPs) through national and EU mandatory disclosure legislation.

The chapter examines the effect of the Directive on consolidating the State duty to protect human rights by imposing an obligation on EU Member States to require certain large undertakings and groups to disclose on human rights. This reinforces State responses to UNGP 3, which articulates that, in meeting their duty to protect, States should 'encourage, and where appropriate require business enterprises to communicate how they address their human rights impacts'.[4] Special attention will be paid to factors that might limit or enhance the effectiveness of the Directive in shaping human rights compliance conduct by business enterprises across the EU.

The non-financial reporting directive: origin and objectives

The following sections will examine the factual origins, the rationale of the EU Commission to issue the proposal for the Non-Financial Reporting Directive, and the objectives of the Directive with regard to fostering improvement in the disclosure and actual performance of business enterprises in relation to human rights.

Legislative history and factual origins

The European Commission first expressed its commitment to issue a legislative proposal on non-financial disclosure in the Single Market Act 2011. The Act was set out to contribute to the objectives of the EU 2020 Strategy to bring the EU on course towards 'smart, sustainable and inclusive growth'.[5] The Act recognizes the importance of transparency in the transition towards a sustainable global economy, and the need to enhance it.[6,7] It identifies a trend towards these objectives, which is visible in new business models integrating these social considerations. The view is that this trend should also be reflected in the single market, which could be achieved by ensuring a level playing field and by supporting initiatives that enhance fairness and contribute to the fight against social exclusion. The Act expressed the commitment of the Commission to present a legislative proposal on the transparency of the social and environmental information provided by companies in all sectors to contribute to the first objective, to level the playing field.[8] The Commission reiterated this commitment in its renewed EU CSR Strategy,[9] and both these initiatives were presented as part of a package of measures, titled the 'Responsible Business Package'.[10] On 16 April 2013, the European Commission issued a legislative proposal to amend the 4th and 7th Accounting Directives on Annual and Consolidated Accounts, 78/660/EEC and 83/349/EEC.[11] The EP expressed its support for a legislative proposal on disclosure of non-financial information in two Resolutions.[12,13] Upon approval by the EP on 15 April 2014 and the Council of the European Union on 29 September 2014, the Directive 2014/95/EU amending Directive 2013/34/EU on non-financial information and diversity information was adopted on 22 October 2014.[14] The date of transposition of this EU Directive into national law is 6 December 2016. After the transit period has passed, business enterprises should start reporting as per January 2017. The EU Commission issued non-binding guidelines for reporting on non-financial information in 2017.[15]

Rationales and objectives

An impact assessment was carried out, which considered the case for improving the transparency of non-financial information, meaning environmental, social and governance information, including information on the diversity in the composition of a government board. The impact assessment pointed to the inadequacy of such non-financial information as the main issue, in terms of both the quantity and quality. The impact assessment recognized the potential of the proposed Directive to increase the transparency and comparability of non-financial information that is available, which in turn could affect the capacity of both business enterprises and other stakeholders to measure, monitor and manage the performance of business enterprises and groups, and their impact on society more generally.[16] An important objective thus was to affect the disclosure practices of large undertakings and groups to an extent that it reaches a sufficient scale and quality to meet stakeholder needs.

The impact assessment indicates that, in the EU context, both national regulation and markets have failed to provide an adequate solution to insufficient reporting on non-financial information. An important reason for why markets have been insufficient to move companies relates to the disputed business case for disclosure. There is no uncontested evidence that the long-term benefits of being more transparent outweigh the short-term costs. These short-term costs can be significant and more discernible and imminent than the long-term benefits of disclosure.[17] This finding supports the notion that companies do not tend to disclose unless they are compelled to do so, by means of market pressure, or if absent, national legislation imposing mandatory disclosure requirements.[18] The enforcement of business disclosure thus is difficult to achieve in practice without State intervention.[19] The assessment also supports the argument that CSR more generally does not flow naturally under the force of market mechanisms only, but depends for its success on effective regulatory intervention to create the conditions for CSR to work.[20]

The previous regime that regulated non-financial disclosure did not impose disclosure obligations on companies.[21,22] The non-financial disclosure by companies in the EU had been partly regulated by the EU regime on non-financial disclosure, which had previously been governed by the Fourth Council Directive 78/660/EEC on the annual accounts of certain types of companies and Seventh Directive 83/349/EEC on consolidated accounts, as amended by Directive 2006/46/EC. Recital 10 of the Preamble of Directive 2006/46/EC noted that 'companies whose securities are admitted to trading on a regulated market and which have their registered office in the Community should be obliged to disclose an annual corporate governance statement' and that '*where relevant*, companies may also provide an analysis of environmental and social aspects *necessary for an understanding of the company's development, performance and position*'.[23] The limiting concepts set out therein were formulated in too open-ended language to impose a clear legal obligation on companies.[24] In the absence of clear obligations, business enterprises perceived the reporting regime as 'voluntary'.[25] The Directive thus had a limited effect of compelling business enterprises to disclose.

The Impact Assessment also notes an increasing number of national disclosure regulations imposing obligations on companies to provide information about their social impacts. Fragmentation in the European landscape resulting from national legislations imposing diverse disclosure requirements on companies turned out not only to be costly for companies operating in multiple countries, but also to complicate efforts to compare and benchmark performances across the internal market. The cross-border nature of business operations called for greater coordination at the EU level. The proposal Directive thus aimed at harmonizing the proliferation of national legislations and to enhance the 'relevance, comparability and consistency' of the information disclosed by companies and groups in the EU and to lift transparency to a similarly high level across the EU.[26]

Disclosure as a regulatory tool

The main rationale for the EU Commission to issue the Non-Financial Reporting Directive thus is to affect and coordinate the regulation by EU Member States of the disclosure of non-financial information by companies with the aim of enhancing the quality and quantity of such disclosure, which had before been inadequate. There is potential for the Directive to serve as a useful regulatory tool that can lead to improvements in the human rights performance of companies. The Directive can illicit disclosure by companies of information that can enable stakeholders (i.e. regulators, NGOs, business enterprises, consumers, investors) to evaluate, compare and hold companies to account for their human rights performance. Business enterprises can be incited to take their responsibility seriously if these stakeholders inflict costs or rewards on them for (non-) compliance. The effectiveness of the Directive in achieving this objective will depend on how Member States will implement the provisions of the Directive and the preparedness of regulators and stakeholders to pressure companies to adhere to the disclosure requirements.[27] The required disclosure has the potential to have positive effects on business respect for human rights in various ways.

First, the disclosure of relevant non-financial information can strengthen accountability by improving the ability of NGOs and civil society actors to monitor business performance. The disclosure requirements thus may legally require and enforce the disclosure of information that would otherwise not be publicly available. Stakeholders rely on the information disclosed to monitor and exert direct pressure on undertakings to meet their responsibility to respect human rights. Consumers, who rely on the disclosed information to make informed purchasing decisions, may exert such pressure. Also, investors find use in the transparency of comparable and accurate information, which they rely on to measure and compare the performance of companies. Enhanced disclosure can result in better-informed investment decisions. It can furthermore empower institutional shareholders in exercising their corporate governance rights to monitor the activities and behaviour of directors, and to intervene where necessary.[28] Research has shown that the availability of information can be critical for leveraging business behaviour through alternative avenues, e.g. transnational private regulation.[29,30]

Second, the implications of the disclosure requirements that undertakings must collect the information to meet these requirements can affect the capacity of business enterprises to measure and monitoring their own risks and performance regarding respect for human rights. While process oriented, the human rights due diligence is linked to performance in that findings must be integrated and acted upon. Better measurement as a result of greater transparency can translate into improvements in policies and processes to discharge their responsibility to respect human rights.[31,32] The pressure that NGOs may exert as a result of their improved monitoring role also can have the positive impact of creating greater human rights awareness within business enterprises and spur improvements in business performance in relation thereto.[33]

The business case for disclosure suggests that transparency can have economic value by facilitating the measurement and monitoring by companies of their risks and opportunities more generally. Disclosure of relevant information also allows companies to meet the demand for information by relevant stakeholders, including consumers, investors and NGOs. In the absence of legal obligations, business respect for human rights in practice largely depends on the voluntary uptake by undertakings of the UNGPs following from social pressure.[34] Disclosure also can make change in business behaviour and markets visible and manageable, and can facilitate the channelling of this change towards the goal of creating a 'sustainable global economy'.[35] Transparency is perceived as 'a "smart lever" to strengthen citizen and consumer trust and confidence in the Single Market and to encourage sustainable economic growth'.[36]

The non-financial reporting directive and the human rights due diligence concept: exploring the links

The next section examines this Directive in detail to determine whether and the extent to which the minimum disclosure requirements articulated in the Directive correspond with the expectations set out in the UNGPs, and specifically regarding the responsibility to communicate set out in UNGPs 17 and 21. Assuming that the Directive does intend to give effects to these two principles, the chapter also examines the way in which and detail to which the Directive defines disclosure requirements related to human rights due diligence.

Mandatory disclosure on corporate respect for human rights

The Directive 2014/95/EU introduces legal requirements for certain large undertakings and groups to disclose information on non-financial issues and, *inter alia*, human rights. It sets a minimum legal benchmark regarding the content of this disclosure, as well as the frequency, form and means of this disclosure. The following section focuses on the disclosure requirements that apply to certain large undertakings individually. Article 19a(1) of the Directive defines the disclosure requirement as follows:

> Large undertakings which are *public-interest entities* exceeding on their balance-sheet dates the criterion of the average number of 500 employees during the financial year shall include in the management report a non-financial statement containing information *to the extent necessary* for an understanding of the undertaking's development, performance, position and *impact of its activity*, relating to, as a minimum, environmental, social and employee matters, *respect for human rights*, anti-corruption and bribery matters.

The Directive applies to 'large undertakings', the size threshold of which is determined by reference to the 'average number of employees, balance sheet total and net turn over'.[37] The criterion of the average number of employees during the financial year is determinant, and should exceed at least 500 on the date of the balance sheets.[38] Only public interest entities are subject to the Directive, which are defined as listed companies, credit institutions, insurance undertakings, and entities designated by Member States as public interest entities.[39] These undertakings must disclose through the formal means of a non-financial statement in the management report. The disclosure requirements extend beyond what is necessary to understand the economic affairs of the undertaking to also include information on the undertaking's impact on public interest issues, including respect for human rights.

Undertakings that are subject to the Directive have an obligation to disclose on respect for human rights only 'to the extent necessary'. This suggests that the non-financial statement should only contain information that is relevant and sufficient for an understanding of the undertaking's development, performance and position and the impact of its activities. The Directive does not further specify the target audience whose understanding of the company should be informed by this information. Also, the Directive does not specify the standard by which to determine when information is relevant and thus 'necessary'. The Directive does note that certain minimum requirements regarding the extent of the disclosure apply and that 'the undertakings subject to this Directive should give a fair and comprehensive view of their policies, outcomes, and risks'.[40] In the absence of further clarification of 'to the extent necessary' for the purpose of the Directive, the company has discretion to decide itself when it is necessary to provide information, at least to a certain extent.

The Directive introduces minimum legal requirements regarding the content of this disclosure. The requirements relate to the type and extent of information that large undertakings subject to the Directive should disclose. Pursuant to Article 19a (1), this information should cover the following:

a a brief description of the undertaking's business model;
b a description of the policies pursued by the undertaking in relation to those matters, including *due diligence processes implemented*;
c the outcome of those policies;
d the principal risks related to those matters linked to the undertaking's operations, including, where relevant and proportionate, its business relationships, products or services which are likely to cause adverse impacts in those areas, and how the undertaking manages those risks;
e non-financial key performance *indicators* relevant to the particular business.[41]

EU Member States must ensure in their national legislation that business enterprises disclose, at a minimum, on: (a) the business model of the undertaking; (b) the human rights policies pursued by the company, including its due diligence processes; (c) the outcome of those policies; (d) the 'principal' human rights risks related to matters that are linked to the undertaking's operations, including 'where relevant and proportionate', its business relationships, products or services, and how the undertaking manages these risks; and (e) relevant non-financial key performance indicators.

There is a discernible conceptual influence of the UNGPs on the text of the Directive. This influence is apparent from the concepts on which the disclosure requirements are construed, in particular, the concept of 'due diligence', as well as the concepts delimiting the content and the extent of the required disclosure.

The requirement that undertakings disclose information that is sufficient to provide a fair and comprehensive overview of their human rights policies, the outcomes of those policies and the risk management implemented to prevent human rights abuses corresponds to the expectation set out in the UNGPs.[42] The Directive also expressly mentions that undertakings should disclose on their due diligence processes implemented. The Directive furthermore extends the scope of the required disclosure beyond the human rights risks that the undertaking may be involved in through its own operations to risks that may be linked to the undertaking's business relationships, products and services. This is important in that it requires undertakings to disclose information on (sub-)subsidiary entities and their supply chains, and the human rights risks relating to their activities that are directly linked to the parent undertaking.[43] These provisions suggest broad alignment between the disclosure requirements as related to human rights and the responsibility to communicate as defined by UNGP 17 and UNGP 21.

There are other elements that point to alignment with the expectations set out under the UNGPs. The requirement that the non-financial statement covers information on *adverse* human rights impacts is a case in point. The disclosure on respect for human rights, after all, is concerned with managing potential adverse human rights impacts. The disclosure must include information on the outcomes of human rights due diligence policies, which requires, in fact, reflection of not only an undertaking's potential but also its actual human rights impact. The Directive appears to orient disclosure primarily to policies and its processes, including human rights due diligence, however, rather than to actual outcomes and impacts.[44] This is by way of exempting undertakings from their obligation to disclose on outcomes if all other obligations under Article 19a 1. have been fulfilled.[45] The Directive calls for the disclosure of information on retrospective management processes, to the extent that business enterprises must provide a description of the due diligence policies they have implemented. It also requires disclosure on forward-looking management processes in that disclosure must cover due diligence processes that are ongoing to manage potential human rights risks.

Conceptual clarity: the due diligence concept

The broad alignment of the disclosure requirements set out in the Directive with the UNGPs should be welcomed, because this increases the likelihood of the Directive having impacts on the disclosure practices and actual human rights due diligence by undertakings in practice. The Directive presents deficiencies, however, in that the disclosure requirements relating to human rights are formulated in ambiguous language. The Directive does not specify the content and the degree of detail of reporting in relation to the 'business model', 'policies' and 'due diligence'.

For instance, there is no exact definition of due diligence in the text of the Directive, nor are its exact requirements in relation to reporting on due diligence implemented relating to human rights defined. The Directive is silent with regards to the specific elements of due diligence that undertakings should report on, and to what extent these correspond to expectations of human rights due diligence as defined by the UNGPs. For instance, there is no provision in the Directive that indicates that the non-financial statement should include information on how the company has integrated the findings relating the outcome of its human rights due diligence in the processes or functions of the undertaking or any action taken in response to these outcomes. The Directive is also silent with regards to the tracking of responses and stakeholder engagement. In the absence of further clarity, the undertaking itself determines the content and detail of the disclosure relating due diligence.

Where the disclosure requirements on human rights risks are concerned, which are articulated under the Article 19a (1) (d), the Directive does not specify what constitutes 'principal' risks. Recital 8 provides some guidance, noting that

> the undertakings which are subject to this Directive should provide adequate information in relation to matters that stand out as being most likely to bring about the materialisation of principal risks of severe impacts, along with those that have already materialised.

The Recital suggests that disclosure should reflect on human rights *matters* that respect for human rights may give rise to, and not just on any matters, but prioritize those matters that stand out as most likely to give rise to '*principal* risks of *severe* impact'. These impacts may be likely to materialize or may have materialized already.

The Directive notes that 'severity' must be judged in relation to the 'scale and gravity' of these impacts.[46] The Directive thus prescribes as a minimum legal requirement that an undertaking has a duty to disclose on human rights risks in the presence of matters reflecting the principal risks of severe human rights impacts. The Directive not only establishes the presence and delimits the scope of the disclosure requirements by reference to the qualification of human rights risks as 'principal' and 'severe', but also by reference to the undertaking's involvement in these risks. Pursuant to the Directive, the non-financial statement must include information on matters reflecting risks that are linked to the undertaking's business relationships, products or services. The Directive thus sets out the requirement that companies report on all their principle risks of severe impacts, irrespective of whether these risks are caused by the entity concerned, or whether these result from the activities of other undertakings that can be linked to the undertaking.

This disclosure obligation is triggered only when such disclosure is '*relevant and proportionate*', however.[47] The Directive does not specify what constitutes 'relevant and proportionate' for the purpose of the Directive. It is reasonable to assume that Article 19a 1.(d) should be contextualized in relation to Article 19a1(b), which requires disclosure on the human rights policies, including the human rights due diligence processes that the undertaking has implemented. Disclosure on matters linked to a company's business relationships, products or services then could be seen as 'relevant and proportionate' where these issues reflect human rights risks that give rise to a due diligence responsibility by the company.[48] Since the Directive fails to define the due diligence concept in the human rights context, however, the disclose requirements that mirror this concept are also ambiguous.

The Directive does not expressly note that the undertakings subject to the Directive should disclose by reference to the UNGPs, although it is mentioned that national implementing measures should permit undertakings to rely on international frameworks, including the UNGPs. The Directive thus leaves flexibility for EU Member States, which must transpose the Directive into national law by 6 December 2016,[49] to decide what is the meaning of '*due diligence*', what constitutes '*principal*' risks and when disclosure on issues is '*relevant and proportionate*' under national law. The Directive leaves discretion to EU Member States as to how to define these concepts, and whether to define these in reference to the expectation set out under the UNGPs, including relating the responsibility of companies to communicate under UNGP 17 to 21. EU Member States are permitted, but not required, to introduce such improvements.[50]

Absent clarity of the concepts, the Directive creates uncertainty and allows for possible divergence between EU Member States as to how their national laws define due diligence and the degree to which these laws ensure large undertakings effectively disclose in reference to the human rights due diligence concept described by UNGP 17 and 21. As will be elaborated below, this discretion undermines the potential of the Directive to generate indirect regulatory effects on business disclosure and human rights due diligence in practice. Where the language of the Directive is formulated in open-ended language, this can also undermine the capacity of the Directive to have 'direct' and 'indirect' effect.

The non-financial reporting directive in the light of the doctrines of 'direct' and 'indirect' effect

It could be argued that an optimal use of the Directive requires that stakeholders (citizens, NGOs, shareholders, etc.) can rely on its provisions when a company does not comply with its requirements. The following section thus aims at ascertaining the exact legal effects the Non-Financial Reporting Directive may have for stakeholders, and right-holders in particular.

This section will focus *first* on the doctrine of the so-called 'indirect effect' of the Directive, according to which national measures should be interpreted in light of EU law, including the Directive. Moreover, given that the provisions of the Directive should be interpreted in accordance with EU protected fundamental rights, and that EU protected fundamental rights also have 'indirect effects', it is argued that an interpretation of the Directive (and its implementing national measures) should be adopted that is most favourable to EU protected fundamental human rights, in particular the right to respect of private life and the right to freedom of expression.

This section will then examine whether the Directive has the so-called 'direct effect'. It is argued that the Directive is unlikely to have direct effect. The following considerations come to the fore: (i) the Directive's provisions are unlikely to be considered by the CJEU as 'clear and unconditional and not contingent on any discretionary implementing measure';[51] and, perhaps more importantly, (ii) attempts to invoke the hypothetical direct effect of the Directive are likely to face the obstacle of the CJEU's refusal to recognize the so-called 'horizontal' direct effect of Directives, *i.e.* to recognize that a Directive can impose obligations in proceedings between individuals.[52]

Indirect effect

The Directive is capable of having 'indirect effect',[53] an effect referred to as 'the principle of interpretation in conformity with Union law'.[54] As noted by Lenaerts and Van Nuffel, pursuant to the doctrine of 'indirect effect', the 'TEU place[d] all public authorities, and therefore also judicial authorities, under a duty to interpret the national law which they have to apply as far as possible in conformity with the requirements of Union law'.[55] More precisely, the CJEU introduced in *Van Colson* the principle of indirect effect, according to which national authorities (including courts) have to interpret national laws 'as far as possible' in conformity with European law.[56] In the subsequent *Marleasing* ruling, the CJEU held that a Directive can have such indirect effect, irrespective of whether the Directive has been transposed. In the case of the Non-Financial Reporting Directive, by operation of such effect, national laws would have to be interpreted in light of this Directive. To be noted is that the effect of the Directive is indirect by reason of this effect being imposed by national law, instead of by the Directive itself.

According to the case law of the CJEU,[57] indirect effect does not apply, as such, before the expiration of the deadline for implementation of a directive (in the case of the Directive, 6 December 2016).[58] However, before that date, and pursuant to the *Inter-Environmental Wallonie* ruling of the CJEU,[59] Member States must not enact any legislation that could seriously compromise the attainment of the result required by the Directive. Consequently, during this period, national legislation must be interpreted, to the extent that is possible, in a manner conducive to avoiding this.[60]

The Non-Financial Reporting Directive defines the objectives of the Directive as follows: 'to increase the relevance, consistency and comparability of information disclosed by certain large undertakings and groups across the Union'.[61] Given that the rationale behind the Directive is to enhance transparency to a similarly high level across the EU, it is necessary for EU Member States to adopt adequate and effective means for the application and enforcement of the Directive, in order for this objective to be achieved.[62] These national implementation measures may not go against the objective of the Directive. This may affect the discretion of national authorities in areas of law different from financial regulation as well. The implementing measures, moreover, must uphold EU protected fundamental human rights when implementing EU Directives, which will be assessed in detail below.

Of particular interest, in relation to indirect effect, is the Directive's provision that requires large undertakings to disclose information 'to the extent *necessary* for an understanding of the undertaking's [...] respect for human rights'.[63] In the light of that provision and, given the importance the Treaties award to fundamental rights (see Articles 2 and 6 TEU), the duty to interpret secondary legislation, such as the Directive, in the light of the Treaties[64] (and the fact that the Treaties themselves have indirect effect),[65] when interpreting the national measures implementing the provisions of the Directive, the requirement to disclose should be widely interpreted in order to further these rights. Moreover, UNGP 3 articulates that, in meeting their duty to protect, States should 'encourage, and where appropriate require business enterprises to communicate how they address their human rights impacts'.[66]

Unlike, as can be seen in more detail in the following section, 'direct effect', the doctrine of 'indirect effect' applies also to scenarios where the interpretation of the Directive can affect the legal position of individuals in a disadvantageous way.[67] Consequently, stakeholders can rely on the indirect effect of the Directive before national courts to make sure corporations fully give effect to the Directive.

The provisions of the Directive should be interpreted in accordance with EU protected fundamental rights including, *inter alia*, the right of respect for private and family life (Article 7 CFREU) and the right to freedom of expression (Article 11 CFREU).

The right to respect for private and family life

Article 7 CFREU establishes that 'everyone has the right to respect for his or her private and family life, home and communications'. This right corresponds to, both in meaning and scope, the right to private life as guaranteed by Article 8 of the ECHR. Pursuant to Article 52(3) CFREU,

> [i]n so far as this Charter contains rights which correspond to rights guaranteed by the Convention for the Protection of Human Rights and Fundamental Freedoms, the meaning and scope of those rights shall be the same as those laid down by the said Convention.

Consequently, the rulings by the ECtHR applying the provisions of the ECHR equivalent to Articles 7 and 11 CFREU (namely, Articles 8 and 10 ECHR) are of the utmost relevance when it comes to determining the scope of the (EU protected) fundamental rights.

The ECtHR held in the 1998 *Guerra* Ruling that Article 8 ECHR created a positive duty on the part of the State to provide information on environmental risks related to the applicants' exposure to chemical emissions by a factory. The denial of this information prevented the individual and his family from assessing the risks to their lives and home. This case law suggests that, under certain circumstances, States may have a positive obligation to make available to the public certain information that would otherwise not become known, in order to secure an individual's right to private life.[68] Article 8 of the ECHR may thus result in the creation of a positive obligation on the part of States to ensure that information about the potential and actual human rights risks of undertakings is publicly available.

The right to freedom of expression

Article 11 CFREU establishes the right to freedom of expression, which 'shall include freedom to hold opinions and to receive and impart information and ideas without interference by public authorities regardless of frontiers'. The scope of this right, which mirrors that of Article 10 of the ECHR, thus includes, *inter alia*, the receipt of information. The Grand Chamber of the ECtHR has established that integral to the right to freedom of expression under Article 10 ECHR is the right to receive information. The right to freedom of expression was initially viewed as creating only a negative obligation for States to refrain 'from restricting a person from receiving information that others wished or might be willing to impart on him'.[69] The Grand Chamber of the ECtHR has held that Article 10 does not give rise to a positive duty for States to collect and disseminate information to the public on their own motion.[70] More recently, however, decisions by sections of the ECtHR suggest the Court may be abandoning this narrow approach. These recent decisions have pointed to a general 'direction of travel'[71] in the case law, departing from the Grand Chamber's narrow interpretation of Article 10 ECtHR and towards the notion that Article 10 gives rise to a positive right of access to information.[72]

The cases in which certain sections have recognized this positive right involved the legitimate gathering of public information by NGOs. More precisely, the ECtHR has held that the activities of NGOs warrant similar protection as those of the press by reason of these NGOs having a similar function to social 'watchdog'.[73] This case law suggests that Article 10 of the ECHR might create (or be on the verge of creating) a right to access public information and a positive obligation on States to make available certain information of public interest. While the Grand Chamber of the ECtHR has not yet confirmed this interpretation, it seems consistent with a substantial body of the Court's case law. This reading would furthermore follow developments in international law, which Article 10 ECHR should be interpreted in accordance with. The right to freedom of expression finds an international equivalent under Article 19 of the ICCPR and Article 13(1) of the American Convention on Human Rights. These provisions have both been interpreted as giving rise to a right to access information held by public bodies.

The effects of the 'indirect' effect of the Directive and EU protected fundamental rights

There is case law of the ECtHR supporting the view that States have a legal obligation to ensure a level of disclosure about the due diligence policies and human rights risks of these undertakings that provides right-holders with the information they need to vindicate their rights. An interpretation of the Directive that is most favourable to giving effect to these rights (and their equivalents under EU law) should be adopted, one that takes this State duty to protect human rights into account. National disclosure obligations, including those deriving from acts of implementation of the Directive, should be interpreted by reference to the Directive and to the CFREU (and, through it, the ECHR).

The Directive permits EU Member States to require further improvements to the transparency of undertakings' disclosure on human rights.[74] However certain provisions in the Directive may restrict EU Member States from doing so. While the Directive sets out certain conditions regarding the modality by which EU Member States must require enterprises to disclose on human rights, these conditions seem more oriented towards ensuring that national implementation measures allow for flexibility in order to ease the burden of disclosure on undertakings, rather than to impose clear disclosure obligations on undertakings. The Directive creates incentives but no obligation for undertakings to rely on international frameworks, *inter alia*, the UNGPs in their disclosure.

The 'comply or explain' modality is an example in point. The Directive provides that an EU Member States should oblige an undertaking to report on its human rights policy and if it does not pursue such a policy to provide in their non-financial statement a 'clear and reasoned' explanation for why they are not doing so.[75] This policy does not amount to a requirement that undertakings pursue a human rights policy in case it is not already pursuing one, but merely, that the undertaking explains why it is not doing so. This explanation must be 'clear and 'reasoned'. It should be noted, in this regard, that research shows that, in practice, undertakings that were subject to the 'report and explain' requirement tended not to disclose as they should, giving invalid, general or false explanations.[76] This prompted the EU Commission to issue guidance and to assist companies in improving the quality of these explanations.[77]

In any event, if transposing the 'comply or explain' modality into national law becomes mandatory for EU Member States, which appears to be the case, the Directive would have the perverse result of preempting EU Member States from adopting a more stringent reporting obligation that would not accept a mere explanation, but that would require companies to adopt a human rights policy and to acquire the level of knowledge it should have about its human rights risks. Disclosure requirements that not only solicit disclosure about the understanding that an undertaking has, but that also require undertakings to be proactive in order to acquire the level of understanding that it should have about its human rights policies and risks, aligns with the *ethos* of the human rights due diligence concept. Human rights due diligence requires business enterprises to enquire and investigate their human rights impacts with the aim of preventing these impacts.

However, the obligations of EU Member States to respect EU protected fundamental rights may require EU Member States to impose more demanding disclosure requirements on undertakings. EU Member States may be under a legal obligation to require improved disclosure from undertakings not only about the understanding they have, but also about the level of understanding they should have on their human rights policies and risks. Adopting such national disclosure regulations mandating greater transparency from undertakings may be necessary for States to secure the right of individuals to receive the information on the basis of which they can assess the risks to their human rights. Since the national implementation measures that introduce more stringent disclosure requirements would extend beyond the minimum requirements of the Non-Financial Reporting Directive, they may be susceptible to control of compatibility with the national standard of human rights protection by national courts. A more demanding disclosure requirement may be necessary in order for States to meet their legal obligations to ensure the right to private life and the right to freedom of expression.

It remains to be seen, in short, how, if at all, the CJEU will interpret the 'indirect effect' of the (not always satisfactory, from the perspective of its content) Directive in the light of the (also indirectly effective and hierarchically superior provisions of the) CFREU and EU protected fundamental rights.

Direct effect

The question arises whether, after the expiration of the deadline for transposition, stakeholders (NGOs, shareholders, individuals, etc.) can rely on the Directive before the national authorities and courts of the EU Member States in order to obtain enhanced disclosure from corporations.

Pursuant to Article 288 TFEU, '[a] directive shall be binding, as to the result to be achieved, upon each Member State to which it is addressed, but shall leave to the national authorities the choice of form and methods'. Consequently, it is implicit in the very nature of an EU Directive that Member States have the discretion to choose the preferred method and form of implementation. Unlike Regulations, in relation to which the literality of Article 288 TFEU expressly provides that they will be 'directly applicable', the TFEU does not contain any provision in relation to whether Directives can be directly applicable. Direct effect is the capacity of Community law to give rise to rights and obligations directly, *i.e.* without the need to be implemented by national law.[78] According to Paul Craig and Gráinne de Búrca, pursuant to the doctrine of direct effect 'provisions of binding EU law which are sufficiently clear, precise and unconditional to be considered justiciable can be invoked and relied on by individuals before national courts'.[79]

The CJEU has recognized that Directives can have direct effect provided that certain general requirements for direct effect are met.[80] The CJEU established these criteria in its seminal *Van Gend en Loos v. Nederlandse Administratie der Belastingen* ruling, noting that, in order for provisions in an instrument of EU law to be directly effective, the provisions should be: (i) precise; (ii) unconditional; and (iii) not dependent on implementing measures.[81] Whether the Non-Financial Directive, or certain of its provisions, create direct effect is ambiguous. It calls for an examination of the criteria outlined in the not always consistent *Van Gend en Loos* case law.[82] An analysis should be done on a case-by-case basis for each provision.

It is argued that the Directive is unlikely to acquire direct effect. The following considerations come to the fore: (i) the Directive's provisions are unlikely to be considered by the CJEU as 'clear and unconditional and not contingent on any discretionary implementing measure';[83] and, perhaps more importantly, (ii) attempts to invoke the hypothetical direct effect of the Directive are likely to face the obstacle of the CJEU's refusal to recognize the so-called 'horizontal' direct effect of Directives, *i.e.* to recognize that a Directive can impose obligations in proceedings between individuals.[84] The CJEU in *Marshall* refused direct horizontal effect for Directives, which it justified by the reason that a Directive is addressed to EU Member States, and cannot 'of itself' impose obligations on individuals.[85] The Directive may still be invoked in proceedings between individuals, however, for the purpose of creating vertical direct effect, if one of the parties is an undertaking that can be designated as an emanation of the 'State'.[86]

The absence of direct effect of the Directive does not mean that stakeholders are completely deprived from invoking it against the corporations under the Directive's reporting obligations.

First, as previously indicated, individuals can invoke the 'indirect' effect of the Directive, and of EU protected fundamental rights, to obtain an interpretation of national law in conformity with EU law. Second, national courts are under an obligation to leave unapplied national rules contrary to the Directive, in certain cases, in proceedings between individuals.[87] Craig and De Búrca refer to this possibility as 'incidental horizontal effects'.[88] Third, while probably remote in practice, individuals retain the possibility, under the *Francovich* case law of the CJEU,[89] to sue the EU Member States for damages if they fail to give full effect to the Directive, including if they fail to obtain from the corporations subject to reporting obligations the levels of disclosure required by the Directive.

Fourth, the CJEU has held more recently that general principles of EU law can bind private parties and that the content of a general principle of EU law can be inferred from a Directive.[90] Given that the Treaties are widely perceived as having 'horizontal' direct effect,[91] and that EU protected fundamental rights have the status of both general principles of EU law and (to the extent that they have been incorporated to the CFREU) primary legislation, the Directive could potentially be very helpful to clarify the scope of directly applicable fundamental rights (be they general principles of EU law or provisions in the CFREU).

Fifth and finally, the possible lack of direct effect of the Directive does not in any manner diminish the obligations, for all EU Member States, to give effect to it. More precisely, if EU Member States fail to require from corporations the information referred to by the Directive, the European Commission, acting on its own motion or after a complaint from a stakeholder, can bring the Member State in question before the CJEU, which can declare that the Member State has breached EU law (see Article 258 TFEU),[92] and even impose a lump sum or penalty payment on the Member State in question if the latter consistently refuses to give effect to the Directive in question (see Article 260 TFEU). Other EU Member States may also bring the matter before the CJEU (see Article 259 TFEU).

All in all, by enacting the Directive, the EU opted for a *type of legal instrument* which has potentially sweeping implications in the rights of stakeholders when it comes to the disclosure obligations of corporations. However, irrespective to the *type* of instrument chosen, and as noted in the preceding section in relation to the 'comply or explain' example, it is uncertain whether the *content* of the Directive will contribute to further the rights of stakeholders.

The non-financial reporting directive: flexibility of action and effectiveness

The following section will examine the discretion that is left to EU Member States in the transposition of the Directive into national law and the potential effects that this discretion may have on the regulatory effects of the Directive in terms of affecting and coordinating business disclosure on human rights in the EU. First, it will examine the flexibilities that are built into the disclosure requirements. Second, it will will assess the form and type of information that companies must disclose, the audience to whom disclosure is owed and the monitoring and verification of compliance with the disclosure obligations.

The disclosure requirements and flexibility

It follows from Recital 3 in the Preamble to the Directive that the EU legislator intended to allow for 'high flexibility of action' considering that account should be had of

> the multidimensional nature of [CSR] and the diversity of the CSR policies implemented by businesses matched by a sufficient level of comparability to meet the needs of investors and other stakeholders as well as the need to provide consumers with easy access to information on the impact of businesses on society.[93]

This disclosure should give stakeholders an understanding of the company's performance in relation to all areas of CSR. Moreover, it should respond to the demands by stakeholders whose interests are engaged in these areas for sufficient or material information related to these respective areas. The Directive provides a non-exhaustive list that includes, apart from respect for human rights, the areas of environmental, social and employee matters, anti-corruption and bribery matters.

There are various provisions in the Directive that permit or require EU Member States to leave a significant degree of flexibility for companies under their national disclosure requirements, as a result of which the disclosure requirements leave considerable discretion for companies to decide how to disclose and what information to include in the non-financial statement.

One example is the 'comply or explain' policy outlined above. This provision requires that States provide business enterprises with the discretion to not disclose on human rights policies if they are not pursuing one and to provide an explanation instead. The Directive does not prescribe how this explanation should be drawn up, which leaves further discretion to companies to decide how to formulate this explanation. There may not be sufficient incentives for business enterprises to provide an informed explanation in the absence of further guidance, as experiences in the corporate governance context have shown.[94]

Another example is that the Directive permits an EU Member State to exempt an undertaking from its obligation to disclose through a non-financial statement, provided that the undertaking publishes a separate report for the same financial year that covers the information required for the non-financial statement. Certain conditions must be met.[95] The separate report should be published with the management report or made publicly available on the undertaking's website, no later than six months after the balance sheet date.[96] This exemption should apply irrespective of whether the undertaking uses a national, Union-based or international framework. EU Member States may also exempt a parent or a subsidiary undertaking subject to the Directive from its obligation to disclose, if this undertaking is included in the consolidated financial statement or separate report of another undertaking.[97]

The Directive also allows for flexibility in the substantive disclosure requirements. This is unsurprising. The requirements to disclose formally may impose a disproportionate burden on certain undertakings. There is support for the view that the design of these requirements should give regard to the circumstances of the undertaking, in terms of its size and the complexity of its actions, the specific risk and challenges that the company faces, and the objective of disclosure. In other words, the flexibility in the disclosure requirements allows for reporting that balances and responds to the circumstances of business enterprises and stakeholder demands, which are specific to the different areas that the concept of CSR encompasses.

Where EU Member States allow too much flexibility for undertakings in meeting their disclosure requirements, this can have the adverse effect of undermining the effectiveness of the Directive in relation to human rights. There is the risk that disclosure requirements on undertakings are eased to an extent that the potential effect of the Directive on improving disclosure practices of companies in the function of human rights protection becomes diluted.

The extraterritorial dimension of the Directive: disclosure on respect for human rights in corporate supply chains

The extraterritorial dimension of the Directive

The Directive provides in Article 19a(d) and Article 29a(d) that undertakings should include in their non-financial statement information about

> the principal risks related to those matters linked to the undertaking's [including, where applicable, the group to which the undertaking belongs] operations including, where relevant and proportionate, its business relationship, products or services which are likely to cause adverse impacts in those areas, and how the undertaking [including, where applicable the group to which the undertaking belongs] manages those risks.

Those undertakings subject to the disclose requirements should thus disclose on the 'principal' human rights risks that are linked to the individual undertaking's or group's operations by their business relationships, services or products. The Directive does not draw a distinction with regards to the location of these 'principal' human rights risks within the EU or in a third State.

Apart from disclosing these principal risks, the undertaking must disclose how these are being managed. The Directive indicates in Recital 6 that the non-financial statement 'should also include information on the due diligence processes implemented by the undertaking, also regarding, where relevant and proportionate, its supply and subcontracting chains, in order to identify, prevent and mitigate existing and potential adverse impacts'.[98] The requirements under Article 19a(d) and Article 29a(d) that companies disclose on how they manage their human rights risks should thus be contextualized in relation to the undertaking's or group's duty to disclose on their due diligence processes implemented.

As noted, the Directive does not indicate the geographical location of these human rights risks. Whether the impacts are located inside or outside of the jurisdiction of the EU Member State in which the company is incorporated, or within or outside the territory of the EU, appears not to be an issue for the applicability of the disclosure obligations. Purposive interpretation, with certain nuances outside the scope of these pages, is of paramount importance in the interpretation of EU law, including secondary legislation such as the Directive is, by the CJEU. As noted by Paul Craig and Gráinne de Búrca, 'the Court [...] examines the whole context in which a particular provision is situated and gives the interpretation most likely to further what the Court considers that provision sought to achieve'.[99] According to consistent case law of the CJEU, the scope of acts of Union institutions needs to be determined by taking into account their wording, context and objectives.[100] Moreover, where a provision of Union law is open to several interpretations, preference must be given to that interpretation which ensures the effectiveness (*effet utile*) of the provision in question.[101]

Hence and, consistent with EU case law,[102] an interpretation of the requirement set out in the Directive should take into account the context and the objectives pursued by this Directive. In this regard, undertakings should include, where 'relevant and proportionate', in their non-financial statement information about existing and potential adverse human rights impacts that are linked to its operations that occur outside the territory of the EU as well.

If the Directive were to be interpreted as drawing a distinction between the human rights impacts of companies within or outside the territory of the EU, then this would be contrary to the objective the Directive pursues in relation to human rights. It should be recalled that the objective of the Directive, as set out in Recital 21, is to 'increase the relevance, consistency and comparability of information disclosed by certain large undertakings and groups across the Union'.[103] Moreover, as can be gathered from Recital 3, such disclosure is meant to 'hel[p] the measuring, monitoring and managing of undertakings' performance and their impact on society'. As regards the extent of disclosure, according to Recital 5, in order for the purpose of the Directive to be achieved, the information included in the non-financial statement should, at a minimum, 'give a fair and comprehensive view' of the company and group's human rights 'policies, outcomes and risks'.[104]

If the company would not be required to, and therefore would not disclose on its human rights risks that are located outside the EU territory, this would suggest that the company does not have such risks, which would be inappropriate. An interpretation that would require business enterprises to report its human rights impacts that occur outside of the territory of the EU as well, and how it manages these seems necessary for the *effet utile* of the Directive. Apart from serving the *effet utile* of the Directive, a purposeful interpretation would be consistent with the expectations set out in the UNGPs, which companies may rely on to comply with the requirements. The UNGPs define human rights due diligence as a regulatory responsibility for business enterprises that transcends the territorial boundaries of a State and extends to the undertaking or group's business relationships, products and services and the human rights impacts directly linked thereto, anywhere in the world.

In order to ensure the effective application of the Directive in light of the objective that companies should provide a 'fair and comprehensive' view of their respect for human rights, the disclosure should thus include information on the company's or group's human rights policies, outcomes and risks, including the potential and actual human rights risks that are located outside the EU and how these are managed. A purposeful interpretation of the Directive in accordance with the aforementioned objective entails that the applicable scope of the disclosure requirements laid down in the Directive extends outside the EU.

The potential extension of the effects of the Directive's application outside the EU would be consistent with a wider trend within EU law. As noted by Scott, 'extraterritoriality is a phenomenon that is both tolerated by the EU and that is increasingly practiced in its name'.[105] More precisely, commentators have noted that the CJEU has not flinched from adopting a purposeful interpretation and recognizing the extraterritorial applicability of certain EU Regulations, *inter alia*, in the area of welfare requirements for animals.

The CJEU delivered a preliminary ruling on 23 April 2015 in the case *Zuchtvieh-Expert GmbH v. Stadt Kempten*,[106] in which the court held that the requirements under Regulation No 1/2005 on the protection of animals during transport and related operations[107] were applicable outside the EU. The Court noted that Regulation No 1/2005 is based on Protocol (No 33) on protection and welfare of animals, which is annexed to the Treaty. The substance of this Protocol is to be found in Article 13 TFEU, which is a provision of general application of the TFEU treaty. Article 13 TFEU indicates that the Community and the Member States, in formulating and implementing the Community's policies on, *inter alia*, agriculture and transport, should have regard to the welfare requirements of animals. The Court also noted that the provisions of the Regulation should be interpreted and applied in accordance with the basic principle established in Recital 5 and 11 of the Regulation in question, according to which 'animals must not be transported in a way likely to cause injury or undue suffering to them, considering that, for reasons of animal welfare, the transport of animals over long journeys should be limited as far as possible'.[108]

The CJEU considered that Regulation No 1/2005 is applicable to all stages of a long journey for animals concerned that commences in the territory of the EU but ends outside that territory, including those stages of the journey that take place on the territory of one or more third countries. The Court furthermore considered that Article 14(1) of the Regulation should be interpreted as meaning that an authority of the place of departure may grant acceptance of transport only if the journal log submitted to that authority is realistic and indicates that the provisions of the regulation will be complied with, 'including for the stages of the journey which are to take place in the territory of third countries'. The authority may require changes to those arrangements to ensure compliance with the provisions of the Regulation throughout the journey.[109]

In addition, the CJEU delivered a preliminary ruling regarding the scope of the prohibition of marketing laid down in provision 18(1)(b) of Regulation 1223/2009 on cosmetic products[110] (the 'Cosmetics Regulation'). This provision of the Cosmetics Regulation prohibits the marketing of products that incorporate ingredients that have undergone animal testing in third countries. The CJEU applied a purposive interpretation and held that this article must be interpreted as prohibiting the marketing of cosmetic products containing some ingredients that have been subject to animal testing outside the EU in order to meet the legislative requirement of third countries and to market the products in those countries.[111] The Court noted that, pursuant to case law, 'when a provision of EU law is interpreted, it is necessary to consider not only its wording but also the context in which it occurs and the objectives pursued by the rules of which it is part'.[112]

The aim of the Directive is to 'comprehensively harmonize the rules in the Community in order to achieve an internal market for cosmetic products while ensuring a high level of protection of human health'. The Court also noted that certain rules of the Regulation are intended to establish a level of animal protection in the cosmetic sector that exceeds that applicable in other sectors. In this light, the Court noted that article 18(1)(b) 'makes no distinction depending on where the animal testing at issue was carried out' and that '[t]he introduction, by interpretation, of such a distinction would be contrary to the objective relating to animal protection pursued by Regulation No 1223/2009 in general and by Article 18 in particular'.[113] The court held that allowing prohibited animal testing outside the EU would seriously compromise the attainment of the objective of the Regulation to actively promote the use of non-animal alternative methods to ensure the safety of products in the cosmetics sector.

The scope of the disclosure requirements

The exact scope of the requirements to disclose on human rights risks laid down in Article 19a(d) and Article 29a(d) is not well defined. However, such scope is important to determine the information companies should include in their non-financial statements. Undertakings may be exposed to legal liability under national law in case they failed to provide this information. The Article indicates that business enterprises should disclose their 'principal' risks and the adverse human rights impacts that are linked to an undertaking's relationships that are 'relevant and proportionate'.[114] The Directive adopts an approach to delimiting the scope of the disclosure obligations, which, as outlined below, aligns with that of the UNGPs, by focusing disclosure on information about matters that pose significant human rights risks.

The UNGPs provide some guidance but also are not unambiguous about the point where the due diligence responsibility of business enterprises ends. The SRSG has noted more generally that the scope of a company's responsibility to respect human rights is 'defined by the actual and potential human rights impacts generated through a company's own business activities and through its relationships with other parties, such as business partners, entities in its value chain, other non-State actors and State agents'.[115] The commentary to UNGP 17 recognizes that it may be 'unreasonably difficult' for business enterprises with complex supply chains involving a large number of entities to conduct human rights due diligence for all these entities.[116] In order to ensure that human rights due diligence does not impose a too heavy burden on companies, business enterprises 'should identify general areas where the risk of adverse human rights impact is most significant [...] and prioritise these for human rights due diligence'.[117]

Human rights issues thus should be prioritized in accordance with the significance of the adverse human rights risks of the company. Accordingly, the duty to disclose in the context of supply chains entails a focus on human rights issues or topics. The relevance of these human rights issues must be determined according to the issues that pose the most significant risks of adverse human rights impacts. Accordingly, it follows that the responsibility to disclose in the context of supply chains, in terms of content disclosure, should be determined in light of the nature and significance of potential adverse human rights impacts.

Recital 8 of the Directive stipulates that companies must disclose on matters that are 'most likely' to bring about the materialization or actual occurrence of 'principal' risks. The Directive aligns with the UNGPs when setting the condition that whether risks reach the threshold of 'principal' risks and thus should be disclosed in the non-financial statement, depends on the severity of these impacts, which relates to their scale and gravity:

> The undertakings which are subject to this Directive should provide adequate information in relation to matters that stand out as being most likely to bring about the materialisation of principal risks of severe impacts, along with those that have already materialised. The severity of such impacts should be judged by their scale and gravity. The risks of adverse impact may stem from the undertaking's own activities or may be linked to its operations, and, where relevant and proportionate, its products, services and business relationships, including its supply and subcontracting chains.

If the formulations of 'relevant and proportionate' would be interpreted in conformity with the concepts of the UNGPs, assessments of what would meet the threshold of 'relevant and proportionate' would be based on human rights. What counts as 'relevant' is information that reflects the human rights risks that arise through business relations and that meet a minimum threshold of 'severity' and 'significance'. The reference to the 'principal risks' suggests that, if such human rights risks exist, business enterprises must prioritize and disclose information that is *most* significant. Important is the target group, in that information must be judged based on its significance to right-holders. That what counts as 'relevant' is information on principal risks that have materialized and the human rights issues that are most likely to materialize into principal human rights risks.

Extraterritorial (indirect) regulatory effects

As a consequence of the disclosure requirements being construed on the due diligence concept and the scope of application extending to operations and adverse human rights impacts irrespective of whether these occurred at home or abroad, the Directive takes on potential *extraterritorial* (indirect) regulatory effects. This is important because the legal responsibilities of business enterprises for human rights often are delimited by national boundaries. The mismatch between the national reach of State legal systems and the activities of business enterprises that reach transnationally and are subject to the regulation of more than one jurisdiction is a well-known regulatory challenge in the area of business and human rights.[118] The extraterritorial indirect regulatory effects of the

Directive can have positive impacts on the human rights performance of individual undertakings and groups. The Directive provides a regulatory response to resolving supply chain challenges that EU businesses are facing in their operations and value chains throughout the EU and third countries.[119]

The parent undertaking that is subject to the Directive must report on all operations and relationships of undertakings within the group, irrespective of geographical location. Consequently, a parent entity must not only consider their own activities, operations and human rights impacts, but also subsidiary entities and business relationships connected to its activities. The Directive in and by itself does not require that undertakings actually exercise due diligence to manage the human rights risks linked to its operations. It merely requires the disclosure of their policies and human rights due diligence or, in case the undertaking does not pursue one, to provide a clear and reasoned explanation for why this is the case.[120] The requirements to disclose human rights nevertheless confirm the existence of and expectation that companies should have a minimum level of understanding and take action as appropriate to its circumstances to manage the human rights risks that are linked to the company's or group's operations through its business relationships.

The Directive recognizes that the legal duty of undertakings to disclose reaches the company's operations and the human rights risks linked thereto, irrespective of whether these operations and risks are located at home or abroad. The process of disclosure potentially promotes internal awareness and drives companies to act, especially if the parent conducts enquiries in order to obtain this minimum level of information. The public disclosure of information may expose the company to external pressure and costs may be inflicted on the company where stakeholders decide on the basis of the company's performance and impacts. In this respect, the disclosure requirements may have the effect in practice of encouraging undertakings and groups to assess and regulate the activities of subsidiary entities or other business relationships down their supply and subcontracting chains to know the potential and actual human rights risks in which they may be involved in order to disclose these risks and how they manage these risks.

Conclusion

The Directive, in short, intends to serve as a regulatory tool that can induce business reporting and performance that corresponds with the expectations of the UNGPs. The focus of the preceding pages was on the potential of the Directive to affect transparency and reporting on human rights by EU businesses in practice and ensure that business enterprises disclose information to which stakeholders can resort in order to meaningfully assess human rights-compliant behaviour against internationally recognized standards, and the UNGPs in particular.[121] More precisely, this chapter explored the connections between the approaches of the Directive to defining the scope of the application, obligation and required substance and the human rights due diligence concept. The previous analysis suggests that the adoption by the EU of disclosure requirements for certain companies on human rights due diligence, while being a welcome development, nonetheless provides only a partial response to the UNGPs, and in certain aspects, may even restrict EU Member States in their implementation of the UNGPs.

The chapter analysed the so-called 'indirect' and 'direct' of the Directive. It concluded with regards to the 'indirect effect' of the Directive that, while EU law mandates national disclosure obligations to be interpreted in the light of the Directive and in the light of EU protected fundamental rights, the content of the Directive itself and, in particular, the 'comply or explain' modality, might not necessarily further the cause of those stakeholders intending to rely on the Directive for the purpose of obtaining enhanced disclosure from corporations. It was argued that the Directive is unlikely to acquire direct effect, not necessarily because it is a Directive, but because its provisions on mandatory disclosure are unlikely to be considered by the CJEU as 'clear and unconditional and not contingent on any discretionary implementing measure'.[122] Perhaps more importantly, to the extent that such direct effect is framed as obligations for (non-publicly owned) corporations vis-à-vis stakeholders (NGOs, shareholders, etc.), it would be hard for the Directive to overcome the CJEU's prohibition of direct effect of Directives.[123]

Which is not to say that the Directive will not have *any* legal effects. Apart from the indirect effects referred to in the preceding paragraph, stakeholders might file a complaint for a breach of EU law before the European Commission in order for the Commission to bring an action against the Member State in question before the CJEU pursuant to Article 258 TFEU. All in all, by enacting the Directive, the EU opted for a *type of legal instrument* which has potentially sweeping implications in the rights of stakeholders when it comes to the disclosure obligations of corporations. However, irrespective of the *type* of instrument chosen, and as noted in the preceding section in relation to the 'comply or explain' example, it is uncertain whether the *content* of the Directive will contribute to further the rights of stakeholders.

More precisely, the Directive does not articulate human rights due diligence to a great level of detail, leaves (too much) flexibility for companies to decide what information to disclose, and creates exceptions that allow business enterprises to abide by the minimum disclosure requirements without actually disclosing any substantive information on their respect for human rights. A prominent example of the Directive's flaws is the 'comply or explain' principle, allowing undertakings not to disclose information regarding their human rights policies in case an undertaking does not pursue one, and to provide a clear and reasoned explanation for why this is the case instead.[124] Also, as noted above, the Directive appears more responsive to mandating disclosure on human rights policies and risks than on actual outcomes. The undertakings may be exempted from their obligation to disclose on actual outcomes if they meet certain conditions.[125] It was argued that too much flexibility for corporations in meeting their disclosure requirements risks easing the disclosure requirements on undertakings to an extent that the potential effect of the Directive on human rights compliant conduct by business enterprises becomes diluted.

This chapter also argued that the Directive, in the light of its objectives and pursuant to well-established case law supporting a purposive interpretation of secondary EU legislation should have certain extraterritorial effects. More precisely, as a consequence of the reporting requirements not drawing a distinction as regard to the location of the human rights impacts and these requirements being construed on the human rights due diligence concept, the Directive carries potential *extraterritorial* (indirect) regulatory effects. The disclosure requirements can serve as a means to induce undertakings to carry out human rights due diligence, which also entails having regard for the conduct of subcontractors and entities in their supply chains that may be causing adverse human rights impacts.[126]

In short, the Directive has provided the conditions and conceptual anchors to foster State practices to lift transparency on human rights to higher levels, but still depends on these EU Member States to take it further. Case law suggests that international human rights law imposes a legal duty on States to do so.

Notes

1 Directive 2014/95/EU of the European Parliament and of the Council of 22 October 2014 amending Directive 2013/34/EU as regards disclosure of non-financial and diversity information by certain large undertakings and groups, 2014/95/EU, 2014 O.J. (L 330) 1 [hereinafter *Non-Financial Reporting Directive*].

2 Directive 2013/34/EU of the European Parliament and of the Council of 26 June 2013 on the annual financial statements, consolidated financial statements and related reports of certain types of undertakings, amending Directive 2006/43/EC of the European Parliament and of the Council and repealing Council Directives 78/660/EEC and 83/349/EEC, 2013 O.J. (L 182) 19 [hereinafter *Accounting Directive*].

3 Ultimately, if reporting is refocused to address a number of key criteria, it can lead to improved human rights performance, thereby creating both internal systems and the accountability mechanisms needed to anticipate and address human rights harms and to communicate these efforts effectively.

Amol Mehra & Sara Blackwell, *The Rise of Non-Financial Disclosure: Reporting on Respect for Human Rights*, *in* Business and Human Rights: From Principles to Practice, 276 (Dorothée Baumann-Pauly & Justine Nolan eds. 2016)

4 Special Representative on the Issue of Human Rights and Transnational Corporations and Other Business Enterprises, *Guiding Principles on Business and Human Rights: Implementing the United Nations 'Protect, Respect and Remedy' Framework*. U.N.Doc. A/HRC/17/31, UNGP 3 (21 Mar. 2011) (by John Ruggie) [hereinafter *UNGPs*].

5 Transparency thus also contributes to the goal set out in Article 3(3) of the Treaty of the European Union to establish an internal market and sustainable development based on 'a highly competitive sustainable market economy'. TEU, Article 3(3). The terms Commission and EU have sometimes been used interchangeably in the

light of the Commission's leading role in EU policies in relation to CSR and business and human rights.

6 *Communication from the Commission to the European Parliament, the Council, the European Economic and Social Committee and the Committee of the Regions: A Renewed EU strategy 2011–14 for Corporate Social Responsibility*, at 12, COM (2011) 681 final (25 Oct. 2011) [hereinafter *A renewed EU CSR Strategy*].

7 *Communication from the Commission to the European Parliament, the Council, the Economic and Social Committee and the Committee of the Regions: Single Market Act Twelve Levers to Boost Growth and Strengthen Confidence 'Working Together to Create New Growth'*, at 5, COM(2011) 206 final (13 Apr. 2011).

8 *Id.* at 14–15.

9 *A Renewed EU CSR Strategy*, *supra* note 6, at 12.

10 *Communication from the Commission to the European Parliament, the Council, the European Central Bank, the Economic and Social Committee, the Committee of the Regions and the European Data Protection Supervisor: 'Responsible Businesses' Package*, COM(2011) 685 final (25 Oct. 2011).

11 This proposal outlined regulatory requirements for certain large undertakings and groups to disclose their non-financial performance as regards, amongst others, respect for human rights, in their annual and consolidated financial statements and related reports. *Proposal for a Directive of the European Parliament and of the Council amending Council Directives 78/660/EEC and 83/349/EEC as Regards Disclosure of Non-financial and Diversity Information by Certain Large Companies and Groups*, COM(2013) 207 final (16 Apr. 2013) [hereinafter *Proposal Non-Financial Disclosure Directive*].

12 In its Resolution entitled 'Corporate social responsibility: accountable, transparent and responsible business behaviour and sustainable growth' of 6 February 2013, the European Parliament expressed its support for the adoption of a legislative proposal

> allowing for high flexibility of action, in order to take account of CSR's multidimensional nature and the diversity of the CSR policies implemented by businesses, matched by a sufficient level of comparability to meet the needs of investors and other stakeholders as well as the need to provide consumers with easy access to information on businesses' impact on society.
>
> Resolution on Corporate Social Responsibility: Accountable, Transparent and Responsible Business Behaviour and Sustainable Growth, Eur. Parl. Doc. P7 TA(2013) 0049 (6 Feb. 2013)

Also *see* Resolution on Corporate Social Responsibility: Promoting Society's Interests and a Route to Sustainable and Inclusive Recovery, Eur. Parl. Doc. P7 TA(2013) 0050 (3 Feb. 2013).

13 The European Parliament has been a staunch supporter of a regulatory approach to CSR. The European Parliament issued a critical report on the theme of business and human rights in 2009, stipulating that a legal turn to CSR was 'most necessary' to advance the business and human rights agenda. Amongst a variety of policy recommendations, the report suggested the development of a legal framework for foreign investment protection that ensures, next to investor protections, accountability for human rights violations, mandatory reporting on human rights performance, regulated benchmarks on CSR and the establishment of accountability mechanisms in EU external relations that target business enterprises directly, rather than only States. It also emphasized that the EU should strengthen accountability for corporate human rights violations by working towards the establishment of 'victim-oriented accountability and redress mechanisms on a global scale', including an EU-wide ombudsman. *European Parliament Business and Human Rights in External Relations: Making the EU a Leader at Home and Internationally*, at 81, EXPO/B/

DROI/2009/2, PE407.014 (23 Apr. 2009), www.europarl.europa.eu/RegData/etudes/etudes/join/2009/407014/ EXPO-DROI_ET(2009)407014_EN.pdf.

14 *Non-Financial Reporting Directive*, *supra* note 1.

15 Communication from the Commission Guidelines on non-financial reporting (methodology for reporting non-financial information), 2017, O.J. (C 215) 1.

16 *Proposal Non-Financial Disclosure Directive*, *supra* note 11, Recital 3.

17 *Id.* at 2–3.

18 Nicola Jägers, *Will Transnational Private Regulation Close the Governance Gap?*, *in* Human Rights Obligations of Business: Beyond the Corporate Responsibility to Respect?, 295, 315 (Surya Deva & David Bilchitz eds. 2013).

19 *Id.* at 295, 315.

20 According to Olivier de Schutter:

> Potentially most important of all, however, is the fact that the 'business case' for CSR produces, at the rhetorical level, a powerful consequence: it serves to create the impression that the development of CSR will make natural progress, in a sort of evolutionary growth driven by market mechanisms, without such progress having to be encouraged or artificially produced by an intervention of public authorities. There is a very thin line between the idea that 'CSR is profitable for business' and the idea that 'CSR may take care of itself'. This consequence should be avoided at all costs. There is a need, clearly identifiable, for a regulatory framework to be established, if CSR is to work. This is not in contradiction with the voluntary character of CSR. On the contrary, it attaches its meaning to voluntary commitments.
>
> Olivier de Schutter, *Corporate Social Responsibility: European Style*, 14 European Law Journal, 219 (2008)

21 *Id.* 219, 232.

22 Earlier proposals to amend the 4th and 7th Council Directive to create obligations for business enterprises to disclose in their annual review on environmental, social, and other aspects relevant to an undertaking of the company's development and position had been abandoned. On this issue, *see id.* 203, 231.

23 Directive 2006/46/EC of the European Parliament and of the Council of 14 June 2006 amending Council Directives 78/660/EEC on the annual accounts of certain types of companies, 83/349/EEC on consolidated accounts, 86/635/EEC on the annual accounts and consolidated accounts of banks and other financial institutions and 91/674/EEC on the annual accounts and consolidated accounts of insurance undertakings, Recital 10, 2006/46/EC, 2006 O.J. (L 224) 1.

24 *Proposal Non-Financial Disclosure Directive*, *supra* note 11, at 12.

25 *Id.* at 12; Jägers, *supra* note 18, 315.

26 *Non-Financial Reporting Directive*, *supra* note 1, Recital 21.

27 Liesbeth Enneking, et al., *Zorgplichten van Nederlandse ondernemingen inzake international maatschappelijk verantwoord ondernemen: Een rechtsvergelijkend and empirisch onderzoek naar de stand van het Nederlandse recht in licht van de UN Guiding Principles*, 624 (Boom Juridisch 2016).

28 Louise Gullifer & Jennifer Payne, Corporate Finance Law: Principles and Policy, 523–540 (2nd ed., Hart Publishing 2015).

29 Nicola Jägers notes how NGOs can use this information to pressure companies to join private or hybrid regulatory initiatives and to comply with the standard set out therein, to which companies have committed themselves when joining. The availability of information becomes of greater importance where the monitoring and verification mechanisms that these initiatives have in place are insufficient in themselves to ensure that relevant information is available to stakeholders. The availability of information, hence, is also critical for the effectiveness of these transnational private initiatives. Jägers, *supra* note 18, at 315.

30 GRI, *Making Headway in Europe: Linking GRI's G4 Guidelines and the European Directive on Nonfinancial Disclosure and Diversity Disclosure*, at 3 (2015).
31 Other benefits for companies related thereto include enhanced trust, brand value and responsiveness to stakeholders. *Proposal Non-Financial Disclosure Directive*, *supra* note 11, § 5.2. A study based on an analysis of the cost/benefit assessment of mandatory reporting requirements showed that European companies perceived identifying and controlling risks an important, although not the most important, benefit of transparency. The companies said that the main benefits of transparency were enhancing the credibility of the company and improving transparency of reporting. Also, enhancing the brand image of products was considered very important, while improvements to internal culture and the ability to react with stakeholders were considered important. *European Commission Disclosure of Nonfinancial Information by Companies (Final Report)*, at 27–30 (Dec. 2011), http://ec.europa.eu/finance/accounting/docs/non-financial-reporting/com_2013_207-study_en.pdf.
32 A *Renewed EU CSR Strategy*, *supra* note 6, at 11.
33 *Proposal Non-Financial Disclosure Directive*, *supra* note 11, at 6.2.3.
34 Jägers, *supra* note 18, 308.
35 *Non-Financial Reporting Directive*, *supra* note 1, Recital 3.
36 *Proposal Non-Financial Disclosure Directive*, *supra* note 11, at 2.
37 *Non-Financial Reporting Directive*, *supra* note 1, Recital 14.
38 *Accounting Directive*, *supra* note 2, Article 3.4.
39 *Id.*
40 *Non-Financial Reporting Directive*, *supra* note 1, Recital 5.
41 *Id.*
42 *Id.* Recital 5, ¶ 2.
43 Recital 6 affirms that 'the non-financial statement should also include information on the due diligence processes implemented by the undertaking, also regarding, where relevant and proportionate, its supply and subcontracting chains, in order to identify, prevent and mitigate existing and potential adverse impacts'. *Id.* Recital 6, 2014 O.J. (L 330) 1.
44 *Id.*
45 *Id.* Article 19a, ¶ 2.
46 This resonates with UNGP 21, which recognizes that severe human rights risks can give rise to an elevated responsibility to disclose – that is, to disclose formally. *UNGPs*, *supra* note 4, GP 21.
47 *Non-Financial Reporting Directive*, *supra* note 1, Article 19a. 1(d).
48 To be noted is Recital 6, which reflects the conceptual influence of the UNGPs on the Directive, indicating that 'the non-financial statement should also include information on the due diligence processes implemented by the undertaking, also regarding, where relevant and proportionate, its supply and subcontracting chains, in order to identify, prevent and mitigate existing and potential adverse impacts'. *Id.* Recital 6.
49 *Non-Financial Reporting Directive*, *supra* note 1, Article 4.1.
50 Recital 1 of the Directive notes 'the possibility for Member States to require, as appropriate, further improvements to the transparency of undertakings' non-financial information, which is by its nature a continuous endeavor'. *Id.*, Recital 1.
51 Case 44/84, Hurd, 1986, E.C.R. 29, ¶ 47.
52 Case 91/92, Faccini Dori, 1994, E.C.R. 3325.
53 *See* P. Craig & G. De Búrca, EU Law: Text, Cases and Materials, 200 (Oxford University Press 5th ed. 2011). *See* further, T. Hartley, The Foundations of European Union Law, at 235 (Oxford University Press 8th ed. 2014) and R. Schütze, European Union Law, at 105 (Cambridge University Press 2015).
54 *See* K Lenaerts & P. Van Nuffel, European Union Law, ¶ 21–007 (Sweet & Maxwell 3rd ed. 2011).

55 *Id.*, referring, *inter alia*, to Case 106/98, Marleasing, 1990, E.C.R. 4135, ¶ 8 and Case 60/02, Criminal Proceedings against X, 2004, E.C.R. 651, ¶¶ 59–60.
56 *See* Case 14/83, Von Colson and Kamann, 1984, E.C.R. 1891.
57 *See* Case 212/04, Adelener, 2006, E.C.R. 6057.
58 *See Non-Financial Reporting Directive*, *supra* note 1, Article 4(1).
59 *See* Case 129/96 *Inter-Environnement Wallonie v. Région Wallone*, 1997, E.C.R. 7411.
60 *See* Case 212/04 Adeneler, 2006, E.C.R. 6057, ¶¶ 107–124. *See* Craig & De Búrca, *supra* note 53, at 200. See further, Hartley, *supra* note 53, at 239 and Schütze, *supra* note 53, at 105.
61 *Non-Financial Reporting Directive*, *supra* note 1, Recital 21.
62 The Directive notes that

> EU Member States should ensure that effective national procedures are in place to enforce compliance with the obligations laid down by this Directive, and that those procedures are available to all persons and legal entities having a legitimate interest, in accordance with national law, in ensuring that the provisions of this Directive are respected.
>
> *Id*. Recital 10

63 Emphasis added.
64 *See*, *inter alia*, Cases 305/05, Ordre des barreaux francophones, 2007, E.C.R. 5305., ¶ 28 and Cases 386/08 Brita, NYR, ¶ 39 and Case 63/09 Walz [NYR], ¶ 22.
65 *See* Case 5–88, Wahchauf, 1989, E.C.R. 2609, ¶ 19. *See* Lenaerts & Van Nuffel, *supra* note 54, ¶ 21–007.
66 *UNGPs*, *supra* note 4, GP 3.
67 *See* Case 106/98, Marleasing, 1990, E.C.R. 4135. The only limit to this applicability would be that individuals would not be able to rely on the Directive in order to obtain the imposition or aggravation of criminal liability on individuals, *see* Case 60/02, Criminal Proceedings against X, 2004, E.C.R. 651. *See* further Craig & De Búrca, *supra* note 53, at 200. See further, Hartley, *supra* note 53, at 204, and R. Schütze, *supra* note 53, at 105.
68 *Guerra and Others v. Italy*, App. No. 14967/89, Eur. H.R. Rep. 1998-I (1998).
69 *Guerra and Others v. Italy*, *id* ¶ 53. Also *see Leander v. Sweden*, App. No. 9248/81, Eur. Ct.H.R (1987), ¶ 74. *Gillberg v. Sweden*, App. No. 41723/06, Eur. Ct. H.R. (2012), ¶ 83.
70 *Guerra and Others v. Italy*, App. No. 14967/89, Eur. H.R. Rep. 1998-I (1998), ¶ 53.
71 *Kennedy v. The Charity Commission* [2014] UKSC 20, [217].
72 *Guerra and Others v. Italy*, App. No. 14967/89, Eur. H.R. Rep. 1998-I (1998).
73 *Youth Initiative for Human Rights v. Serbia*, App. No. 48135/06, Eur. Ct. H.R. (2013), ¶ 20.
74 *Non-Financial Reporting Directive*, *supra* note 1, Recital 1.
75 *Id.*
76 *See* Dániel Gergely Szabó & Karsten Engsig Sørensen, *New EU Directive on the Disclosure of Non-Financial Information (CSR)*, 12 European Company and Financial Law Review 3, 307–340 (2015).
77 Commission Recommendation of 9 April 2014 on the quality of corporate governance reporting ('comply or explain'), 2014 O.J. (L 109) 43.
78 Or, more precisely, without the need, in the so-called 'dualist' countries from the perspective of classic International law, to adopt a domestic measure giving effects to the provision in question from International/European law. *See* Schütze, *supra* note 53, at 76.
79 *See* Craig & De Búrca, *supra* 53, at 181 and 200. See further, Hartley, *supra* note 53, at 235 and R. Schütze, *supra* note 53, at 209.
80 *See* Case 41/74, Van Duyn, 1974, E.C.R. 1337.

81 *See*, *inter alia*, Case 26/62, Van Gend en Loos, 1963, E.C.R. 1 (1963); Case 2/74 *Reyners v. Belgium*, 1974, E.C.R. 631; Case 43/75, *Defrenne v. Sabena*, 1976, E.C.R. 455; Case 36/74, *Walrave v. Association Union Cycliste International*, 1974, E.C.R. 1405; Case 126/86, *Zaera v. Instituto Nacionale de la Seguridad Social*, 1987, E.C.R. 3697.

82 Lenaerts and Van Nuffel indicate that the CJEU 'has not invariably formulated the test in the same way', *see* Lenaerts & Van Nuffel, *supra* note 54, ¶ 21–056.

83 This is how the test for direct effect was formulated in Case 44/84 Hurd, 1986, E.C.R. 29, ¶ 47.

84 Case 91/92 Faccini Dori, 1994, E.C.R. 3325.

85 Case 152/84 *Marshall v. Southampton*, 1986, E.C.R. 723. *See further*, Schütze, *supra* note 53, at 98.

86 An undertaking that is subject to the Directive may qualify as a 'State' by application of the *Foster* criteria. The CJEU in *Foster v. British Gas* held that 'State' ought to be construed widely, and encompasses within its scope

> a body, whatever its legal form, which has been made responsible, pursuant to a measure adopted by the State, for providing a public service under the control of a State and has for that purpose special powers beyond those which result from the normal rules applicable in relations between individuals.

See Case 188/89 Foster, 1990, E.C.R. 3313, for a recent confirmation of the test *see* Case 180/04, Vasallo, 2006, E.C.R. 7235. *See* Schütze, *supra* note 53, at 100 and Craig & De Búrca, *supra* note 53, at 196.

87 *See*, *e.g.* Case 194/94 *CIA Security International SA v. Signalson*, 1996, E.C.R. 2201 and Case 443/98, Unilever, 2000, E.C.R. 7535.

88 *See* Craig & De Búrca, *supra* note 53, at 200, *see* further Schütze, *supra* note 53, at 101.

89 *See* Cases 6/90 and C-9/90 Francovich and others, 1991, E.C.R. 5357, ¶¶ 39–41.

90 *See* Case 144/04 *Mangold v. Rüdiger Helm*, 2005, E.C.R. I-9981.

91 *See* Case 435/05 *International Transport Workers' Federation and Finnish Seamen's Union v. Viking Line ABP and OÜ Viking Line Eesti*, 2007, E.C.R. I-10779. *See* further Craig & De Búrca, *supra* note 53, at 189.

92 This was the case, *e.g.* in Case 205/98, *Commission v. Austria*, 2000. *See* further K. Lenaerts, et al., EU Procedural Law, ¶ 5–05 (Sweet & Maxwell 2014).

93 *Non-Financial Reporting Directive*, *supra* note 1, Recital 3.

94 Directive 2013/34 EC applies a similar 'comply or explain' principle, setting out the requirement that companies provide in their corporate governance statements an explanation of the part of the corporate governance code they depart from. Research showed that, in practice, undertakings that were subject to this requirement tended not to disclose as they should, giving invalid, general or false explanations. *See* Szabó & Sørensen, *supra* note 76, at 12. This prompted the EU Commission to issue guidance and to assist companies in improving the quality of these explanations. Commission Recommendation of 9 April 2014 on the quality of corporate governance reporting ('comply or explain'), 2014 O.J. (L 109) 43.

95 *Non-Financial Reporting Directive*, *supra* note 1, Article 19a 4, Recital 6. In the case of the parent undertaking, this report must refer to the whole group. *See* id. Article 29a 4.

96 *Id.* Articles 19a.4. 29a.4.

97 *Id.* Articles 19a.3. 29a.3.

98 *Non-Financial Reporting Directive*, *supra* note 1, Recital 6.

99 *See* Craig & De Búrca, *supra* note 53, at 64. *See* further Hartley, *supra* note 53, at 72,73, and Schütze, *supra* note 53, at 206–207.

100 *See*, Case 280/04, Jyske Finans, 2005, E.C.R. I-10683, ¶¶ 31–44.

101 *See*, Case 434/97, *Commission v. France*, 2000, ECR I-1129, ¶ 21.
102 Case 592/14, *European Federation for Cosmetic Ingredients v. Secretary of State for Business, Innovation and Skills*, 2015 E.C.R. 081/10 [31].
103 *Non-Financial Reporting Directive*, *supra* note 1, Recital 21.
104 *Id.*
105 Joanne Scott, *Extraterritoriality and Territorial Extension in EU Law*, 62 American Journal of Comparative Law 1 (2014). *See* further Note, *Developments in the Law of Extraterritoriality*, 124 Harvard Law Review 1226 (2011).
106 Case 424/13, *Zuchtvieh-Export GmbH v. Stadt Kempten*, 2015 E.C.R. 259.
107 Council Regulation (EC) No 1/2005 of 22 December 2004 on the protection of animals during transport and related operations and amending Directives 64/432/EEC and 93/119/EC and Regulation (EC) No 1255/97, 2005, O.J. (L 3) 1, at 1–44.
108 *Id.* ¶ 3.
109 *Id.* ¶ 56.
110 Regulation (EC) No 1223/2009 of the European Parliament and of the Council of 30 November 2009 on cosmetic products (Text with EEA relevance), O.J. (L 342), 59.
111 Case 592/14, *European Federation for Cosmetic Ingredients v. Secretary of State for Business, Innovation and Skills*, 2015 E.C.R. 081/10.
112 *Id.* ¶ 31.
113 *Id.* ¶ 41.
114 *Non-Financial Reporting Directive*, *supra* note 1, Art. 19a. 1(d).
115 Special Representative on the Issue of Human Rights and Transnational Corporations and Other Business Enterprises, Business and human rights: further steps toward the operationalization of the 'protect, respect and remedy' framework, § 58, U.N. doc. A/HRC/14/27 (9 Apr. 2010) (by John Ruggie).
116 *Id.* Commentary to GP 17.
117 *Id.*
118 Peter Muchlinski, *Implementing the New UN Corporate Human Rights Framework: Implications for Corporate Law, Governance, and Regulation*, 22 Business Ethics Quarterly 145, 145 (2012).
119 European Commission, Responsible Supply Chain Management: Potential Success Factors and Challenges for Addressing Prevailing Human Rights and other CSR issues in Supply Chains of EU-based Companies, 88 (2011).
120 *Non-Financial Reporting Directive*, *supra* note 1, Art. 19a.2., Art. 29a.2.
121 *UNGPs*, *supra* note 4, GP 21.
122 Case 44/84, Hurd, 1986, E.C.R. 29, ¶ 47.
123 Case 91/92, Faccini Dori, 1994, E.C.R. 3325.
124 *Non-Financial Reporting Directive*, *supra* note 1, Article 19a.2., Article 29a.2.
125 *Id.* Recital 6.
126 According to Buhmann, human rights reporting may function along the lines of 'reflexive law', meaning that 'the process of developing the report will generate insight on stakeholder views and social expectations as well as the firm's performance, which companies may apply for self-regulatory purposes'. K. Buhmann, *Defying Territorial Limitations: Regulating Business Conduct Extraterritorially through Establishing Obligations*, *in* EU law and national law in Human Rights and Business: Direct Corporate Accountability for Human Rights, 281, 292 (Jernej Letnar Černič & Tara Van Ho eds. 2015).

Conclusion

This book examined the interaction between CSR, human rights and the law. It focused on the shared definition of the corporate responsibility to respect human rights, as defined by the UNGPs, which the HRC 'endorsed' in 2011. This responsibility is recognized to exist, not as a legally binding standard founded in international human rights law, but rather as a standard of conduct founded on social expectations, more specifically 'a standard of expected conduct acknowledged in virtually every voluntary and soft-law instrument related to corporate responsibility'. While this norm is thus not legally binding in a strict legal sense, this 'soft' norm is not without legal effects. The UNGPs place corporate respect for human rights at the centre of a system of polycentric governance, which is intended to maximize the effectiveness of human rights, not only, but not in the least by crystalizing into new legislation.

The SRSG's 'principled pragmatism' deliberately intends to transcend classic legality with a focus on the effectiveness of human rights. As noted by Mares, the SRSG saw in the notion of 'polycentric governance', 'the way forward to advance the cause of human rights in the global economy'.[1] According to the SRSG, in application of the notion of 'polycentric governance', there are three systems that develop CSR standards: (i) the public governance system, encompassing law and policy; (ii) the corporate governance system, reflecting risk management and (iii) the civil governance system, reflecting social expectations of stakeholders.[2] In a nutshell, the SRSG concluded, 'the [UNGPs] prescribe paths for strengthening and better aligning these governance systems in relation to business and human rights. They aim to generate a mutually reinforcing dynamic that produces cumulative change'.[3]

As also noted by Mares, the SRSG aimed at moving 'to a critical mass by leveraging as many sources of authority as possible and getting them to interact in a process of cumulative progress' since 'if one would be tempted to boil down to one word [the SRSG]'s mandate, that word would be "leverage". The SRSG's quest, then, for cumulative progress would be explained as an effort to maximize that leverage through the activation and combination of all sources of leverage"'.[4] The UNGPs thus provide an authoritative framework that, once embedded in policy and practise, should foster a new regulatory dynamic under which the public and private governance systems (public, civil and corporate) become better aligned and perform mutually reinforcing roles in relation to business and human rights. According to the SRSG, 'a more comprehensive and effective global regime' may evolve out of this dynamic, 'including specific legal measures'.[5]

Also according to the SRSG, 'the successful expansion of the international human rights regime to encompass business enterprises must activate and mobilize the full array of rationales and institutional means that affect corporate conduct. That is what the [UNGPs] seek to do.'[6] The General Principles of the UNGPs thus establishes a link between the UNGPs and these objectives, by stating in its third paragraph that

> these Guiding Principles [...] should be read, individually and collectively, in terms of their objective of enhancing standards and practices with regard to business and human rights so as to achieve tangible results for affected individuals and communities, and thereby also contributing to socially sustainable globalization.[7]

A broad convergence exists around the UNGPs, which provides a foundation that future efforts can built on.[8,9] This book has argued that the corporate responsibility to respect human rights, as it is currently conceived, should further evolve. Consequently, while this norm may not be legally binding in its inception, this responsibility is expected to acquire: (i) normative force, through its recognition and acceptance by State and non-State actors; and (ii) effectiveness, through the UNGPs' embedding in the regulatory ecosystem of business and human rights. This book set out the scenario of the corporate responsibility to respect acquiring such binding-ness and normative force, including the (selective) translation of such responsibility into 'hard' (legally binding) norms. And indeed, the UNGPs are crystallizing in a number of developments at the national, supranational (EU) level and international level that endorse the approach of the SRSG.

The UNGPs did not alter the existing obligations of States. The UNGPs also do not expect States to depart from their existing classic legal duties to protect in relation to human rights. It is a matter of legal obligation for States to adopt the necessary rules and regulations to ensure that business enterprises respect human rights in practice. International human rights law imposes a positive obligation on States to adopt such legislative measures as necessary in particular circumstances. In fact, according to UNGP 1, 'States must protect against human rights abuse within their territory and/or jurisdiction, including business enterprises. This requires taking appropriate steps to prevent, investigate, punish and redress such abuse through effective policies, legislation, regulations and adjudication.'[10]

National authorities can refer to the human rights due diligence concept when revisiting rules and regulations for the purpose of realigning them with the expectation that business enterprises respect human rights by reference to universally recognized human rights standards and principles. The human rights due diligence concept has certain unique qualities that lends itself for usage as a regulatory concept and legal standard of conduct in different areas of law.[11] The concept can give direction to national authorities when revisiting dominant conceptualizations in, for instance, tort law, corporate law or transparency law in order to address gaps in human rights protection. In the light of the preceding considerations, the corporate responsibility to respect human rights may be viewed as reconceptualization of existing obligations under various areas of law at national and sub-national levels.

The book identified and examined a wide range of regulatory measures (voluntary and mandatory) that EU Member States, the EU and other non-State actors have adopted in their efforts to actively implement their duties and responsibilities under the UNGPs. These range from transnational laws at national and EU level in the area of non-financial disclosure to soft law mechanisms by State and non-State actors at all levels. Some of these regulatory measures entail a restatement of the human rights due diligence concept, or aspects thereof in 'hard' law. These developments as referred to in the next paragraphs become particularly significant when considered in combination, thereby indicating that the corporate responsibility to respect human rights has begun to crystallize into a more binding norm.

At EU level, a number of EU Directives have been adapted (or are currently under negotiation), which are of particular relevance for regulating the conduct of business in relation to human rights in various areas. This book departs from the observation that the EU has a legal obligation to consider seriously taking all actions that are within its competences to promote business respect for human rights. This obligation can be derived from the CFREU and the objective that the EU has set 'to make the fundamental rights provided for in the Charter as effective as possible'. This book has analysed, *inter alia*, the EU Directive on non-financial disclosure.

This Directive is partially successful in re-enforcing State adherence to their existing obligations. The study on this Directive is illustrative of the legal (transformatory) effects that the enforcement of human rights due diligence in law can have, in terms of driving conceptual improvements in different areas of existing law at all levels (as well as generate transnational effects). The analysis undertaken in this book concludes that the aforementioned EU Directive does not define or fully adopt the corporate responsibility to respect human rights, nor are the UNGPs expressly mentioned therein, or if the case, only in passing. This book has highlighted some of these gaps.

In short, the SRSG itself noted about the corporate responsibility to respect that 'this unorthodox formulation initially was the most controversial conceptual move I made because it was not considered to be fully "rights-based"'.[12] However, as set out in detail throughout this book, not fully 'rights-based' is far from being tantamount to 'decoupled from rights'. On the one hand, the UNGPs do not alter pre-existing (national and international) obligations and in fact, award a primordial importance to these when it comes to the State. Though the UNGPs do not, in and of themselves, create new legal obligations, they certainly reinforce the importance of State adherence to existing obligations. On the other hand, to the extent the UNGPs, by placing CSR at the centre of a polycentric system of global governance, succeed in bringing compliance – and achieving changes in the behaviour of the corporate world in relation to human rights, CSR has already had the (often legal, in the positivistic sense of the word) effects indicated above, and is bound to have more and more, legal status – and renewed (both legal and non-legal) effects.

Notes

1 Radu Mares, *A Rejoinder to G. Skinner's Rethinking Limited Liability of Parent Corporations for Foreign Subsidiaries' Violations of International Human Rights Law*, 73 Washington and Lee Law Review Online, 117 (2016).
2 *Id.*
3 John Ruggie, *Opinion: Business and Human Rights – The Next Chapter* (7 Mar. 2013).
4 Radu Mares, *Decentering Human Rights From the International Order: The Alignment and Interaction of Transnational Policy Channels*, 23 Indiana Journal of Global Legal Studies, 173 (2016).
5 John Gerard Ruggie, Just Business Multinational Corporations and Human Rights, 78 (W.W. Norton & Company 2013).
6 *Id.*
7 Special Representative on the Issue of Human Rights and Transnational Corporations and Other Business Enterprises, *Guiding Principles on Business and Human Rights: Implementing the United Nations 'Protect, Respect and Remedy' Framework*. U.N.Doc. A/HRC/17/31, GP 23a (21 Mar. 2011) [hereinafter *UNGPs*] (by John Ruggie).
8 *Id.* GP 23a.
9 Ruggie, *supra* note 3.
10 As indicated in paragraph IV of the Preamble of the UNGPs, '[n]othing in these Guiding Principles should be read as [...] limiting or undermining any legal obligations a State may have undertaken or be subject to under International law with regard to human rights'. *UNGPs*, *supra* note 7, GP 23a.
11 Jonathan Bonnitcha & Robert McCorquodale, *Is the Concept of 'Due Diligence' in the Guiding Principles Coherent?* (2013), *available at* http://papers.ssrn.com/sol3/papers.cfm?abstract_id=2208588.
12 Ruggie, *supra* note 5, at 44.

Index

For Product Safety Concerns and Information please contact our EU representative GPSR@taylorandfrancis.com
Taylor & Francis Verlag GmbH, Kaufingerstraße 24, 80331 München, Germany

www.ingramcontent.com/pod-product-compliance
Ingram Content Group UK Ltd.
Pitfield, Milton Keynes, MK11 3LW, UK
UKHW021612240425
457818UK00018B/520

* 9 7 8 0 3 6 7 4 5 9 0 5 5 *